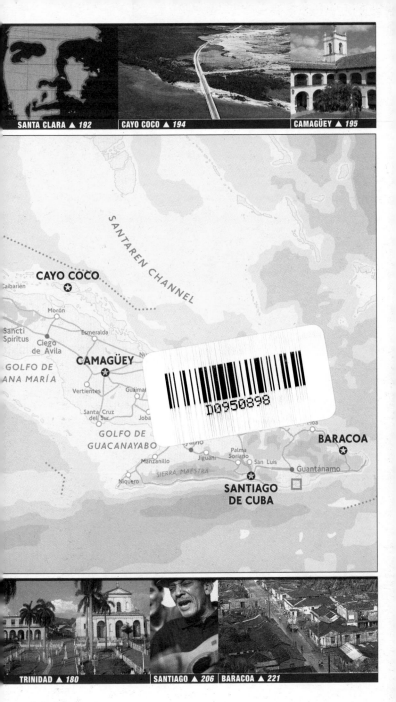

SANTAREN CHANNEL

Caibarién

CAYO COCO ✪

Morón

Sancti
Spíritus   Esmeralda

Ciego
de Ávila

CAMAGÜEY ✪

GOLFO DE
ANA MARÍA

Vertientes   Guáimar

Santa Cruz
del Sur   Joba

GOLFO DE
GUACANAYABO

Manzanillo   Jiguaní   Palma
Soriano   San Luis   Guantánamo

Niquero   SIERRA MAESTRA

**SANTIAGO
DE CUBA** ✪

BARACOA ✪

Guantánamo

D0950898

Lavish 18th- and 19th-century palaces, built here by the wealthy sugar magnates. Visit Plaza Mayor.
SANTA CLARA
Follow in Che's footsteps. Visit the Plaza de la Revolución.
CAYO COCO
One of Cuba's loveliest cays, near the second largest barrier reef in the world.
CAMAGÜEY
The city of the tinajones (clay jars). Admire these receptacles in the patios of colonial houses here.
SANTIAGO DE CUBA
A taste for celebration. The home of one of Cuba's carnivals, this city has a passion for rhythm. Visit Parque Céspedes and Calle Heredia.
BARACOA
The oldest city in Cuba. A small port perched on the easternmost tip of the island. Visit the Museo Municipal.

The mini-map pinpoints the itinerary within the wider area covered by the guide.

The itinerary map shows the main sites, the editor's choices and the places of special interest.

● ▲ ◆
The above symbols within the text provide cross-references to a place or a theme discussed elsewhere in the guide.

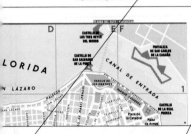

PLAYAS DEL ESTE • VARADERO

D | E | F

CASTILLO
LOS TRES REYES
DEL MORRO

FORTALEZA
DE SAN CARLOS
DE LA CABAÑA

CASTILLO
DE SAN SALVADOR
DE LA PUNTA

CANAL DE ENTRADA

PARQUE DE
LOS MÁRTIRES

CASTILLO
DE LA REAL
FUERZA

Plaza de
la Catedral

Plaza
de Armas

LORIDA

N LÁZARO

1. CASTILLO DE LA REAL FUERZA
2. PALACIO DEL SEGUNDO CABO
3. PALACIO DE LOS CAPITANES GENERALES
4. EL TEMPLETE
5. CASA DEL CONDE DE SANTOVENIA

PLAZA DE ARMAS ★

This is the oldest and finest square in the city. A simple parade ground in the 16th century, by the end of the 18th century it had been enlarged to become the administrative and political center of Havana, lined with the baroque façades of stylish palaces. The square was redesigned in 1934, reflecting the Romantic spirit of the 19th century. Kapok trees, royal palms break up the geometry of avenues that meet at the foot of the STATUE OF CARLOS MANUEL DE CÉSPEDES, sculpted in 1955 by Sergio López Mesa (*bottom right*). Like the Havana citizens of days gone by, who used to come here in their famous *volantas* (carriages) to listen to musical concerts, you can take a leisurely stroll in this square while enjoying the music that is still performed under the arcades.

CASTILLO DE LA REAL FUERZA ● 78. In 1538, as part of the program to fortify the city, the governor Hernando de Soto ordered the construction of the first defense works opposite the narrow pass marking the entrance to the bay. Completed in 1540 but destroyed in 1555 by the French pirate Jacques de Sores ● 33, ▲ 206, the original fortress was replaced by the existing building between 1558 and 1577. Constructed to a square plan and flanked at each corner by four bastions, its symmetrical design was the work of military engineer Bartolomé Sánchez who was the first designer to adopt Italian Renaissance principles in the Americas. The city's governors occupied the top story of the fortress from 1590 until their move to the Palacio de los Capitanes Generales ▲ 124. The first story now houses the MUSEO DE LA CERÁMICA. From the top, there is a picturesque view over the two fortresses which guard the other bank of the canal ▲ 146.

PALACIO DEL SEGUNDO CABO. Together with the Palacio de los Capitanes Generales, this palace forms the finest architectural complex on the square, a symbol of colonial power at the end of the 18th century. It was built by royal order between 1770 and 1791 to house the Casa de Correos (post office). It subsequently became the treasury and the home of the vice-governor in 1854, hence its name (Palace of the Second Lieutenant), then the seat of the Senate and the justice courts. It now houses the Instituto Cubano del Libro. Designed by J. A. de Armona, built by Antonio Fernández de Trevejos and refurbished in 1829 by Govantes and Cabarrocas, the building is a remarkable illustration of what is known as 'Cuban baroque' ● 82, a more restrained style than its European counterpart. The delicate outline of the windows and the intricate work on the pilasters of the portico enliven an austere façade. The narrow COURTYARD enclosed by a blind arcade on the first story with blue windows and huge white louvered shutters, is definitely worth a look.

EL TEMPLETE ● 86. This small Greco-Roman style temple was inaugurated on March 19, 1828, to commemorate the first mass celebrated on the site when the hamlet of San Cristóbal de la Habana was transferred here in 1519. The Doric portico supports a pediment engraved with an inscription instructing the Cuban people to preserve the memory of this place. Inside, three paintings by the French artist Jean-Baptiste Vermay (c. 1786–1833) also illustrate these events. A *ceiba* (kapok tree) marks the spot where the original ceremony took place. Beside it stands a column, erected in 1754, topped by the Virgen del Pilar, patron saint of Spanish sailors.

CASA DEL CONDE DE SANTOVENIA
This 18th-century house prefigured the neoclassical style of the 19th century. Once a residence of the Count of Santovenia, in 1867 it became the city's first hotel, the *Santa Isabel*, now lavishly restored and reopened. Its façade, punctuated by the columns of the portico, is graced by a first-story balcony with large openings. The polychromatic windows and the beautiful wrought-iron railings around the windows and the balconies add a graceful touch.

OLD HAVANA: UNESCO
WORLD HERITAGE SITE ✪
Try to visit Old Havana between 8am and 2pm to avoid the heat and the crowd of tourists. For an introduction to the history and artistic heart of the capital, you should visit the Museo de la Ciudad, Plaza de Armas, and the Museo de Arte Colonial, Plaza de la Catedral.

123

At the beginning of each itinerary, the distance, the suggested means of travel and the time it will take to cover the area are indicated beneath the maps:
→ Distance
▭ By car
▣ By foot
▥ By boat
◷ Duration

★ The star symbol signifies sites singled out by the editor for special attention.

✪ This symbol indicates places of special interest.

03

● Encyclopedia section

CUBA

KNOPF GUIDES

● Encyclopedia section

NATURE The natural heritage: species and habitats characteristic to the area covered by the guide, annotated and illustrated by naturalist authors and artists.

HISTORY The impact of international historical events on local history, from the arrival of the first inhabitants, with key dates appearing in a timeline above the text.

ART AND TRADITIONS Customs and traditions and their continuing role in contemporary life.

ARCHITECTURE The architectural heritage, focusing on style and topology, a look at rural and urban buildings, major civil, religious and military monuments.

AS SEEN BY PAINTERS A selection of paintings of the city or country by different artists and schools, arranged chronologically or thematically.

AS SEEN BY WRITERS An anthology of texts focusing on the city or country, taken from works of all periods and countries, arranged thematically.

▲ Itineraries

Each itinerary begins with a map of the area to be explored.

✪ SPECIAL INTEREST These sites are not to be missed. They are highlighted in gray boxes in the margins.

★ EDITOR'S CHOICE Sites singled out by the editor for special attention.

INSETS On richly illustrated double pages, these insets turn the spotlight on subjects deserving more in-depth treatment.

◆ Practical information

All the travel information you will need before you go and when you get there.

SIGHTSEEING A handy table of addresses and opening hours.

USEFUL ADDRESSES A selection of the best hotels and restaurants compiled by an expert.

APPENDICES Bibliography, list of illustrations and general index.

MAP SECTION Maps of all the areas covered by the guide, followed by an index; these maps are marked out with letters and figures making it easy for the reader to pinpoint a town, region or site.

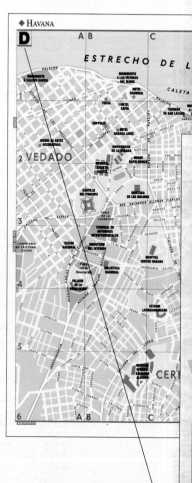

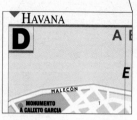

Each map in the map section is designated by a letter. In the itineraries, all the sites of interest are given a map reference (for example: **D** B2).

▲Cuban itineraries

◆Practical information

HAVANA ▲ 119

An itinerary in the capital of Cuba which follows the city's historic development and expansion westward. It begins in Old Havana (Habana Vieja), the historic center, then crosses Centro Habana and the Prado, an esplanade much loved by the inhabitants of Havana, the Vedado with its stately eclectic mansions, the Plaza de la Revolución and the residential quarter of Miramar. It concludes on the other side of the bay with the fortresses of Habana del Este.

WESTERN CUBA: PINAR DEL RÍO PROVINCE ▲ 151

A nature-oriented itinerary that takes in the lush Sierra del Rosario, the famous Viñales Valley with its unique limestone landscape, Vuelta Abajo, the home of Cuba's world-famous tobacco, the southern part of Pinar del Río province and the Guanahacabibes Peninsula with its beautiful national park. It then loops back to Havana via the north coast of the province, which boasts some superb dive sites.

THE NORTH COAST, FROM HAVANA TO CÁRDENAS ▲ 163

An itinerary which makes the most of the beaches along the 'Cuban Riviera'. It begins in Cojímar, Ernest Hemingway's home from home, and runs alongside the Playas del Este to Varadero, the largest seaside resort on the island and the most popular destination for tourists. It also lingers in two cities that owed their onetime prosperity to the sugar industry: Matanzas, 'queen of rumba' and Cárdenas, 'queen of rum'.

CENTRAL CUBA ▲ 171

An itinerary which stays close to the vast central plain of the island and takes in some prestigious colonial cities. It begins in the Zapata Peninsula, with its national park, and heads through Cienfuegos, Trinidad, Sancti Spíritus and Santa Clara, Che Guevara's memorial city. It also takes a little detour to the Sabana-Camagüey archipelago before finishing in the tour in the colonial town of Camagüey.

ORIENTE ▲ 197

Oriente, or the head of the 'great green lizard', as Cuba is often described. This itinerary charts Cuba's history of rebellion. It begins in Holguín, climbs toward the major seaside resort of Guardalavaca, reaches the Sierra Maestra, following in the footsteps of Fidel Castro and Che, crosses the festive, cross-cultural city of Santiago de Cuba, and passes one of the island's most arid regions to reach Baracoa, the first colonial city.

THE ARCHIPIÉLEGO DE LOS CANARREOS ▲ 223

A seaside itinerary beginning in the extensive Archipiélego de los Canarreos (Isle of Youth) and going as far as Cayo Largo. It starts at Nueva Gerona, in the north of the island, visits the Presidio Modelo (Model Prison), then heads along a magnificent isolated beach of white sand on the south coast as far as the impressive coral reef in the southwest. It finishes in the silence of the wind-swept cayos.

Numerous specialists and academics have contributed to this guide. All the information contained in this book has been checked by Paul Estrade (Encyclopedia section) and Juan Luis Morales Menocal (Itineraries).

Encyclopedia section

YVES COHAT
Co-author of 'The Cayos and the Coral Reef'; author of 'The Pelagic Environment'. PhD; specializes in the sea and fishing.

PAUL ESTRADE
Author of the pages on José Martí. Qualified Spanish teacher. PhD; professor emeritus at the Université Paris-VIII. Specializes in the Spanish West Indies and the work of José Martí. Founder and president of the France-Cuba Association.

LOUIS FAHRASMANE
Author of the sections on 'Sugarcane Farming' and 'Making Sugar and Rum'. Works as a researcher at the national institute for agronomic research in Guadeloupe and specializes in sugarcane.

CARMEN GONZÁLEZ DÍAZ DE VILLEGAS
Co-author of 'Popular Cults of African Origin' and 'Carnival'. Cuban. She worked at the Ministry of Foreign Affairs in the African countries department, then at the Africa and Middle East research center until 1990.

GUILHEM LESAFFRE
Co-author of the Nature section. Naturalist, author of ornithological works.

CATHERINE BLAKE
Author of 'Cuba as Seen by Writers'.

Writer and editor. specializing in travel and literature She has an MA in Literature from Cambrige.

JEAN-CLAUDE RIBAUT
Author of 'Tobacco', 'Cigars and Rum' and 'La Fábrica Partagás'. Food critic for Le Monde.

MARIE-THÉRÈSE RICHARD HERNÁNDEZ
Author of 'Cuba as Seen by Painters'. Ph.D.; senior lecturer at the University of Cergy-Pontoise and at the Institute of Political Sciences in Paris; author of a thesis on Cuban painting during the Republican era.

EDUARDO LUIS RODRÍGUEZ
Author of the Architecture section and 'Public Buildings of the Republic'. Cuban architect, critic and historian. Director of the journal Arquitectura Cuba.

MARYSE ROUX
Co-author of the Nature section, 'Popular Cults of African Origin' and 'Carnival'; author of 'Montuna Chicken'. Geographer. She lived in Havana from 1986 to 1998.

MAYA ROY
Author of 'Music and Dance', co-author of 'Carnival'. University lecturer, author of a book and articles on music in the Spanish Caribbean, assistant producer at Radio France Internationale (RFI3). Devised and produced numerous radio broadcasts in Paris and the provinces until 1996.

EDUARDO TORRES-CUEVAS
Author of 'Chronology', 'The Indo-Cubans' and 'Slavery'. Cuban. Full professor of history at Havana University, director of the social sciences journal Debates Americanos and the Don Fernando Ortiz school of higher education.

Itineraries in Cuba

JUAN LUIS MORALES MENOCAL
Author of the introduction to Havana. Cuban architect who has lived in Paris since 1993. After working in Cuba, he founded the Atelier Morales and was responsible for the decor of the Havanita Café and Little Havana restaurants in Paris.

JOSÉ DOS SANTOS LÓPEZ
Author of 'Havana' and 'The north coast, from Havana to Cárdenas'. Journalist since 1969, vice-president of the Prensa Latina agency for ten years.

GÉRARD DE CORTANZE
Author of 'Ernest Hemingway in Cuba'. Novelist and essayist, regarded as one of the leading authorities on Hispanic affairs.

ANDRÉS ESCOBAR SOTO
Co-author of 'Western Cuba'. Cuban. Journalist and editor at Prensa Latina agency in Havana, former press correspondent in France, Spain and the Lebanon.

MARYSE ROUX
Co-author of 'Western Cuba'. Geographer. She lived in Havana from 1986 to 1998.

JAMES CLEMENT
Author of 'The Bay of Pigs' and sections on Cienfuegos, Sancti Spíritus, Santa Clara, Remedios, Morón, Cayo Coco, Cayo Guillermo and Camagüey. Graduate in languages from Bristol university, where he was president of the Spanish and Latin-American society. He worked as a tourist guide in Cuba.

JEAN ORTIZ
Author of 'Santa Clara, Che's Memorial Town'. Journalist in Latin America from 1977 to 1981. Senior lecturer at the university of Pau; specializing in Cuban affairs.

FRANÇOIS MISSEN
Author of sections on Trinidad and 'Oriente'. Writer and journalist specializing in Cuba.

MONIQUE PEAINCHAU
Author of 'The Archipiélago de los Canarreos'. Lives in Havana and teaches at the Alliance Française.

Practical Information

MONIQUE PEAINCHAU
Author of 'Practical Information'. Lives in Havana. Teaches at the Alliance Française.

JEAN-CLAUDE RIBAUT
Author of 'Hotels and restaurants'. Food critic for Le Monde newspaper.

**This is a Borzoi Book
published by Alfred A. Knopf**

Copyright © 2000 by Alfred A. Knopf

All rights reserved under International and Pan-American Copyright Conventions. Published in the United States by Alfred A. Knopf, a division of Random House, Inc., New York, and simultaneously in Canada by Random House of Canada Limited, Toronto. Distributed by Random House, Inc., New York.

www.randomhouse.com

Originally published in France by Nouveaux-Loisirs, a subsidiary of Editions Gallimard, Paris, 1999. Copyright © 1999 by Editions Nouveaux-Loisirs

Knopf, Borzoi Books, and the colophon are registered trademarks of Random House, Inc.

ISBN 0-375-706-585 (pb)

TRANSLATED BY
Sue Rose

EDITED AND TYPESET BY
Book Creation Services Ltd, London

SPECIAL THANKS TO
David Bigelman, Dominique Colombani, Coralia and Bertrand Lamotte, Una Liutkus (Havanatour), Mario Veranes Castañeda, María Helena Martine Zequeira, his Excellency Eumelio Caballero and Madame Gloria de Dios, at the Cuban embassy in Paris.

CUBA

■ **PRODUCTION**
Béatrice Méneux,
assisted by Isabelle Dessommes, Catherine Ianco *with the collaboration of* Emmanuelle Lepetit

■ **PRACTICAL INFORMATION**
Sylvie Gendrot, Elsa Schifano, Nicolas Christitch

■ **LAYOUT**
Isabelle Roller, Olivier Brunot (Nature)

■ **PICTURE RESEARCH**
Natalie Saint-Martin

■ **ILLUSTRATIONS**
COVER: Henri Galeron
NATURE: Frédéric Bony, Marc Duquet, Guilhem Lesaffre with François Desbordes, Claire Felloni, Pascal Robin
ARCHITECTURE: Bruno Lenormand
assisted by Philippe Candé, Jean-François Péneau, Claude Quiec, Jean-Sylvain Roveri, Jean-Claude Senée, Amato Soro
ITINERARIES: Maurice Pommier, Frédéric Bony
PHOTOGRAPHY: Éric Guillemot, Patrick Léger
PRACTICAL INFORMATION: Maurice Pommier
MAPS: Vincent Brunot
CARTOGRAPHIC COMPUTER GRAPHICS: Editorial graphics, Paul Coulbois, Patrick Mérienne

Printed in Italy by Editoriale Lloyd

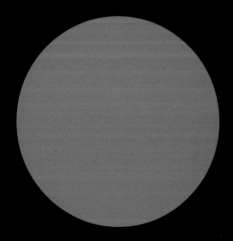

Encyclopedia section

Tobacco leaves have a long way to go before they can be rolled by the skilled *torcedores*: at the factory, where work methods have barely altered since the beginning of the 20th century, the strippers remove the midribs one by one with remarkable dexterity; the leaf halves are then graded for the first time and arranged on a round tub with padded sides, nicknamed 'the turtle' by Cubans.

Santiago de Cuba, as typified by this market and
these faces in the 1920s to 1930s, described
so evocatively by the Cuban poet, Nicolás
Guillén: 'The spirit of Cuba is cross-cultural.
And it is this spirit that will give our skin its
true color. One day, we will even talk of the
Cuban color.'

On July 26th, 1959 Camilo Cienfuegos organized a procession to commemorate the sixth anniversary of the attack by Fidel Castro and his men on the Moncada Barracks in Santiago de Cuba.

Nature

The island of Cuba curves in a shallow arc along a central rolling plain, which at times climbs to higher upland areas. Western Cuba is dominated by the Cordillera de Guaniguanico mountain range, eastern Cuba by the Sierra Maestra and the massifs of Sagua-Baracoa while the Sierra del Escambray rises on the south central coast. Cuba has a humid tropical climate: a hot, wet season between May and October and a cooler, drier season between November and April. The island is influenced by the northeasterly trade winds, which bring heat and humidity, and the continental anticyclone, which has a cooling effect. Although the distribution of Cuba's tropical forests and savannas is closely linked to its climate, local variations in soil and vegetation are often determined by its mountainous terrain and stony bedrock.

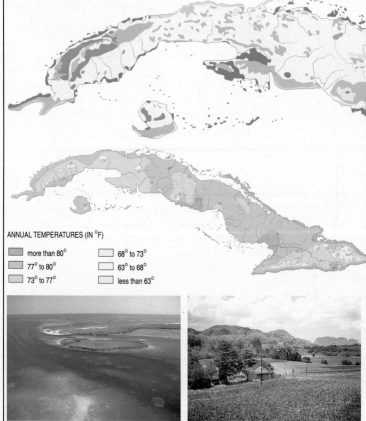

ANNUAL TEMPERATURES (IN °F)

more than 80° 68° to 73°
77° to 80° 63° to 68°
73° to 77° less than 63°

THE ARCHIPELAGO. Cuba's archipelago and the relief of its coast was formed by the change in sea levels during the Quaternary Period. This, and the effect of the currents that washed along the sand of the estuaries and beaches, led to the formation of *cayos* (cays).

'MOGOTES' ▲ *156*. Occurring on a smaller scale than in tropical Asia, *mogotes* are hillocks formed of residual limestone bedrock that are found in a deeply eroded karst terrain. Here in Cuba, they look over the tobacco fields.

SUGARCANE PLANTATIONS ● 48. Fields of sugarcane stretch as far as the eye can see in the flat open countryside. Forming a checkerboard pattern with other crops, scrub, savanna and prairie, they monopolize the best land: the red soil of the chalky plains. The sugar refinery, which smokes during the *zafra* (harvest), is never far away.

THE SIERRAS. These vast sierras occupy about one third of the island and stand witness to a complex geological history. They are covered with different layers of vegetation that give way, in the valleys, to shrubby thickets, then mixed forest and pine forest. Endemic species, such as the Mayarí pine, grow in the eastern sierras.

ANNUAL RAINFALL (IN INCHES)

- more than 85
- 70 to 85
- 55 to 70
- 40 to 55
- 40 to 55
- 30 to 40
- less than 30

VEGETATION

- Mangrove
- Manigua costera and common xerophyllum (bear grass)
- Xerophyllum growing on the *mogote*
- *Cuabal y charrascal*
- Pine forest
- Semi-deciduous forest
- Rainforest
- Mountain
- Cultivated areas

THE TROPICAL FOREST. Directly influenced by the northeasterly trade winds, the dense mountainous regions of Moa and Baracoa have an annual rainfall of 120 inches, half of which occurs during the dry season. The only real tropical forest in Cuba is found here.

THE CACTI. The foehn (dry wind) and the orientation of the sierras have made the southern coast between Punta de Maisí and Guantánamo semi-arid. This area supports cacti and prickly shrubs, which are also found more sparsely on the north central coast.

17

■ THE SAVANNA

AMERICAN KESTREL
The local breed is recognizable by its red plumage. This small raptor can often be seen hovering in the air on the lookout for prey.

The word 'savanna' is derived from the indigenous word *zabana*, which refers to a treeless plain. This wide-open expanse carpeted by grass and bushes is dominated by pine trees and palms that grow singly or in clumps. When uncultivated, it is colloquially known as *monte*, a name it shares with the denser, more shrubby vegetation of the uplands. It now occupies around forty percent of Cuban territory. The areas with poor soil, the home of thorn bushes, have been abandoned by farmers; cattle are put out to pasture on the lush grasslands. Fields of sugarcane, tobacco and even maize alternate with food crops on the richer soil.

Royal palm

Turkey vulture

Mango tree

Tobacco plant

Sugarcane

CUBAN AMAZON PARROT
(*Cotorra*)
With the return of the wet season, these parrots engage in noisy mating displays and perform acrobatic feats in the branches.

RED-TAILED HAWK
With the turkey vulture, this large raptor is one of the most common birds in Cuba. It hovers in circles, gliding on the thermals.

TURKEY VULTURE
Very common in Cuba, these vultures fly over exposed areas to locate the scraps and dead animals on which they feed.

WHITE-WINGED DOVE
Taking their name from the markings of their outspread wings in flight, these doves often gather in small flocks.

MOURNING DOVE
This bird prefers wide-open areas. Not easily frightened as a rule, it may come close enough for you to be able to admire the metallic sheen of its neck.

COMMON GROUND-DOVE
No bigger than a human fist, this bird is frequently seen on roadsides. When disturbed, it flies off quickly.

ANOLE LIZARD
While basking in the sun, this lizard changes color if it sees a female of the species or a rival, affording a marvelous display of blues and greens.

ANTILLEAN PALM SWIFT
This small, erratic flier is often seen near palms as it builds its nest at the top of these trees.

Banana tree

Cattle egrets

MANGO TREE
The oldest trees bear several tons of mangoes; each fruit hangs on the end of a long, supple and robust stalk before ripening.

BANANA TREE
Although it may look like a tree, this is in fact an herb. Its false trunk is composed of leaf sheaths tightly rolled around one another.

TOBACCO PLANT
This is a member of the Solanaceae family, as is the potato, and will only grow to its optimum height if planted in rich soil ● *68.*

SUGARCANE
Despite its size, which can reach up to 16 feet, this is a gramineae or grass, belonging to the same family as wheat or rice.

■ THE TROPICAL RAINFOREST

BLACK ANOLE
When disturbed, this lizard extends its small white dewlap which, when folded up, is concealed beneath its throat.

Cuban Amazon parrot

When the Spanish conquerors arrived in Cuba, about two thirds of the island was covered, to varying degrees, by tropical forest. Vast areas were cleared, providing wood (for ship repairs and buildings, then fuel for the sugar mills and the railroad) and making room for crops, in line with the rapid development of the sugarcane industry. The settlers exhausted the forests on the plains – only a few kapoks and coral trees remain – except at high altitudes, where some precious species grow alongside tree-ferns. In the sierras, the tropical forest managed to survive in

optimum conditions. It is dense and abounds in a wide variety of indigenous plant species, including deciduous and evergreen trees.

RED-LEGGED HONEYCREEPER
The metallic sheen of this nectar-loving bird's blue plumage is only visible in broad daylight.

CUBAN EMERALD
(*Zunzún*)
This hummingbird is found in clearings surrounded by flowering trees. It is also fond of flower gardens.

RED-LEGGED THRUSH
This sociable bird, a prodigious songster, makes an active contribution to the forest's musical background.

CUBAN TODY
(*Cartacuba*)
The tiny toadies perch motionless before suddenly darting out after an insect.

CUBAN SOLENODON
Cuba is home to one of the two species of this small, mainly nocturnal mammal, which weighs around two pounds.

CUBAN CONURE
(*Periquito*)
Identifiable by its long tail, this small parakeet is only found in Cuba and frequents the savanna.

CUBAN TROGON
(*Tocororo*)
This jewel-like bird is regarded as Cuba's national bird because its colors are identical to those found on the island's flag.

CUBAN RED-BELLIED WOODPECKER
This bird often walks up and down the smooth trunk of palm trees in search of insects and larvae.

Tricolore heron

Cuban
red-
bellied
wood-
pecker

Red-legged thrush

F. Desbordes

■ THE PINE FOREST

GREAT LIZARD CUCKOO
Well-camouflaged on the ground despite its size, this bird's long shape and brightly colored wings attract attention in flight.

Very little of the pine forest exists in its natural state; it can only be found at a certain altitude and is conspicuous for its flora, much of which is endemic. Recent pine forests resulting from Cuban reforestation programs take the form of stereotypical stands, with dense, rectilinear trunks. The older pine forests, however, have either preserved their appearance or are beginning to revert to their original state. On the slopes of some of the sierras, the pines soar above banana, coffee and cacao trees. Elsewhere, the undergrowth is characterized by varied vegetation.

OLIVE-CAPPED WARBLER
Unlike the American warblers, which spend the winter here, this bird does not migrate.

YELLOW-HEADED WARBLER
This species of warbler is only found in Cuba, where it frequents the pine forests in particular.

NORTHERN MOCKINGBIRD
Perched on fences or telephone lines, this bird watches eagerly for insects or starts imitating the song of other birds.

CUBAN GREEN WOODPECKER
This multicolored bird with its harsh call never goes unnoticed. It is only found in Cuba.

COMMON NIGHTHAWK
(*Querequeté*)
Not active during the day, this bird takes flight in the late afternoon, tracing elaborate patterns against the sky and splitting the air with its grating cry: 'téré-téré'

CUBAN PINES
There are four species of endemic pine in Cuba, including the Sierra Maestra pine, the Mayarí pine and the male pine.

male

STRIPE-HEADED TANAGER
The beautiful plumage of this small-sized bird is as enchanting as its very melodious song.

LOGGERHEAD KINGBIRD
(*Pitirre*)
Easy to spot perched on wires and stakes, this tyrant keeps a careful lookout for large insects.

CUBAN BULLFINCH
From afar, the male of this seed-eating passerine appears to be all black. The white band on its wing can only be seen from up close.

Cuban
trogon

Cuban pine

Tree-fern

Cuban green
woodpecker

Great
lizard
cucko

F. Desbordes 95

23

PIED-BILLED GREBE
This bird alternately floats
like a cork or dives to feed
underwater.

By far the most extensive swampland in the Antilles, Cuba's swamp areas are a valuable natural resource. Although some swamps are still used as hunting preserves, many are assiduously protected. These habitats often cover the coastal margins of limestone plains where poor surface and underground drainage have caused the water to stagnate. Crisscrossed by canals, generally carpeted by luxuriant floating vegetation and lined with mangroves ● 26, the swamps form a tranquil environment abounding in a wide variety of seabirds, fish, turtles and, occasionally, crocodiles and manatees.

Purple gallinule

Northern jacana

ANHINGA
A consummate diver, this web-footed bird is as at home in the water as it is soaring across the skies.

Manjuarí

female

male

OSPREY
This bird spends long periods sitting on a branch on the lookout for fish, which it catches by swooping down low over the water.

GREEN HERON
This small heron may be seen on the banks. It stands patiently for long periods before harpooning a fish.

WOOD DUCK
The male's brightly colored, intricately patterned plumage makes this duck one of the most eye-catching of its kind.

Osprey

Green heron

Cuban turtle

CARIBBEAN COOT
This bird's shrill call
is much less discreet
than its sober black
plumage.

PURPLE GALLINULE
This bird is an expert at foraging
through the tangle of riverside
vegetation, which also provides a
refuge if danger threatens.

NORTHERN JACANA
This bird's outsize feet
enable it to walk across
the floating carpet of
water lily leaves.

■ THE MANGROVE

1 Black mangrove **2** Gray mangle
3 White mangle **4** Red mangrove

1 2 3 4

The boundary between land and
sea in Cuba is the kingdom of the mangroves.
This dense area of vegetation perched on the coastline
is a fragile natural habitat of great biological worth. All
varieties of indigenous fish swim through the submerged tangle
of roots, while a wide range of bird species make use of the thick
foliage as a nighttime refuge,
building their nests here. Open
expanses of shallow water between
the clumps of mangrove provide a
virtually inexhaustible source of food
for a myriad of wading birds
throughout the wet season.

Over time, the mangrove has
become an enclosed habitat.

Greater flamingos

Cormorants

Royal terns

Roseate spoonbills

HUTIA ▲ *161*
With the exception of one
relatively common species,
hutias, large arboreal
rodents, are now a
protected species.

WHITE-CROWNED PIGEON
From dawn, their repetitive
cooing can be heard from the
top of large trees lining the
mangrove, where they gather
in small flocks.

WHITE IBIS
Easily recognizable by its long
curved beak, this bird likes to
perch on top of mangrove
trees. Only the adults have
white plumage.

26

Red mangroves

Black mangrove

Gray and white mangroves

The mangrove swamp is composed of various species of mangrove tree, including the mangle, and they each have different ecological requirements. In the rear, the gray and white mangroves are less tolerant of water and salt, unlike the black mangroves and particularly the red mangroves, which grow happily in the water.

Frigatebirds

MAGNIFICENT FRIGATEBIRD
In flight, the frigatebird's long angled wings and forked tail offer remarkable maneuverability.

Black buzzard

White ibises

TRICOLORED HERON
This largely sedentary heron is conspicuous as much for its graceful shape as for the beauty of its plumage.

ROSEATE SPOONBILL
Although both adults and young of this species have flattened beaks, only the adults have the distinctive pink feathers.

GREATER FLAMINGO
The plankton this bird feeds on by filtering the salt water contains carotenes which give the feathers their trademark color.

THE *CAYOS* AND THE CORAL REEF

The largest islands in the Sabana-Camagüey archipelago, to the north of Cuba, were separated from the coast by the rise in sea level after the last period of glaciation.

The *cayos* (cays) are sandy islets that lack fresh water and form an intricate border along the coast of Cuba. They provide support, at the edge of the underwater talus slope, for the growing coral reefs. Behind them, the coast has formed many indentations in the *seboruco*, the ancient emerging reef on which fossils have been found of the polyps, the animals which join together to form coral areas. The smallest *cayos* are nothing more than 'resting places' frequented by birds, particularly during migration. The large *cayos*, however, are home to vast colonies of birds, and of reptiles such as iguanas and lizards.

Scad

BROWN PELICAN
However clumsy this bird is on land, it soars through the air with ease once it has managed to get off the ground.

breeding plumage

Staghorn coral

winter

ROYAL TERN
A strong and acrobatic flyer, this bird skims over the waves before diving to catch any fish it spots.

RUDDY TURNSTONE
This bird, which benefits from short legs and robust feet, runs fearlessly over the sharp-edged reefs to catch its prey.

SEMIPALMATED PLOVER
A small migratory wader, this bird searches for plankton in the small pools left by the sea spray.

Blue tang

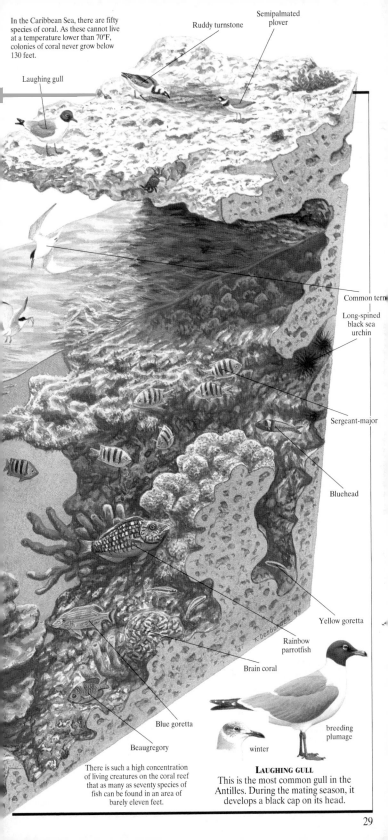

In the Caribbean Sea, there are fifty species of coral. As these cannot live at a temperature lower than 70°F, colonies of coral never grow below 130 feet.

Laughing gull

Ruddy turnstone

Semipalmated plover

Common tern

Long-spined black sea urchin

Sergeant-major

Bluehead

Yellow goretta

Rainbow parrotfish

Brain coral

Blue goretta

Beaugregory

There is such a high concentration of living creatures on the coral reef that as many as seventy species of fish can be found in an area of barely eleven feet.

LAUGHING GULL
This is the most common gull in the Antilles. During the mating season, it develops a black cap on its head.

winter

breeding plumage

29

■ OCEAN LIFE

The warm waters off the coast are home to a
particular type of fauna whose life cycle takes place mainly in
deep water, even if certain individuals occasionally come closer
to the coast and 'stray' onto the reefs. These marine species
include several fish that defend themselves fiercely and
energetically, such as the sailfish, which gives sports fishing
enthusiasts the chance to engage in some Homeric battles.

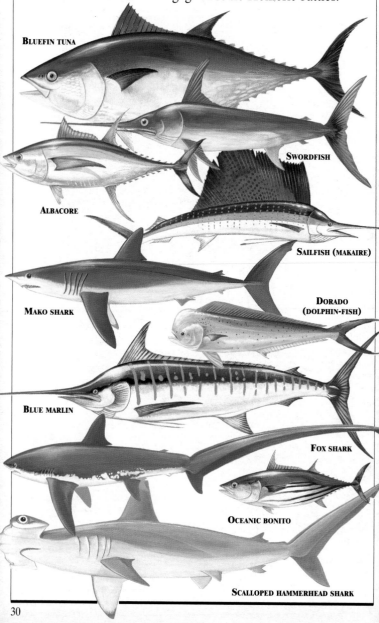

BLUEFIN TUNA

ALBACORE

SWORDFISH

SAILFISH (MAKAIRE)

MAKO SHARK

DORADO
(DOLPHIN-FISH)

BLUE MARLIN

FOX SHARK

OCEANIC BONITO

SCALLOPED HAMMERHEAD SHARK

History

| 1492 Recaptured by Spain | 1519 Hernán Cortés leaves Cuba to conquer Mexico |

| 8000 BC | 5000 BC | 1000 BC | 0 | 1500 | 1525 |

| 8000 BC First inhabitants in the Cuban archipelago | 4500 BC Second wave of settlers | 500 BC Third wave of migration | 1492 Christopher Columbus discovers Cuba | 1510 Start of the conquest of Cuba |

THE PRE-HISPANIC PERIOD

Archeological excavations have uncovered traces of human settlers in the Cuban archipelago dating as far back as 10,000 years. When the Europeans arrived in 1492, the island's communities had reached various stages of development. The Guanajatabey ● 34, a Mesolithic culture, were the oldest community, and survived by fishing and gathering.

The most advanced community was that of the most numerous peoples in South America, the Arawak, who had settled here around AD 500. Residing on all the Caribbean islands down to the mouth of the Orinoco River in Venezuela, they were known as the Tainos ● 34. Their flourishing civilization, which revolved around yucca farming and a tribal social structure,

led to further settlement and the development of many farming implements. The Tainos were also the leading artists in the Antilles, as can be seen by their highly elaborate pottery and

cult objects (*zemí* ● 34, *above*, a fertility deity). By the time the Europeans arrived, there were still an estimated 100,000 indigenous peoples living in Cuba.

THE FORMATION OF CREOLE SOCIETY: COLONIZATION

THE ISLAND IS DISCOVERED

In 1492 Christopher Columbus, named Admiral of the Ocean Seas by Queen Isabella of Castile, made his voyage of discovery to the Indies. On his maiden voyage, the local inhabitants of the first island he discovered told him about a large island called Cuba. On October 28, 1492, Columbus landed at the Bay of Bariay

▲ 201, on the north coast of modern Holguín Province. He originally thought he had reached Asia, confusing Cuba with Cipango (Japan). It was only ten years later, when sailing round Cuba, that Nicolás de Ovando confirmed that it was actually an island, and not a continent as was first thought.

THE CONQUEST

In 1510, Diego Velázquez landed in Cuba with 300 men and began the conquest of the island in the name of the Spanish Crown. His main objective was to find gold. In 1511, he founded the colony's first towns (modern Baracoa, Bayamo, Trinidad, Sancti Spiritus, Havana, Camagüey and Santiago de Cuba). Many social injustices were committed against the aboriginal population during this period of conquest. Hatuey, the *cacique* (chieftain) from Santo Domingo, led the Indo-Cuban resistance in the region of Bayamo. He was burned at the stake by the Spanish in 1512 ▲ 221. Under the *encomienda* system, the Spanish landowners were allotted a number of Indian laborers who were forced to work their land. By 1524, their numbers had fallen to 893 as a result of harsh treatment, epidemics and intermarriage.

THE DEFENDER OF THE INDIANS
The Dominican friar Bartolomé de Las Casas (1474–1566), who arrived at the start of the conquest, witnessed the massacre of the so-called Caonao Indians. He devoted his writings and his religious activities to gaining them the status of royal subjects. He achieved his goal in 1542, with the New Laws (*Leyes Nuevas de Indias*), which also abolished the *encomienda* system. Las Casas was accused of promoting slavery, in America – wrongly, since this practice dated back to the conquest.

1532 Pizarro conquers Peru	1728 Foundation of Havana's San Gerónimo Royal and Pontifical University

1530 1575 1600 1650 1740 1760

| 1542 *Leyes Nuevas de Indias* (New Laws) | 1553 Havana becomes the island's de facto capital; this is made official in 1607 | 1697 Peace of Ryswick: end of piracy and privateering |

CUBA AT THE MEETING POINT OF THE SEA ROUTES

One of the main reasons for the conquest was the gold mines, but they were soon exhausted and new expeditions to the continent were organized, such as the one led by Hernán Cortés to Mexico in 1519. The people were mobilized and the island was soon emptied. This caused radical changes to the agricultural economy. Although tobacco farming continued, cattle breeding became much more widespread, and was soon the island's main resource as leather was highly prized throughout Europe. In the early 17th century, the island's economy was given a boost by the growth of Havana's harbor. Its geographical location made it a vital stopover for Spanish fleets laden with goods from the colonies and heading towards Cádiz (fortifications of

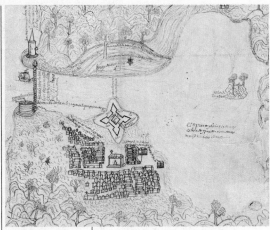

Havana harbor in 1567, above). Because of the Spanish Crown's monopoly, Santiago and Havana, which became the de facto capital of the island in 1553, were the only two ports entitled to trade. The colonists had to resort to smuggling to survive.

SMUGGLING AND TRADE WARS (16TH–17TH CENTURY)

were in the pay of various governments, who were were a far more common and serious concern. Certain buccaneers, such as the Dutchman Piet Heyn, and free-booters (*opposite*) also worked for European trading houses in collaboration with the island's colonists. In 1697, the Peace of Ryswick finally put an end to piracy and privateering. In order to protect its trade routes and the larger cities that were connected with them, such as Havana, the Spanish Crown decided to build a large system of fortifications ● 78 in the Caribbean. This soon became one of the most striking architectural achievements of the 18th century in the region.

THE DEVELOPMENT OF A CREOLE WAY OF LIFE

By the mid-18th century Havana was the third-largest city in the New World, the center of trade with the Indies and the most important strategic location for defending the Spanish sea routes. The island's population soared by 80 percent during the first half of the 19th century. The Creoles – the name given to people born on the island, regardless of their origins – developed their own way of life, from the marriage of two cultures, Spanish and African (the latter first arrived as slaves in 1522) and certain

elements of the indigenous culture (including a great respect for nature). The Virgin of Charity (*Virgen de la Caridad del Cobre*) ▲ 218, a statue found at El Cobre in 1605 by two mulattos and a young black slave, was to become the island's patron saint. The 18th century also saw the creation of a genuine Creole aristocracy which asserted its power by building grand palaces and founding major cultural institutions on the island, such as the Havana University in 1728 ▲ 142.

In the 16th and 17th centuries, rival European nations which were opposed to Spain's monopoly of America began a trade war. Random piracy, which brought Frenchman Jacques de Sores ▲ 122, 206, to fame, was, however, only an annoying, marginal problem for the Cubans. It was privateers such as British sailors Francis Drake and Henry Morgan ▲ 206, who

In 1492, the Cuban archipelago was populated by around 100,000 indigenous peoples belonging to various ethnic groups. Settlements were concentrated along the coast and at river mouths. The Guanajatabey, a nomadic people who arrived from North America in 6000 BC, occupied the western part of the island. They were gatherers by nature and used shells to make tools. The Siboney, probably from Central America, settled in the south of Cuba in 2000 BC, creating a Neolithic culture. They were partially assimilated by the Tainos, the largest and most advanced ethnic group, who arrived in the eastern part of the country around AD 500. The Tainos were a peace-loving people and as a result did not resist the Spanish, who conquered the island with ease.

'ZEMÍS' ● *32*
Taino culture revolved around the worship of
their ancestors and their belief in spirits.
Zemís, idols carved from stone or wood,
were an integral part of everyday life.
Linked to fertility (triangular *zemí*,
opposite) and the creation of the
earth and mankind, they
were used in a
variety of
funerary
practices.

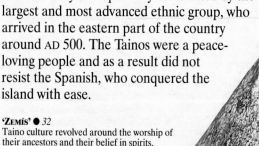

Although tobacco was smoked to attain a state of ecstasy in religious ceremonies, it 'played an important role in mythology, magic, medicine, tribal rituals, politics, wars, farming and fishing' (Fernando Ortíz ● 42).

TOBACCO ● 68

One habit that struck the early Spanish settlers as unusual was the Indians' inhalation of a whitish smoke through their noses: they placed the dried leaf of the tobacco (*cohiba*) in hollow, Y-shaped wooden sticks and burned it. They also rolled leaves, lit them and inhaled the smoke through their mouths, in the same way a cigar is smoked today.

YUCCA FARMING

This crop contributed to the development of Taino farming techniques. It was used to make various products such as *casabe* (cassava), hot dishes and drinks. The local farmers sowed it in pairs: one farmer dug holes in the ground using a *coa* (long pointed stick), while the other farmer planted the yucca seeds.

ARCHIVO NACIONAL
PLANO GENERAL
DE LA
JURISDICCIONDECIENFUEGOS
DEDICADO
A su Gobernador Político y Militar
EL SOR BRIG.D.RAMON M.DE LABRA
por los Agrimensores publicos
D.JOSÉ M.SAINZ Y RUEDA Y D.JOSÉ NADAL
1847.

The Tainos, who lived in organized villages and survived by farming, were easily conquered by the Spanish. The Enlightenment ideal of the 'Noble Savage' was modeled on the Taino people.

THE TAINO VILLAGE

This could consist of as many as fifty dwellings in different shapes and sizes: circular huts with conical roofs or rectangular houses with pitched roofs and porches. This latter type of structure, the *bohío*, was reserved for the highest-ranking dignitaries. It has remained the traditional abode of the Cuban peasant (the Cuban countryside at the end of the 19th century, top left). The *batey* was the space in the center of the village used for religious festivals. This term, which was extended to the community itself, now refers to the villages of sugar mill workers.

Black slavery in Cuba began with the Spanish conquest and was abolished in 1886. During this period, more than 850,000 slaves were brought to the island, 90 percent of them between 1762 and 1869. They came from more than twenty-five ethnic tribes over a vast area in West Africa (between the southern Sahara and Angola). The price of slaves varied depending on their status: *bozal* (born in Africa), *criollo* (born in Cuba of African parents), or *rellollo* (of Creole parentage). By 1842, only 22 percent of slaves, generally the *bozales*, worked on the sugar plantations. The others were employed in the arts and crafts industry, the coffee plantations or as domestic servants. Their traditional customs and beliefs played a vital role in the formation of the island's society, culture and religion.

THE 'BARRACÓN'

As many as four hundred slaves might work on a single large sugar plantation. They were housed in a rectangular building called a *barracón*, with only one barred door. According to the account given by a *cimarrón* (runaway slave) recorded by Miguel Barnet ● *106*, the *barracón* was divided into 'rooms' with 'a hole in the wall' or 'a barred skylight'; in the inner courtyard, 'women washed the whole family's laundry in tubs'.

AFRO-CUBAN WRITERS

Juan Francisco Manzano (1797–1854) was the first black Cuban writer. Formerly a slave, in 1837 he bought his freedom with funds set up by intellectuals who admired his work. Gabriel de la Concepción Valdés, known as Plácido (1809–44), was a free mulatto whose poetry evoked Creole sensibilities. Accused of conspiracy, he was executed in 1844.

A DAY IN THE LIFE OF A PLANTATION SLAVE

'At four-thirty in the morning they rang the Ave Maria [...] At six they rang another bell called the line-up bell, and everyone had to form up in a place just outside the barracoon. [...] Then off to the cane-fields until eleven when we ate jerked beef, vegetables and bread [...] At half-past eight they rang the last bell for everyone to go to sleep, the silence bell.' (*The Autobiography of a Runaway Slave.* Esteban Montejo, Ed. Miguel Barnet, 1968)

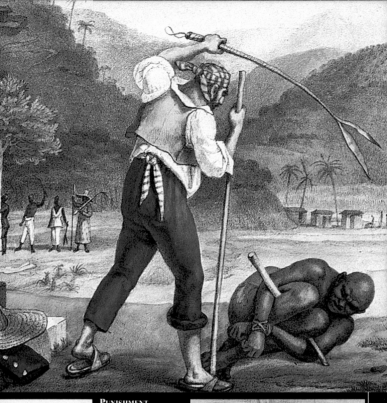

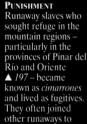

PUNISHMENT

Runaway slaves who sought refuge in the mountain regions – particularly in the provinces of Pinar del Río and Oriente ▲ *197* – became known as *cimarrones* and lived as fugitives. They often joined other runaways to

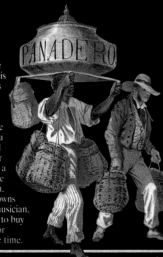

form communities called *palenques*. If they were recaptured, they were usually subjected to a variety of cruel punishments such as the stocks, a plank of wood with two or four holes in which the slave's limbs were confined for days, or even weeks (above).

EMANCIPATION

In the early 19th century, Alexander von Humboldt wrote that 'In no part of the world, where slavery exists, is manumission so frequent as in the island of Cuba'. He went on to comment that there was a world of difference between the slave who served in the house of a wealthy man in Havana and Kingston or who worked for himself and paid his master a stipulated daily sum, and the slave in the sugar plantation. Slaves who worked in the towns (coachman, cook, mason, musician, painter, etc) found it easier to buy their freedom by working for themselves during their free time.

CHRONOLOGY

1776 Havana: center of operations against the English during the American War of Independence

1791 Slave revolt in Haiti

1808 Spanish war of independence

1760   1770   1780   1790   1800   1810

1762 English occupy Havana

1789 Free trade among black slaves

1791 Haitian French arrive in Cuba

1808 First Cuban conspiracy

SLAVERY AND THE FORMATION OF CUBAN SOCIETY

CUBA, THE WORLD'S LEADING SUGAR PRODUCER

In the last thirty years of the 18th century, following the English occupation of Havana in 1762, Cuban society changed drastically. Havana harbor opened up to direct trade with England and its North American colonies. In 1763, Spain recaptured Havana and launched a program of economic reform to finance the island's defense. A vast number of slaves ● 36 (more than 600,000 between 1763 and 1867) were brought to the island from Africa and immigration soared: around 400,000 Americans and Europeans also arrived. The latter devoted themselves to running small farms, trade and other urban business ventures. Cuba became the leading international sugar producer (in 1827) and exported the best tobacco in the world, as well as precious woods and coffee. Coffee farming, which began in earnest in the 1770s, benefited from the techniques introduced by the French, who arrived in the eastern part of the island after the slave revolt in Haiti in 1791 ▲ 199. Cuba also benefited from steam engines (for the sugar mills ● 50) and the railroad was introduced here even before it reached the Spanish mainland. Existing towns were soon modernized and new ones were quickly founded, such as Cienfuegos ▲ 178, built by French settlers from Louisiana.

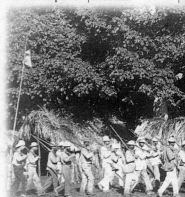

CUBA: INDEPENDENCE OR ANNEXATION?

The political upheavals of the time left their mark on the island. The Creoles actively participated in the American War of Independence. Between 1816 and 1826 the Spanish colonies threw off the yoke of the Spanish mainland. After 1823, Cuba was subject to the *facultades omnímodas* (complete control) of the captain generals, giving rise to a desire for independence. Theories concerning the island's annexation were formulated in the United States, winning support among Creole landowners. From 1860, following the British abolition of the slave trade in 1820 and then the American Civil War (1861–5), slavery declined. In 1867, moves for political and economic reform failed.

BIRTH OF A CUBAN CULTURE

A far-reaching cultural movement emerged at the end of the 18th century. The desire to assert Cuban identity found expression in the works of charismatic figures such as the poet José María de Heredia ▲ 212, Félix Varela, head of the Philosophy department at the Seminario de San Carlos y San Ambrosio ▲ 128, the novelist Cirilo Villaverde and the musician Esteban Salas. *Filosofía Electiva*, by Agustín Caballero, the first Cuban work of philosophy, introduced elements of European ideology into Cuban thinking. As Cuban philosophy developed so too did a flourishing social life. In 1820 Havana had more than thirty dance halls. Black people and mulattos, whether they were free or slaves, played a key role in this development, as can be seen by the success of the black musician Brindis de Salas ● 52, the mulatto painter Vicente Escobar and the mulatto poet Plácido.

1812–26 Spanish colonies in America gain independence except for Cuba and Puerto Rico	1846–8 War between the United States and Mexico	1870-1 Franco-Prussian War. Treaty of Paris		

1815   1870   1890   1900   1902

1823 Cuban separatist conspiracy	1868–78 Ten Years' War	1886 Abolition of slavery	1895–8 War for independence	1899–1902 North American occupation of Cuba

THE WARS FOR INDEPENDENCE

THE TEN YEARS' WAR (1868–78)

From 1867, the Cuba and Antilles Grand Orient Masonic lodges played a vital role in molding Cuban independence groups. On October 10, 1868, at *La Demajagua* ▲ 205, Carlos Manuel de Céspedes freed his slaves and proclaimed independence. The first Assembly of the Republic at arms was convened at Bayamo, and the Cuban national anthem ▲ 204 was sung for the first time. In 1873, an invasion of the western part of the island was planned, but failed. On February 10, 1878, revolutionaries from Central Cuba signed the Pact of Zanjón with the Spanish. General Antonio Maceo (opposite) ▲ 215 and several officers rejected it in the *Protesta de Baraguá* on March 23, 1878. This call to arms ended in failure; Maceo went into exile. The Spanish authorized the first political parties (1878) and abolished slavery in two stages: the law of 1880 which turned slaves into 'apprentices' and the final abolition decree which was passed in 1886.

THE 'MAMBISES'

This Congolese word meaning, according to Fernando Ortíz ● 42, 'despicable, good-for-nothing' referred to those who joined the ranks of the independence movement: major landowners, black or white peasants, former slaves, Chinese from the eastern regions. Their only weapons were their machetes.

AMERICAN OCCUPATION (1899–1902)

During the American occupation at the turn of the 20th century, the island's entire legal and administrative systems were modified: a new Constitution was promulgated in 1901 and the United States Congress imposed the Platt Amendment on Cuba as a condition of independence. This constitutional amendment authorized the United States to intervene in the island's political and military affairs and obliged the latter to allow the installation of military bases on some of its territory (Guantánamo ● 46, ▲ 220).

THE WAR FOR INDEPENDENCE (1895–8)

February 24, 1895, marked the outbreak of the war for independence, organized by the Cuban Revolutionary

Party, led by José Martí ● 40. In April the latter landed on the eastern part of the island with Antonio Maceo and Máximo Gómez (above), but died in battle on May 19. In October Maceo decided to march westward, and he carved out a trail of victories before reaching Mantua in January 1896. The Spanish sent General Valeriano Weyler to Cuba, where he herded the entire peasant population into camps. According to some research, 380,000 prisoners died as a result of starvation, epidemics and the unsanitary conditions. On December 7, 1896, Maceo died in combat. At the end of 1897, in a bid to end the war, Spain granted Cuba its autonomy, but it was rejected by the independence movement, which believed it was on the verge of victory. In February 1898 the American battleship USS *Maine* was blown up in Havana harbor (90 percent of trade at that time was with the United States). This event served as a incentive for the United States to intervene in the Spanish-Cuban war. The Spanish surrendered in July 1898. The Cubans were not invited to the signing of the Treaty of Paris on December 10, 1898, marking the end of Spanish sovereignty in Cuba and the start of an American military government, to administer the country.

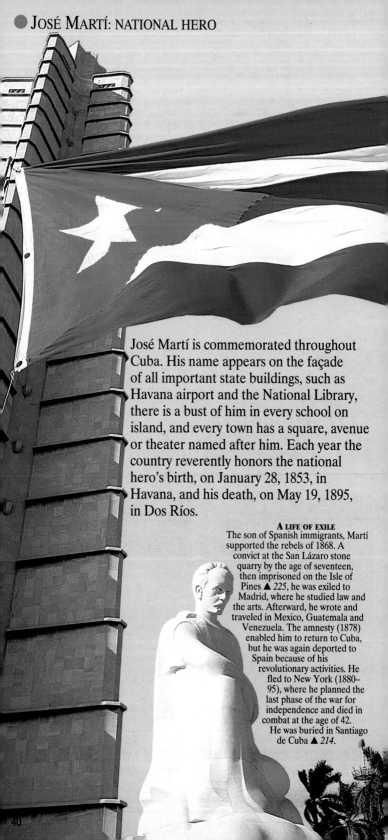

José Martí is commemorated throughout Cuba. His name appears on the façade of all important state buildings, such as Havana airport and the National Library, there is a bust of him in every school on island, and every town has a square, avenue or theater named after him. Each year the country reverently honors the national hero's birth, on January 28, 1853, in Havana, and his death, on May 19, 1895, in Dos Ríos.

A LIFE OF EXILE
The son of Spanish immigrants, Martí supported the rebels of 1868. A convict at the San Lázaro stone quarry by the age of seventeen, then imprisoned on the Isle of Pines ▲ 225, he was exiled to Madrid, where he studied law and the arts. Afterward, he wrote and traveled in Mexico, Guatemala and Venezuela. The amnesty (1878) enabled him to return to Cuba, but he was again deported to Spain because of his revolutionary activities. He fled to New York (1880–95), where he planned the last phase of the war for independence and died in combat at the age of 42.
He was buried in Santiago de Cuba ▲ 214.

> 'Anything that drives a wedge between people, classifies them, isolates them or confines them is a sin against humanity.' 'The Fatherland demands sacrifices. It is an altar not a pedestal.'
>
> José Martí

THE ARCHITECT OF INDEPENDENCE
The founder of the Cuban Revolutionary Party (CRP), Martí applied lessons learned from the Ten Years' War ● *39* and the *Guerra Chiquita* ('Little War') ▲ *207*. He planned the last War of Independence (1895–8), also known as 'Martí's War', but was killed in the first days of fighting.

A PIONEERING WRITER
José Martí left behind a substantial body of poetry (including *Ismaelillo*, *Versos Libres*, *Versos Sencillos*), articles, reviews, speeches, essays and public and private correspondence. Many believe that his energy, touching sincerity, dazzling use of metaphors and rejection of all foreign fashions and models helped pave the way for contemporary Latin American literature.

The preliminaries for the two Havana Declarations, revolutionary manifestos dated 1960 and 1962, and that of the Constitution of 1976 were inspired by the ideas and activities of the spiritual father of the Revolution, José Martí. The poet Nicolás Guillén wrote: 'Fidel has accomplished... what Martí promised'. An even more deeply revered figure than Che or Castro, Martí embodies the spirit of the entire Cuban nation, even for its opponents. His memorial still stands proudly in Havana (left) ▲ *145*.

THE FATHER OF CUBAN DEMOCRACY
Martí lost no time in pointing out the various dangers that American expansionism posed for Latin America. Following in Bolívar's footsteps, he urged all Latin American nations to join forces against these perils. Martí's social awareness and his ideological beliefs, radically opposed to racism, dictatorships, militarism and clericalism, gave birth to the concept of a democratic republic, which was completely unprecedented in this part of the world.

THE FINCA DEL ABRA
House of the Sardá family on the Isle of Pines, where Martí was kept under house arrest before being exiled to Europe.

1910 Mexican Revolution begins

1914–18 World War One

1917 Russian revolution

1902   1905   1910   1915   1920   1925

May 20, 1902 Republic of Cuba established

1906 'Little August War'. Second American occupation of the island

1914–18 Rise in sugar prices

1917 Liberal uprising in Cuba

1925 Start of Gerardo Machado's dictatorship

A CULTURE IN SEARCH OF AN IDENTITY

III Festival de Habaneras

aniversario 469 DEL 10 AL 15 DE NO
1519/1988
de la fundación de la ciudad

During the second half of the 19th century, a large number of Spaniards immigrated to Cuba, particularly from Galicia, the Canaries, Andalusia and Valencia. New technology was brought in to modernize the public utility companies and sugar refineries. Benefit and mutual-aid societies were founded. The number of newspapers and journals increased. Theaters put on seasons of opera and *zarzuela* (Spanish operetta), dances were organized in vast open-air spaces or 'gardens', and music acquired a distinctly Cuban character: the typical band, the *charanga a la francesa* ● 54, incorporated Cuban and African instruments. The invention of the *danzón* ▲ 166 revealed a new feeling and sound. The *habanera* also became a popular genre. During the first years of the 20th century, new rhythmic dances were created: the *son*, *conga*, *rumba* and *bolero* ● 54.

THE FIRST REPUBLIC (1902–33)

POLITICS AND SOCIETY

REBIRTH OF NATIONAL CONSCIOUSNESS
A wide-ranging cultural movement emerged in the 1920s–1930s. The aims of the new generation of artists, intellectuals and politicians were twofold: more extensive political and social reforms and total independence from the United States. Among the intellectuals who initiated this movement, special mention should be made of Ramiro Guerra, Jorge Mañach, Raúl Roa and Fernando Ortíz (1881–1969). Ortíz, an ethnologist, was the first to study the sectors on the fringes of Cuban society and culture, in particular the African influence.

On May 20, 1902, the Republic of Cuba – circumscribed by the Platt Amendment – was proclaimed. Tomás Estrada Palma was elected president. A year later, in 1903, the United States established a new trade agreement: the new Republic had to pay higher prices for American products and export most of its products to the United States. The first years of the century were characterized by extreme political instability and increased government corruption. Conservatives and Liberals vied for power and resorted to electoral fraud, which led, on several occasions, to armed clashes: the 'Little August War' in 1906, after which the Americans occupied the island until 1909, and the *Chambelona* or Liberal uprising of 1917. However, some major democratic advances were made under Liberal president José Miguel Gómez: the separation of the

Church and the State, the civil register (of births, marriages and deaths), the divorce law, free and non-denominational state-run schools, freedom of expression and association. The Cuban economy stagnated after the boom at the end of the 1910s. The country became the fourth-largest investment center of the United States, which controlled industry and agriculture. The recessions of 1921 and 1929 hit the island particularly hard, and Liberal president Gerardo Machado (above), supported by the United States, established a dictatorship (1925–33) to curb any attempt to stir up political unrest. Several important figures took part in

the fight against this regime: Julio Antonio Mella, founder of the Cuban Communist Party in 1925, led the movement for university reform and was assassinated in Mexico in 1929; Rubén Martínez Villena, a poet, was one of the leaders of the Cuban Communist Party. Following a general strike, Machado was overthrown on August 12, 1933. The country was to undergo some major political changes.

1929 Stock market crash in New York: start of the Great Depression	1939-45 World War II				

1930	1935	1940	1945	1950	1952

| | 1933 Gerardo Machado overthrown. First coup by Fulgencio Batista | 1939–45 Declaration of the new Cuban constitution | 1942 Cuba joins forces with the Allies | | March 10, 1952 Second coup by Fulgencio Batista |

THE RESTRUCTURING OF THE REPUBLIC (1933–52)

POLITICS AND SOCIETY

On September 4, 1933, army officers instigated a coup d'état and, joining forces with the student movement (below), overthrew the interim government of Ramón Grau San Martín, who had succeeded Machado. Worried at this turn of events, the United States threatened to send in its troops. But the new leader, Fulgencio Batista (opposite), reassured Cuba's concerned neighbor and held the reins of power as chief of staff of the army until 1940. The far-reaching political and popular movement of 1933 led to new advances: the abolition of the Platt Amendment (1934), women's suffrage (1935), the eight-hour work day (1940), improvement to the road infrastructure and the

pronouncement of a new constitution in 1940. The latter made provision for agrarian reform, the nationalization of natural resources and parliamentary elections. Batista, with support from the United States, eliminated the far right and part of the left and, in 1940, was elected president. Because of popular support, two members of the Cuban Revolutionary Party (the Partido Auténtico), Grau San Martín and Prío Socarrás, were elected in succession, in 1944 and 1948. In 1947, in an attempt to combat administrative and governmental corruption, Eduardo Chibás broke away from the Auténtico Party and created the Cuban

People's Party (known as the Partido Ortodoxo). Shortly before the next elections in 1952, Batista, realizing he had little chance of

beating the candidate from the Ortodoxo Party, organized a new coup d'état, with the assistance of the Cuban military.

1952	1954	1956	1958	1960	1961

1953 Fidel Castro
attacks the
Moncada barracks

November 20, 1954
Elections legalize
Batista's presidency

1959 Castro wins victory.
Agrarian reform. Beginning
of dispute with United States

1961
Literacy campaign. Bay of
Pigs invasion

THE REVOLUTION AGAINST THE DICTATORSHIP (1953–9)

The armed fight against Batista's dictatorship began on July 26, 1953: lawyer Fidel Castro led a group of 160 rebels in an attack on the Moncada barracks at Santiago de Cuba. After the assault failed, Castro was imprisoned on the Isle of Pines (now the Isle of Youth) ▲ 224. Freed in 1955, then

exiled to Mexico, Castro organized the 26th of July Movement and masterminded the expedition aboard the yacht *Granma*, which was joined by Ernesto 'Che' Guevara ▲ 192, an Argentine doctor at the hospital in Mexico. On December 2, 1956,

Castro and eighty-one companions landed in Oriente Province. Decimated by loyalist troops at Alegría de Pío, the group took refuge in the mountain ranges of the Sierra Maestra ▲ 202. From his hideout, Castro launched a guerrilla war against the dictator's army with the active support of a large majority of the Cuban population. The international media also gave him the opportunity to explain his struggle to the world at large. In February 1957, he agreed to meet Herbert Matthews,

a journalist from the *New York Times*. Matthews was the first to introduce the international public to the *Barbudos* (bearded ones) dressed in green combat uniforms and their charismatic leader. The sympathy elicited by his article forced the United States to reduce their support for Batista. In February 1958, Radio Rebelde, the rebel radio station, began to broadcast from La Plata, high in the Sierra Maestra. During the summer of that same year, after thwarting the major offensive by

Batista's army, Castro set up a second eastern front in the Sierra del Cristal, led by his brother Raúl Castro. Then, under the command of Juan Almeida, he set up a third eastern front, east of the Sierra Maestra. Following in the footsteps of Máximo Gómez and Antonio Maceo, he sent men led by Ernesto 'Che' Guevara and Camilo Cienfuegos to conquer the western part of the island. They successfully defeated Batista's troops in several large cities in Las Villas Province. At the end of December 1958, Che Guevara joined battle in the capital of this province, Santa Clara. After the city was captured, Batista and his main collaborators secretly left the country, defeated, on January 1, 1959.

THE FIRST STEPS

On January 1, 1959, a general strike against the militia and the political system inherited from Batista's regime began in response to a call from Castro. On January 2, the rebels entered Havana. On January 7, the Republic's Fundamental Law

was declared. It centralized legislative and executive powers in the hands of the Council of Ministers. A first set of laws was passed, including nationalization of American-owned electricity and telephone companies, reduction of rents, agrarian reform

breaking up the *latifundia* (large estates) and redistributing the land among the peasants, educational reform, and the abolition of racial discrimination. The departure of thousands of opponents handicapped the economic future.

THE ATTACK ON THE PRESIDENTIAL PALACE
On March 13, 1957, students in Havana belonging to the Revolutionary Directorate attempted to capture the Presidential Palace. Thirty-five were killed, including José Antonio Echevarría, the founder of the Directorate in December 1955 and president of the University Students' Federation. The resulting crackdown was severe: the number of raids, tortures and murders escalated in the days that followed.

ESTUDIO - ZAFRA
PASTOREOS - VIANDAS
CUMPLIREMOS

1963 American military intervention in Vietnam escalates

1968 Vatican II council. Soviet invasion of Czechoslovakia.

1973 Coup in Chile and assassination of President Allende

1962   1964   1966   1968   1970   1974

1962 Cuba is suspended from OAS Cuban missile crisis.

1964 Cuba joins the non-aligned countries. The embargo is enforced

1967 Assassination of Che Guevara in Bolivia

1972 Cuba joins Comecon

THE YEARS OF REVOLUTION (1959–74)

CONFLICT AGAINST THE BACKDROP OF THE COLD WAR

The program of reforms, the nationalization of American-owned companies and Cuba's new independence aroused the hostility of the United States. After various attempts at intimidation, a de facto embargo was imposed on Cuba in the fall of 1960. The United States reduced its purchases of Cuban sugar and stopped sales of oil to the island. Cuba then signed a pact with the USSR, which supplied the island with oil and bought part of its sugar stock, thereby guaranteeing its economic survival. The year 1961 saw the launch of the literacy campaign but also the breakdown of diplomatic relations with the United States. The US recalled their ambassador, then landed at the Bay of Pigs ▲ 176. Castro proclaimed that the revolution was socialist in character. In January 1962, the United States suspended Cuba from the OAS (Organization of American States), and enforced restrictive trade sanctions which only Mexico and Canada refused to enforce. The general embargo increased the pressure on the island's struggling economy. In October, the Cuban missile crisis, caused by the installation of Soviet nuclear missiles in Cuba, threatened

THE CDR
Mass organizations played a vital role in the spread of revolutionary ideas. The best known are the Committees for the Defense of the Revolution (CDR), founded in 1960. There is one of these bodies in each block of houses and their activities range from the organization of vaccination programs to elections and civil and political surveillance.

world peace. Their removal without consulting the Cubans humiliated Castro, and cracks started to appear in Cuba's relationship with the USSR. Driven by severe economic difficulties (the

United States embargo was tightened in 1964), *El Comandante* forged closer links with the Russians, even to the point of supporting the Soviet invasion of Czechoslovakia in 1968.

CUBA, A HOTBED OF REVOLUTIONARY ZEAL
From the early 1960s, Cuba was involved in the armed revolts that shook the American continent and Africa, in particular Angola (1975–88). The Tricontinental Conference (which was held January 3–14, 1966) and the summit of non-aligned countries, held in Havana in 1979, confirmed its role as leader. Che Guevara symbolized this revolutionary zeal. In 1965, he left for the Congo to support the battle for liberation. In 1966, he waged guerrilla war in Bolivia. He was captured by the army and murdered on October 9, 1967.

THE VICISSITUDES OF THE ECONOMY

The first ten years of the Revolution were very hard. Cuba endeavored to abandon the sugar monoculture ● 48, but poor management of human resources and technical methods forced it to change course. In 1963, a new agrarian reform allowed the state to take possession of more than two-thirds of the arable land, which was redistributed among the peasants, who formed cooperatives. In 1965, after a lucrative agreement with the USSR, sugar became a priority once more. In 1968, the so-called Great Revolutionary Offensive nationalized some 55,000 companies and prohibited private businesses, further precipitating economic decline. In 1970, the country made a collective effort to obtain a record sugar harvest, which was to finance its expansion. Its failure (8.5 million tons were harvested instead of the expected 10 million tons) resulted in recession. Two years later, Cuba joined the economic community of socialist countries, Comecon (Council for Mutual Economic Assistance). Cuba remains, however, an influential member of the non-aligned movement.

● CHRONOLOGY

1989 Fall of the Berlin Wall. American invasion of Panama

1992 The Torricelli Act tightens the American blockade

1996 Helms-Burton law (United States)

1975	1980	1985	1990	1995	2000

1975 Cuban troops in Angola

1976 Third Constitution

1988 Retreat of Cuban troops from Angola

1991 Start of the 'special period'

1995 Start of economic reforms

1997 Che's body brought back to Cuba

1998 Visit by the Pope

THE YEARS OF REVOLUTION: 1975–99

THE PROCESS OF INSTITUTIONALIZATION

THE MARIEL EXODUS

In April 1980, the Carter administration finally promised to grant asylum to all Cuban refugees and hundreds of would-be emigrants sought shelter in the Peruvian embassy. Castro allowed anyone to leave who wanted, including the mentally ill and common criminals. In the following months, more than 120,000 *marielitos* set sail for Miami from Mariel.

In 1975, the First Congress of the Cuban Communist Party (which was re-formed in 1965) supported the institutionalization process. The latter led to the first 'socialist constitution'. Proclaimed in 1976, after a referendum, it replaced the Fundamental Law of 1959 and ratified the achievements of the Revolution. For the first time since 1959 Cuba had a parliament, the National Assembly of People's Power, which elected the first Council of State, the collegial body governing the country. From this time Castro was to hold concurrently the positions of president of the Council of State and the Council of Ministers, first secretary of the CCP and head of the army.

THE 1980S

A new wave of emigration hit the island: in 1980, thousands of Cubans arrived in Miami via the port of Mariel. In 1986, *perestroika* was instituted in the USSR. In Cuba, the so-called program of 'Rectification' was already underway. Promoting a greater degree of openness and decentralization, it resulted in a vast anti-corruption campaign in 1989. This targeted all sectors of society and ended in the contested trial of General Arnaldo Ochoa Sánchez, sentenced to death for corruption and drug trafficking.

THE 'SPECIAL PERIOD'

In 1991, after the USSR and the Soviet bloc were dissolved, the island lost four-fifths of its market outlets. Castro then announced a program of austerity measures for a 'special period' of five years. It was a time of scarcity: oil, electricity, public transport and agriculture suffered. The state took various steps. The island set its sights on tourism, which generated a high revenue. In 1994, possession of the dollar was legalized. The *agromercados* (farmers' markets intended for private sales) were reopened. Private enterprise was permitted and controlled by taxation on dollar profits. In August 1994, following rioting in Havana, Castro allowed nearly 35,000 *balseros* to leave the island on board makeshift rafts (or *balsas*, hence their name) ▲ 220. In 1996, a new period of growth began. The mixed economy flourished, despite the Helms-Burton law. Voted by the US Congress, this threatened to impose sanctions on all Third World countries trading with Cuba and provoked an international outcry. On October 8, 1997, the mortal remains of Che ▲ 192 were brought back to Cuba amid great popular excitement. The following year, Pope John Paul II visited Cuba in February. This visit eased relations with the Catholic Church and proved to be an excellent public relations exercise. In 1999, faced with the rise in juvenile delinquency and political disputes, the central government cracked down on crimes likely to undermine the economy and national independence.

GUANTÁNAMO NAVAL BASE ▲ 220

The Guantánamo Naval Base served as a look-out post for the entire Caribbean. The government would like this area, given in 1903 to the Americans, to revert to Cuban ownership. This could happen as soon as 2002: as the length of the lease was not specified in the transfer contract, it could automatically expire after 99 years.

Art and traditions

Sugarcane (*Saccharum officinarum*) was first introduced to Cuba in 1512 by the Spanish colonizers. Cuban sugar production began to increase in the late 16th century and was given a further boost, two centuries later, by the collapse of the Haitian sugar industry. In the 19th century, unused land favorable to the cultivation of sugarcane, the use of innovative new technology and the construction of the railroad all helped to make the Cuban sugar industry the undisputed market leader in the Caribbean. Cuba currently has 156 sugar mills and remains one of the leading sugar exporters in the world.

THE 'MACHETEROS'
The men who cut down the sugarcane use a *machete* and are thus known as *macheteros*. These workers are extremely efficient: one *machetero* can cut down as many as 400 *arrobas* per day, the equivalent of 4.5 tons of sugarcane. They are financially rewarded if they bring in a better harvest than the year before.

SUGAR BYPRODUCTS
Various useful and ecologically friendly products are generated when the sugarcane is processed. These include *bagasse* or cane trash, a fibrous waste matter used as fuel or turned into paper pulp, cattle feed and chipboard; molasses, a syrupy liquid with a 50 percent sugar content; evaporation scum, used as a soil nutrient; and *vinasse*, a liquid waste that can be spread back over the fields as manure.

SUGARCANE
Sugarcane is most successfully grown in tropical and subtropical areas. It is a giant, hardy grass which looks something like a reed. The sugarcane's stem, formed from a series of nodes and internodes, is the productive part of the plant where the sucrose is stored, making up some 10 to 18 percent of the total plant.

FROM PLANTING TO HARVESTING

1. PLANTING

Planting begins by laying seedlings measuring 12 to 16 inches long with 3 or 4 nodes in furrows at a distance of 12 to 16 inches apart, and covered with a thin layer of moist soil. Between 3 and 8 tons of seedlings are needed for approximately 2.5 acres.

2. GROWTH

In early growth, buds appear on the seedling and sprout primary stems. Secondary and tertiary stems appear as the plant sprouts suckers. The clump of cane formed in this way will have between

5 and 20 stalks when mature. The buds on each stalk then produce a series of nodes and internodes and this is how the sugarcane grows.

3. MATURITY

Mature sugarcane stalks reach heights of between 6 to 16 feet and measure between ½ an inch to 2 inches in diameter. In some plant varieties, the cane will flower before maturity is reached, while sucrose accumulates in the stem.

4. BURNING THE FIELDS

This widespread practice, which burns off the long, sharp, sword-shaped leaves of the plant, helps to make the *macheteros'* work easier.

5. HARVESTING

Harvesting (*zafra*) takes place from the end of December to June, 11 to 18 months after planting, or one year after the previous harvest if the sugarcane has been allowed to regrow (if the cane is not pulled up, it grows back again naturally). Harvesting these days is generally carried out by machine in the plains but it is still done manually in the valleys. There are three stages: cutting the stalk as close as possible to the ground, because its lower sections are the richest in sugar; cutting the leafy top of the stalk, which encourages the sucrose to crystallize; and finally, stripping the stalk, which involves removing all the dry leaves attached to it. The canes must be transported as quickly as possible, because as soon as they are cut the sucrose begins to decompose, a process that is further speeded up by the heat of the Caribbean climate.

PROCESSING THE SUGARCANE: MAKING SUGAR AND RUM

The first implements used in the 16th century to extract sugarcane juice (*guarapo*) were *trapiches* (mills), driven by horses, oxen or slaves.

Hydraulic energy, twice as powerful, began to be used shortly after in the *ingenios* (sugar mills), which numbered 120 in 1760. In 1838, the first steam-powered machines led to a substantial increase in the sugar mills' production and performance. As a result, two separate sectors were created, dividing agricultural and industrial activities. Growth of the industry also coined new words, such as *central* (giant sugar mill) and *colono* (sugarcane farmer). By the time the Spanish parliament outlawed slavery in Cuba in 1880 – it was one of the last countries where it disappeared, in 1886 – industrialization had already relieved the slaves of many of their tasks.

SUGAR PRODUCTION

There are several steps in the extraction of sucrose from the sap of the sugarcane:

1. The sugarcane is delivered to the sugar mill yard, having been weighed and cleaned beforehand.

2. The cane is shredded into a homogenous mass. It is then put through roller mills where it is crushed and forced against a countercurrent of water, a process known as 'imbibition'.

3. The juice produced by the crushing process is purified or clarified by filtering and the addition of chemicals.

4. Evaporation removes 75 percent of the juice's water, transforming it into a brown syrup.

5. The syrup is heated in earthenware cauldrons, initiating the crystallization process.

6. The heated mass is dried in centrifugal baskets, producing sucrose crystals. A ton of sugarcane produces around 220 pounds of sucrose.

The Bacardí family ▲ *212* was responsible for the fame of Cuban *ron* (rum). The latter is now marketed under the name Havana Club ● *66*.

Rum production: the distillery

Rum is produced in several stages:

1. Fermentation is a natural phenomenon during which time the yeasts, present in the raw material, transform the sucrose and other fermentable sugars into ethanol.

2. Distillation involves separating out the pleasant aromas and flavors and eliminating them from the less pleasant tastes found in the fermented mixture. This was originally done by alembics (old distilling apparatus) but these were replaced by distillation columns in the 19th century.

3. During the maturing or aging process, which can last several weeks or even several years, the unprocessed distillate acquires a distinctive flavor as a result of the various slow-acting chemical reactions. The coloration of the distillates is the most spectacular stage of the process.

4. The final stage in rum production is dilution, which reduces the rum to commercial strength. It is then bottled and ready for drinking.

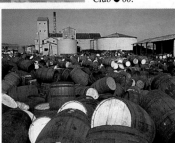

A sugar mill in the 19th century

'When operating, the sugar mill is a hive of activity. It echoes with shouts, everything denotes movement. Here handcarts are unloading sugarcane, there machines are working, snorting noisily from time to time, emitting a shrill whistle; the smoke of the furnaces, carried by the wind, mingles black spirals with the white vapors escaping from the cauldrons.'
Régis de Torbriand, 1853

Music has been an integral part of life in Cuba from the colony's early days. Churches and brass bands were the first 'schools of music' where the Cubans learned European instruments and singing techniques. From the mid 19th century, classically trained composers used the instruments and rhythmic patterns of popular musical genres and created a more serious and distinctive Cuban sound.

Cuban musical theater adapted the extremely popular Spanish *zarzuela* (operetta) into its own entertainment by introducing typical characters from Cuban society. In the early 20th century, Cuba's African heritage influenced the harmonic innovations used in classical music and vocalists achieved much success with songs of African origin. However, for financial reasons, many instrumentalists were forced to perform in symphony orchestras as well as dance bands.

IGNACIO CERVANTES
(1847–1905)
The pianist and composer Cervantes wrote *danzas* for piano based on Creole quadrille rhythms, thereby continuing the work of Manue Saumell (1817–70), described by Carpentier ● *109* as the 'father of the Cuban quadrille'. Amadeo Roldán (1900–39) went a step further by incorporating Afro-Cuban themes and instruments, which had only been used in dance music, into the symphonic orchestra.

HABANERA

DE LA ZARZUELA

"EXPOSICION"
o
EL SUBMARINO

POR

I. Cervantes.

EDITORES

OBISPO 127   HABANA
ES PROPIEDAD

BRINDIS DE SALAS
(*below*)
Brindis de Salas (1852–1911) was a Cuban violin virtuoso, nicknamed the 'Black Paganini'. He won first prize at the Paris Conservatoire and was appointed chamber musician to the court of William II. Showered with honors in his early career, he ended his days in poverty and died in Buenos Aires.

COMIC THEATER
A Cuban-style musical theater emerged in the late 18th century and became a popular form of entertainment. Sketches and satirical songs (*tonadillas*) were also sandwiched between acts in the European music hall tradition. The genre was peopled with stereotypical peasants (*left*), mulattos and black people playing everyday musical instruments. However the popularity of the satirical *guaracha*, full of sexual and political innuendo, and the *guajira*, depicting rural life, waned at the end of the 19th century and merged with the street song.

THE 'HABANERA'
A type of song with piano accompaniment, the *habanera* first appeared in 1841 in Havana and soon became popular in Mexico and Spain. The *Souvenirs de Cuba*, a *habanera* composed by Cervantes for his operetta, became a huge success.

ERNESTO LECUONA
(1896–1963)
Lecuona was a brilliant classical pianist who was widely admired by his contemporaries, including Ravel and Gershwin. He was received rapturously in Paris in 1928 and went on to give concerts all over the world. Lecuona composed many semi-classical pieces which were clearly Afro-Cuban in inspiration (*La Comparsa*, *Danzas Afro-Cubanas*), as well as songs (*Siboney*). He also composed specifically Cuban operas, including *El Cafetal*, whose heroine was called Africa, *María La O*, taken from the name of a famous mulatto woman and, with the collaboration of Eliseo Grenet, *Nina Rita o La Habana en 1830* in which Rita Montaner (1900–58) sang *Mamá Inés*. Rita was, along with Esther Borja, one of the composer's favorite sopranos: both also had very successful careers as singers of popular music. In Paris in 1928, during Josephine Baker's heyday and at the height of the craze for black artists, Rita was a triumph at the Palace Theater with her Afro songs and the *Manisero* by Moisés Simons. On her return to Cuba, Rita hired Ignacio Villa, a compatriot from Guanabacoa, as her pianist and singer. His dark skin earned him the affectionate nickname of *Bola de Nieve* (Snowball) and his voice was regarded as a musical phenomenon. The pair were hugely successful in Paris in 1953 (*above*).

LECUONA'S CUBAN BOYS
This jazz-style dance band (*below*), founded by Ernesto Lecuona in 1931, was an 'ambassador' in Europe of tropical dance rhythms.

The Cuban melting pot combines music from the Spanish provinces with rhythms introduced by Africans brought over as slaves. The tradition of poetry in song has not only found expression in the *punto guajiro* of the peasants of western and central Cuba and in the traditional *trova* of the east, but also in the *rumba*, sung and danced in the poverty-stricken, overcrowded districts of Havana and Matanzas. The *danzón* (1879), an instrumental genre, was all the rage until the 1920s. It derived from the Creole version of the quadrille, popular in the French courts and salons at the time of the early days of the colony. It then developed under the influence of the *son*, which was to embody the very soul of Cuba.

THE 'PUNTO GUAJIRO'

This musical genre developed in western and central Cuba. Its history is linked to the early tobacco plantations which were mainly farmed by immigrants from the Canary Islands. At popular festivals (the *guateque* ▲ 152) a singer (*repentista*) would improvize on a given theme in octosyllabic ten-line stanzas (*décimas*), accompanied by a lute (*above*), a guitar and a Cuban *tres* (guitar with three sets of double strings). The music clearly revealed African influences.

'DANZÓN' BANDS

Criticized initially for being indecorous, the *danzón* ▲ 166 was the first dance performed by a closely linked couple. It was played by bands (*orquesta típica*) predominantly comprised of brass instruments, as well as violins, clarinets, double bass, drums and *güiro*. At the turn of the 20th century the *charangas a la francesca* emerged: these bands substituted piano and flute for brass and the Creole *paila* replaced the drums. The use of a *tumbadora* (tall drum), singers and rhythms inspired by the *son* gave the

soul.' Ignacio Piñeira

The Trio Matamoros in 1928 (*right*): Miguel Matamoros, Rafael Cueto and Siro Rodríguez (two guitars, *maracas*, claves and three-part harmony).

THE TRADITIONAL 'TROVA' ('VIEJA TROVA')

Santiago de Cuba is the birthplace of the *trovadores*, writers-composers-performers of a popular style of poetry in song that appeared at the end of the 19th century. These self-taught troubadours accompanied themselves on the guitar as they sang of their joy and sorrow in verse. Subtlety, sensitivity and simplicity of expression explain the huge popularity enjoyed in Europe today by the Cuarteto Patria, Compay Segundo or the performers at the Casa de la Trova in Santiago ▲ 209. Pepe Sánchez (1856–1918) is famous for composing the first *bolero* (1883) and the *trova* was to influence the *son*: the Trio Matamoros is the best example of the genre.

THE 'SON'

Hailing from the mountains of Oriente ▲ 205, the *son* was to have a profound impact on Cuba's dance music. The vocal part alternated the soloist's improvization with the chorus' refrain. The *tres*, *bongós* and *marímbula*, an instrument of Bantu origin played by plucking its metal tongues (*bongós* on top of a *marímbula*, *above*), were accompanied by the guitar, claves and *maracas*: the *Sexteto Habanero* (1919) included all these instruments. Over the years the *son* has evolved: trumpets (*Septeto*) and piano were added and the vocals sung by several singers. The *son* can be played in many rhythms.

THE RUMBA

If the traditional *tumbadoras* are not available, the *rumba* can be played with any percussion instrument. The solo vocalist begins a wordless melody, then develops his theme in *décimas* while the chorus replies, often in several voices. There are three styles of rumba, *yambú*, *columbia* and *guaguancó*, the last two of which are still played. In the *columbia* a male dancer stands alone in front of the drum (*quinto*). The erotic *guaguancó* mimes the man's possession of the woman.

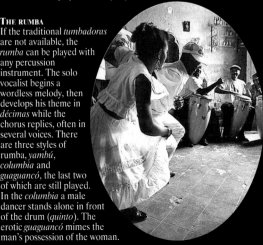

danzón a more modern sound. In 1960, the Estellas Cubanas *charanga* orchestra (*above*) was founded by Félix Reina (*far left*). From left to right are the violins, *tumbadora*, flute, *paila*, *güiro*, double bass, singers and, in the center, pianist Raúl Valdés.

The development of the record, radio and film industry meant that Cuban music was now exported around the world and thus continually evolved. Old and new rhythms gained international appeal, such as the *cha-cha-chá* and jazz and the beat of American music merged with the basic Cuban beat. The trade embargo of the 1960s then put a stop to commercial expansion. Young people in Cuba identified as much with the songs of the Nueva Trova as rock music. They embraced a new style of dance music which incorporated modern technology with elements of ritual music, traditional rhythms or those derived from other sources, such as rock, funk and rap.

BENNY MORÉ (1919–63)
This popular singer (*left*), nicknamed the 'Wild Man of Rhythm', was a self-taught musician. In 1953, on his return from Mexico where he worked with Pérez Prado, he founded a jazz band, the Banda Gigante, with whom he created some memorable hits.

LOS VAN VAN

Founded in 1969 by the bassist Juan Formell, Los Van Van (*below*) gave dance music a new lease of life with the *songo* and its use of brass and strings. Very popular with Cubans of all ages, the band has created a distinctive style whose success has much to do with its charismatic vocalists and often witty lyrics that provide a hard-hitting social commentary on Cuba.

'TIMBA' OR 'SALSA'?

Young Cubans generally prefer the name *timba* to the expression *salsa cubana*, because it distinguishes it more clearly from the *salsa*, which is not Cuban in origin. The *timba* is also accompanied by a less structured, very erotic dance.

NG LA BANDA

The symbol of a new, slightly rebellious generation, this band of performers (*above*), conducted by J-L. Cortés, was founded in 1988. Young Cubans rave about the group, which tackles subjects such as religion and racism and mixes rap with Cuban music.

MAMBO

The term refers to a section of the *danzón*. Pérez Prado, a Cuban pianist who emigrated to Mexico, used it to describe his own syncopated rhythm, which was all the rage with dancers during the 1950s.

● POPULAR CULTS OF AFRICAN ORIGIN
SANTERÍA

The *Regla de Ocha Ifá*, known as *santería*, the *Reglas de Palo* and the Abakuá secret society are the most widespread cults of African origin in Cuba. Brought over by Africans imported as slaves, these beliefs provided them with a spiritual refuge, giving them the strength to deal with being uprooted from their homes. Each cult pays tribute to their ancestors, but does not exclude other types of worship, including Catholicism. *Santería* is a polytheistic religion whose divine beings or *orishas* are deified ancestors. The *santeros* (believers) call on them to solve their everyday problems.

THE YORUBA PANTHEON

This once large 'family' of *orishas* has been reconstructed from the memories gathered together by slaves from the kingdoms of Dahomey, Togo and the Yoruba region of Nigeria. Only powerful symbolic deities have been retained. This non-hierarchical family all form an integral part of Olofi, the supreme being, who is believed to govern the universe and everything within it.

'ORISHAS' AND CATHOLIC SAINTS: COMPROMISE OR CONCILIATION?

During the colonial period, the slaves, who had been converted to Christianity, took advantage of public holidays dedicated to Catholic saints to celebrate their *orishas*. As a result, a relationship developed between the two. The *santeros* go to pay homage to the saints at masses and parades: the Virgen de Regla ▲ 147, Yemayá (*below*), the Virgen de la Caridad del Cobre ● 33, ▲ 218 and Ochún are honored on September 8.

THE MAIN 'ORISHAS'

Each deity has specific attributes. CHANGÓ (*above, right*), lord of thunder, lightning and drums, symbolizes virility. Dressed in red and white, he holds a scepter topped with a double-headed axe, similar to his head-dress. His Catholic equivalent is Santa Bárbara. YEMAYÁ is the emblem of the nurturing sea and motherhood. She wears blue and white (*above*). OCHÚN personifies fresh water, femininity and love. Her color is yellow. ELEGUÁ (*head, above right*), is guardian of the gate and the crossroads and lord of the future. His colors are red and black; he corresponds to Saint Anthony of Padua. OBBATALÁ symbolizes creation, peace and harmony. Dressed in white from head to toe, he is associated with the Virgen de la Merced (Virgin of Mercy). Garbed in violet, BABALÚ AYÉ is god of illness and healing, similar to Saint Lazarus. OGGÚN, lord of metals, personifies the different stages of life development. His colors are green and black and is associated with Saint Peter. The *patakies* recount the life story of the *orishas*. Each deity, often related to each other, appears in about twelve of these stories, but few of them are known by believers.

The Oracles

Santeros use divination to solve everyday problems, particularly those linked to health. In the case of straightforward questions, they themselves can interpret the *oddún* (prophecies) from the simplest oracle, the *obi*, which is read with four pieces of dried coconut shell. Occasionally, the *obi* will send them to consult two other oracles: the *diloggún*, composed of sixteen *oddún*, interpreted with a collection of shells, and the *Ifá*, the principal and most complex oracle in *santería*. In this case, Orula, god of knowledge and divination, speaks through the picture of the *Ifá* or the chain of the *ekuelé* and his words are conveyed by the *babalawo* (priest). He is the only human being authorized to interpret this oracle. When they leave the *babalawo's* house, *santeros* pay a fee of several pesos.

This represents a pact of mutual respect, veneration and obedience between the guardian *orisha* and a believer. Before the seven-day ceremony, the believer receives the warrior

Initiation

orishas, including Oggún, Ochosí, the bowman, (*below left*) and Eleguá, who offer him protection. After the sacrifice of an animal corresponding to the believer's *orisha*, he receives, behind closed doors, the attributes of his saint (such as jewelry and

stones). Then the initiate (*yabo*) puts on ceremonial attire and his family and friends pay their respects. After consulting the oracle, the *babalawo* lays down a life path of conduct for him; for a year, the *yabo* (*above*) must wear only white.

The 'Canastillero'

The *canastillero* is a piece of furniture (*below*) on which the *santero* keeps dishes of attributes that symbolize the power of the *orishas*. The *santero* usually has five dishes, arranged in a hierarchical order: one dedicated to the *orisha* he or she received and four others: Obbatalá, Yemayá, Ochún and Changó. The believer places various offerings of flowers, fruit and occasionally animals, depending on the choice of oracle, on his *canastillero*.

● POPULAR CULTS OF AFRICAN ORIGIN
THE *REGLAS DE PALO* AND THE ABAKUÁ SECRET SOCIETY

The *Reglas de Palo* were originally observed by slaves from the kingdom of Manicongo, a territory that was made up of part of modern Zaïre, the Republic of the Congo and northern Angola. They are known as *mayombe*, *brillumba*, *chamalongo* and *kimbisa*. Of the last three, which have assimilated elements of spiritualism or of other cults (such as *santería*, for example), *kimbisa* is the most distinctly fused with other forms of Christianity. The Abakuá secret society was imported to Cuba by the communities from Calabar, who had originally settled in southeast Nigeria. Its members (*ñáñigos*) were all male because the slaves were often warriors or hunters by origin. The spiritual basis of this hermetic brotherhood differed from the popular religiosity of the *Reglas de Palo* and *santería*: it was a monotheistic cult with a strict moral code.

THE BASIS OF THE 'REGLAS DE PALO'

The spiritual life of the *palero* revolves around the *nganga*, which combines, in an indivisible whole, the life force of the human being, alive or dead, and that of nature. The belief is based on the power of the dead person's protective energy, which can be used to achieve any goal. The *nganga* (below) which takes the form of a receptacle, such as a gourd or a cauldron, contains the bones of a dead man (*nfumbe*) and the following elements taken from the natural world: water and earth gathered from different places, stones, grass, picks, claws, nails and the bones of various animals. Together these items form a type of microcosm.

'KIMBISA': THE FUSION OF SEVERAL CULTS

Kimbisa, which originated in Havana, was founded in the 19th century by the mulatto Andrés Petit, who was a member of the order of Saint Francis as well as being a spiritualist, *palero* and *santero* ● 58. Petit merged the different concepts and rites of these African religions because he believed that following several cults at the same time made him more pious. Petit, who also belonged to the Abakuá secret society, allowed the initiation of the first group of white people in 1863, at Guanabacoa ▲ 147. Most followers of *kimbisa* now are *santeros*, *paleros* and often spiritualists, and are today led by the Frenchman Alan Kardec.

THE FOUNDING MYTH OF THE ABAKUÁ SECRET SOCIETY: THE 'SIKANEKUE'

According to the legend of the peoples of Calabar, Princess Sikán went one day to fetch water from the river and unintentionally caught in her pitcher the sacred fish, Tanze, who was the mouthpiece for the supreme god, Abasí. On Tanze's death, the witch doctor and the men of Sikán's tribe decided to sacrifice the princess and use her skin to make a sacred drum, the first *ekwé*, so that the god had a new means of expressing himself. Even today, the sacred voice can only be heard in the secret room of the Famba, and only the *ekobios*, the initiates, are admitted. The *ekwé* must remain out of sight at all times.

> 'Serge Diaghilev could never have dreamed up a ballet so complete, so functional yet so decorative and so perfect.'
> Alejo Carpentier, speaking about Abakuá ceremonies

THE ABAKUÁ TRADITION OF MUTUAL AID

Abakuá societies operated as mutual aid associations, particularly for buying slaves' freedom. They are still committed to social justice: although many of the members frequented Masonic lodges and participated in the wars for independence ● *39*, afterward they often gave direct support to the revolution. In 1902, they were used as scapegoats during the trade union disputes in the harbors of Havana, Matanzas and Cárdenas. Even today, members of the Abakuá feel it is their duty to provide their brothers with moral and financial aid.

ABAKUÁ CEREMONIES

Diabolitos or *iremes* (*left* and *above*), representations of the spirits of the ancestors, appear in the open-air sacred enclosure. They do not sing but they dance to the rhythm of the *enkríkamo* drum. Their gestures and colors of their costume – a fully hooded hessian outfit decorated with geometric patterns and fringed at the cuffs and ankles – indicate their social position and the type of ceremony (such as initiatory or funerary).

THE 'ENKRÍKAMO' DRUM

As well as the sacred *ekwé* drum, four other small drums are used in Abakuá rituals. The *enkríkamo* drum (*above*) is topped with three bunches of cock's feathers (collection in the museum at Guanabacoa ● *147*).

Despite the levels of austerity linked, since 1991, to the island's economic problems, the carnivals in Havana and Santiago are major events in Cuba's festive calendar. During the colonial period, Epiphany was the only time that slaves belonging to *cabildos de nación* (ethnic brotherhoods) were allowed out during the day with their costumes, masks and drums. This parade, banned in 1884, was authorized again after the abolition of slavery, in the form of *comparsas*. These processions of musicians, singers and dancers each represent their neighborhood. Every year they choose a theme which they carefully orchestrate, choreograph and decorate, enabling each area to be identified.

THE CARNIVAL PARADE
The *comparsas* follow a strict order: standard-bearers and people carrying *farolas* (giant lanterns), dancers and singers, then musicians playing the *conga*. The band is composed of drums, metal percussion instruments (*cencerro*, square bell and *llantas*, truck wheels) and brass (trumpets, trombones and saxophones).

TRADITIONAL HAVANA 'COMPARSAS'
Created in 1908 in the Jesús María district (Cerro), the El Alacrán *comparsa* (the Scorpion) stages the massacre of the scorpion after the death of the grass snake, a story dating from the time of the old *cabildos*. The masks portray village people or typical characters. The Los Marqueses *comparsa*, founded in 1937 in the Ataré district, portrays the aristocracy during the colonial period. The La Jardinera *comparsa*, created in 1940 in the Jesús del Monte district, takes garden art as its theme (*below*). The Los Guaracheros *comparsa*, in Regla ▲ *147*, represents *guaracha* players ● *52*.

SANTIAGO CARNIVAL

This carnival, famous during the 1930s to the 1960s (*far left*), is derived from the *fiestas de mamarrachos* or *máscaras* (masquerades), held toward the end of the 17th century in honor of Saint James (Santiago), the city's patron saint. Festivities last for three days from around July 26. The carnival is famous for its *congas* which lead an ever-growing throng through the city's streets. More recently, the *paseos* have played popular hits of the year.

THE LOS HOYOS 'COMPARSA'

Created in a working-class district of western Santiago, this is Cuba's most famous *comparsa*. Its director, Sebastián Herrera, known as 'Chan' (*above*), remains keen to pass on the traditions of this legendary group.

DRUMS

The most common type of drum is the *bocúe*, shaped like a flattened cone and fairly tall. There are three sorts, each producing a different sound: the *fondo*, the *requinto* and the *quinto*. The *galleta* has a narrow frame and the wider *pilón* provides the basic beat.

THE 'CORNETA CHINA'

Descended from the Chinese immigrant communities of the 19th century, this instrument (*left*) with its whiny timbre symbolizes Santiago's carnival. Its melody starts the *conga* and the *comparsa*.

THE CABILDO CARABALÍ OLUGO

Derived from the *cabildos de nación* which grouped together slaves from former Calabar ● 60, the Cabildo Carabalí Olugo (*below*) was created at the end of the 19th century. The *comparsa* of this secret society, which also operates as a mutual aid society, can be seen at the carnival.

● 'MONTUNA' CHICKEN

Pork and poultry are widely eaten throughout Cuba. Both meats are usually served with an accompaniment of beans and peas, an ancient legacy from Spain, as well as root vegetables. Rice, a popular accompaniment to any meal, is often served with black beans: this is a customary dish in Cuba, nicknamed *moros y cristianos* (Moors and Christians) because of the contrast between the black and white colors. Rice served with kidney beans is another typical example of Cuban cuisine. 'Montuna' chicken is a traditional country recipe that remains popular all over the island.

Ingredients
- one chicken (2.2 lb)
- 3 onions
- 8 cloves of garlic
- ginger
- lard or chicken fat
- a tablespoon of vinegar
- a tablespoon of flour
- basil and parsley
- salt and pepper
- sugarcane syrup (*guarapo*) or, if not available, sweet white wine

Ingredients for garnish:
- 2 green plantain bananas
- 1 lb of yams
- 4 potatoes
- 1 lb of taros (or *malangas*)
- white rice

Ingredients for the Creole sauce (*mojo*)
- 7 fl oz of oil
- diced bacon
- 10 cloves of garlic
- 1 Seville orange (or one orange and one lime)

1. Cut the chicken into pieces and place at the bottom of a casserole. Add salt and pepper.

2. Slice the three onions finely.

3. Crush the eight cloves of garlic with a little ginger. Add chopped parsley and basil.

4. Cover the pieces of chicken with the mixture of onions, garlic, parsley and basil; add a little lard or chicken fat and a tablespoon of vinegar. Cover and cook over a low heat.

5. When the pieces of chicken are golden brown, take them out of the casserole and thicken the sauce with a tablespoon of flour.

6. Put the chicken pieces back in the casserole and add a little sugarcane syrup or white wine. Continue to cook over a low heat until the flesh is falling off the bones.

7. Peel and cut the taros, potatoes, yams and green plantain bananas into large chunks. Cook in salted water in separate saucepans. When cooked, pour them all into one large salad bowl.

8. To prepare the Creole sauce or *mojo*, brown the diced bacon in oil followed by the ten crushed cloves of garlic. Stir well with a spatula; be careful not to let the garlic burn. Pour over the root vegetables.

9. Combine the glaze from the still hot pan with the juice of a Seville orange (or the juice of an orange and lime mixed together). Pour the liquid over the root vegetables.

10. Serve with white rice.

● CIGARS AND RUM

CIGARS FOR ALL TASTES

There are cigars for all tastes and (almost) all pockets. You can choose between a mild morning robusto (Epicure N° 2 from Hoyo de Monterrey), a more highly flavored corona gorda (Exhibition N° 3 from Romeo y Julieta) or a strong, fragrant double corona, such as the Prominente, produced by the San Luis Rey label. They are best smoked while enjoying a glass of rum or fortified wine. There are many imitations of these cigars, so it is best to buy them from factory shops such as Partagás and La Corona. Americans still cannot import these cigars.

CUBA, HOME OF THE COCKTAIL

The Club des Cantineros de Cuba, a school that awards diplomas for 'Master Cocktail Makers', was founded as early as 1914. But the golden age of the Cuban cocktail was the 1920s: many barmen from Paris, the Canary Islands and the United States (then at the height of Prohibition) learned their trade in Havana. The famous Cuban barman, Constante, an authority on cocktails based at the *Floridita*, invented the frozen daiquiri as well as Hemingway's Special for the writer *(below)*.

Cuban *ron* is appreciated for its sweet, delicate, dry, slightly spicy flavor and its translucent appearance.

TWO TYPES OF RUM

The Carta Blanca (white label) is used as the base for cocktails such as the Mojito, daiquiri and Cuba Libre. The Carta Oro (gold label) is a rum which has been aged for three, five or seven years and is enjoyed like a cognac.

'MOJITO': half a spoonful of sugar, the juice of half a lime, several mint leaves. Mix, then add ice, two centiliters of rum and sparkling water in a tall glass.

DAIQUIRI: four centiliters of white rum, two centiliters of lime juice. Mix with crushed ice. Garnish with a slice of lime.

HEMINGWAY'S SPECIAL: two centiliters of rum, a spoonful of grapefruit juice, the juice of half a lime, a spoonful of maraschino and crushed ice. Mix.

Tobacco
Jean-Claude Ribaut

● TOBACCO FARMING

The wrapper (*right*) is the leaf that envelops the Havana,
the part of the cigar that can be seen; it is wrapped around
the filler, a distinctive blend of leaves whose secret is
guarded closely by the different factories.

Two varieties of tobacco are grown in the
five tobacco-producing regions of Vuelta
Abajo, Semi Vuelta, Partido, Remedios
and Oriente. The *corojo* is generally used
for wrapper leaves, which range from
light (*claras*) to dark (*coloradas*). There
are six choices of leaves on the plant
and their respective positions
determine the order in which
harvesting is carried out. The *criollo*
provides the filler leaves: four of the
five leaves used to fill most
Havana cigars.

PLANTING
Tobacco is a winter
plant: from October
to January, the
planters (*vegueros*)
sow seedlings
obtained from the
nursery; they grow to
their ideal height in
about forty-five days.

GROWING WRAPPERS UNDER 'TAPADOS'
To protect the wrapper leaves from sunshine
and insects, the *corojo* plants are grown under
fine sheets of cotton fabric (*tapados*). This
encourages the wrapper leaves to become
soft, smooth and pliable.

THE HARVEST
Harvesting lasts from
January to the end of
March. The lowest
leaves (*libres de pie*)

are gathered first,
two by two, using a
machete; a week
later, the two leaves
just above them (*uno*

y medio) are
gathered, and so on,
until the top leaf of
the plant (*corona*) is
harvested last.

Centro gordo

Corona

Centro fino

Centro ligero

Uno y medio

Libre de pie

THE PLANT AND ITS SEEDS
Nicotania tabacum was discovered at the same time as America. It is a member of the Solanaceae family, as is the potato. The seed (*above*) is planted in a sand and ashes mix and replanted after forty-five days' irrigation.

DRYING
All leaves are strung up in twos on poles and arranged in rows in tobacco barns (*casas del tabaco*) which face west and are covered in palm leaves. They are then left to dry. After fifty days, the leaf loses 85 percent of its water and acquires a golden color.

FIRST STAGE OF FERMENTATION
The leaves are stored in bundles (*gavillas*) for one to three months. The remaining moisture in the leaves causes fermentation, reducing the resin and nicotine content and giving the leaves a uniform color. When the temperature exceeds 95°F, the bundles are dismantled and the leaves aired.

'The Indian leaf, comfort of the thoughtful, the delight of dreamers, architects of the air, bosom full of the fragrance of the winged opal.' José Martí

69

After the leaves have been dried and fermented, they are stored in the tobacco factory (*fábrica*). They are then moistened, stripped of their midribs, graded and weighed under the expert supervision of the tobacco master – there is one per factory – who, similar to a cellar master, is responsible for deciding the right blend for each type of Havana. The leaves are then given to the rollers (*torcedores*). This repetitive work is carried out every day in the factory workshop (*galera*) by a large labor force.

1. TRANSPORT TO THE FACTORY
Before leaving for the factories, each bale is identified by a sheet listing the variety of tobacco, the *vega* (plantation) of origin, and the amount of time the tobacco has been fermented and matured.

2. SECOND STAGE OF FERMENTATION
After the leaves are graded, they are again fermented for sixty days under strict supervision. This removes traces of ammonia and chlorine and encourages aromas to develop.

CLASSES AND GRADES
Leaves are graded according to the position on the plant and color. Depending on the factory, there are between eleven and fifteen grades and over seventy-five colors in each category.

3. HUMIDIFICATION
Wrapper leaves are individually separated and sprayed with water. This moistening process (*moja*) restores their elasticity.

4. STRIPPING AND SMOOTHING

After fermentation, the factory strippers flatten out the crumpled leaves. They then sort the

leaves into the individually required sizes and begin to strip out the remaining part of the leaves' midrib.

SKILLED WORK

The workers begin classifying the leaves in the workshop. This operation, repeated several times, is carried out to a complex set of rules and requires great dexterity. Specialists spend five years training.

5. GRADING

The leaves are graded once again for different use in the cigars (either binder or filler), as well as for their size, color and texture and for the considered 'quality' of the tobacco (*right*).

6. WEIGHING

The specific character of a Havana cigar depends on its percentage of *ligero* leaves (strength), *seco* leaves (aroma) and *volado* leaves (burning quality). It is therefore essential to weigh the mixture (*liga*).

7. BLEND

The success of the *ligada* (blend) depends on the sound judgment and competence of the factory head, the blend master. He is the only one who knows the recipe for each cigar in every variety and brand.

71

● ROLLING THE HAVANA

The wrapper: pliable
corojo leaves ● 68.

The roller (*torcedor*) is ultimately responsible for the quality of a Havana. Firstly, he lays the *ligero*, the leaf that gives the cigar its strength, in the palm of his hand. He surrounds it with the *seco* and *volado* leaves, depending on the quantities established by the blend master, and lastly adds the binder. The skill hinges on manual dexterity: to ensure the cigar draws easily, the leaves must not be too tight or too loose. The wrapper leaf forms the *torcedor*'s signature, but it does not alter the flavor of the Havana.

THE 'GALERA'
The workshop, the heart of the factory (*left*), is often located upstairs. In this large room, the rollers (*torcedores*) sit at desks in front of the lector's platform; the more productive the worker, the nearer he sits to the platform. Traditionally, the lector reads out literary texts or describes events of the Revolution.

THE FIRST STAGE OF ROLLING
The roller arranges the various leaves in his palm so that he can roll them. Once the filler leaves are rolled, he envelops them in the binder leaves.

THE 'BUNCH'
Produced after the first stage of rolling, the 'bunch', wrapped in the binder composed of *volado* leaves, is slightly longer and fatter than the final product.

PRESSING
The 'bunch' is then pressed into a mold for about twenty minutes.

THE ROLLING OF THE WRAPPER
The roller cuts the wrapper with the *chaveta* (semi-circular knife), then deftly rolls it around the bunch; the rounded end of the leaf is folded in such a way as to seal the Havana.

CUTTING THE HAVANA
The Havana is cut to the right size with the use of an adjustable guillotine.

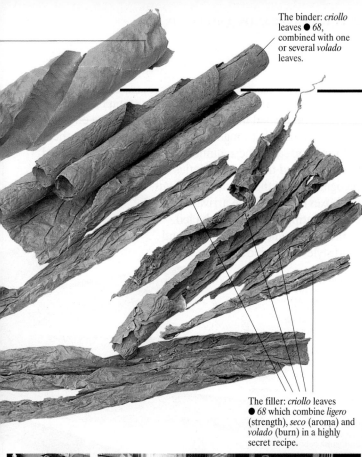

The binder: *criollo* leaves ● *68*, combined with one or several *volado* leaves.

The filler: *criollo* leaves ● *68* which combine *ligero* (strength), *seco* (aroma) and *volado* (burn) in a highly secret recipe.

SORTING BY COLOR
The *escogida*, or the art of sorting colors, is carried out on large tables. The head colorist lays out the Havanas and applies a code to the cigars peculiar to each factory. Havanas are usually sorted into six color categories, ranging from a dark red shade to pale green, known individually by the terms *sangre de toro*, *colorado*, *colorado claro*, *colorado pariso*, *pariso verde* and finally *pariso verdoso*.

THE COOL ROOM
This is where the Havanas are stored so that they lose their moisture.

PACKAGING
The Havanas are laid in boxes, the darkest on the left and the lightest on the right.

QUALITY CHECK
Quality checks are carried out on a sample of the cigars produced by the *torcedores* (who can roll as many as 120 Havanas a day). These checks focus on the Havanas' weight, smoothness and length. The *cepo*, a small perforated wooden board, is used to check the correct diameter of each cigar.

After a long period of anonymity, cigars stamped 'Cuba' or 'Havana' flourished in the early 19th century: the end of the Spanish monopoly brought about a rapid increase in the number of brands on sale. These numerous, sometimes short-lived brands created their own varieties of Havana (they are recognizable by their bands and *vistas*, the prints that appear on the boxes). In 1860, the arrival of color printing presses in Cuba led to the rise of a new, imaginative and vivid style of graphic art.

Robusto

Pirámide

Prominente

Julieta

Mareva

VARIETIES
Each of these five varieties (*opposite*) are sold under an original name which is associated with a brand. Their names are given by the *galeras*, in accordance with the usual nomenclature used by the factories. There are over thirty different names. Havana buffs distinguish between some fifteen current varieties with names that differ from those given by the *galeras*.

'VISTA' ▲ *160*
The highly ornate graphic design of the brand's *vista* is intended to prevent imitations.

BANDS
The ring of paper that fastens the wrapper leaf changed, around 1830, from a simple binder to a richly emblazoned band. They are often commemorative or promotional, and are occasionally a true work of art. These bands now function as the brand's imprint or logo.

EL REY DEL MUNDO
Founded in 1882, this Havana brand (*above*) is represented by a *vista* showing a king (*rey*) crowned with feathers on a throne pulled by a donkey, a ram, an elephant and a horse.

Architecture

Eduardo Luis Rodríguez

Map of Camagüey, (*above*). The Plaza de Armas, Havana, (*below*).

THE FIRST COLONIAL TOWN-PLANNING PROGRAM

The first settlements founded by the conquistadors between 1512 and 1515 had irregular streets running from a central square, on one side of which

stood the parish church. This layout did not form part of a town-planning program; the conquistadors merely adapted procedures in their native towns to the topography of the area concerned. This resulted in an irregular style of urbanization, best exemplified by the historic center of Camagüey. Although Havana features an almost regular street layout, it also boasts a fortified building, the Castillo de la Real Fuerza, which was built on the Plaza de Armas.

The Law of the Indies (1573), which systematized the building of cities and their growth, stipulated a harmonious network of narrow, shady streets and functional squares. Havana did not expand beyond its city walls until the end of the 18th century and, in the early 20th century, it saw the Hispanic influences replaced by the American model. After 1959, town-planning programs drew their inspiration from the Soviet model, creating housing developments that interrupted the city's continuity.

THE DEVELOPMENT OF HAVANA ▲ *141*

The inner-city area of Havana from 1519.

Expansion outside the walls (from the 18th century).

New residential areas: Carmelo (1859) and Vedado (1860).

Urbanization of the ramparts sector (1865).

MAP OF HAVANA IN 1898

Because of the bay, the city of Havana was forced to expand westward. In 1818, a development plan designed by Antonio María de la Torre standardized construction outside the city walls. The plans drawn up by Luis Yboleón Bosque ▲ *141* for the new quarters of Carmelo and Vedado, with their wide tree-lined boulevards, were quite revolutionary in their emphasis on quality and style.

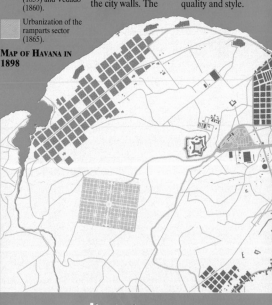

SHADY PORTICOS, PLAZA VIEJA, HAVANA ▲ *130*

Military engineer Juan Bautista Orduña came up with the plan for developing this area, formerly the site of the glacis, moat and city walls, which were demolished in 1863. This quarter ▲ *132* represented an architectural transition between the inner-city area and the quarters outside the city walls and, until the late 20th century, all the important institutions were gathered in this sector.

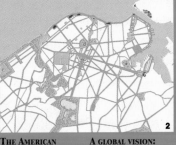

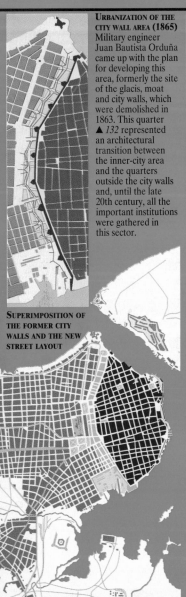

SUPERIMPOSITION OF THE FORMER CITY WALLS AND THE NEW STREET LAYOUT

THE AMERICAN MODEL: THE COUNTRY CLUB (1914) ▲ *120*
The American architect Sheffield A. Arnold designed this elegant residential quarter as a garden city around a golf course (1). This countrified setting, comprising vast plots of land bounded by curved streets and avenues, was intended for the city's wealthy families as well as its cosmopolitan community.

A GLOBAL VISION: DEVELOPMENT SCHEME FOR HAVANA (1925–30) ▲ *136*
The French landscape architect J. C. Nicolas Forestier came up with an ambitious plan to enlarge the city, inspired by Haussmann's ideas (2). He superimposed the traditional urban framework on an assemblage of large parks and broad avenues. The plan was only partially realized ▲ *145*.

BETWEEN RECONSTRUCTION AND RENOVATION: JOSÉ LUIS SERT'S PROJECT (1955–8)
This famous Catalan architect devised a comprehensive regulatory scheme (*opposite*) for Havana designed to provide solutions to all the problems likely to arise in a modern city, particularly with respect to urban traffic and open spaces. However, he did not place enough importance on the traditional urban layout and architecture of the dilapidated historic quarters. This project was never carried out.

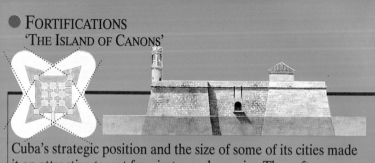

Cuba's strategic position and the size of some of its cities made it an attractive target for pirates and corsairs. They often completely destroyed the towns and villages they attacked, so at least one fortress was needed to defend a city. The official creation, in 1561, of the Fleet System marked the beginning of Havana's prosperity and at the same time whetted the appetites of potential attackers: a string of defense systems was therefore constructed to protect the capital.

CASTILLO DE SAN PEDRO DE LA ROCA DEL MORRO

FIRST DEFENSE SYSTEM
Built in Santiago de Cuba by Juan Bautista Antonelli, this 17th century *castillo* ▲ *217* is one of the finest examples of Renaissance military architecture. It was built to a bastioned plan which formed stepped batteries closing off the bay on the seaward side and a low-built fortification comprising a moat and a glacis, facing inland.

THE FIRST FORTRESSES
(The Castillo de la Real Fuerza ▲ *122*, Havana, 1558–77, *above*. Rebuilt in 1632, the same year as the construction of the Giraldilla.) This fortification, whose design is attributed to engineer Jerónimo Bustamante de Herrera, was built by Bartolomé Sánchez and Esteban Calona. This was the first bastioned fortress in the Americas. The triangular bastions are composed of casemates which facilitated low crossfire and removed the blind spots that interfered with a close defense. Their terrace roofs formed platforms for high-angle fire.

THE FIRST FORTRESSES
1 Fuerza Vieja, 1539 (demolished).
2 Castillo de la Real Fuerza, 1558–77.

FIRST DEFENSE SYSTEM, FROM 1589
3 Castillo de San Salvador de la Punta, c. 1589–1600.
4 Castillo de los Tres Reyes del Morro, 1589–1630.
5 Fortress of La Chorrera, c. 1645.
6 Fortress of Cojímar, c. 1645.
7 Fortress of San Lázaro, c. 1665.
8 City walls, 1674–1797.

SECOND DEFENSE SYSTEM

The construction of new fortresses was a direct result of the capture of Havana by the English in 1762 ● *38*. S. Abarca and A. Crame designed this second system, of which the most impressive example is the fortress of San Carlos de la Cabaña ● *147*. Completed in 1774, it covers an area of more than 2300 feet and includes all the classic elements of defense: 1) bastioned ramparts; 2) ravelins; 3) tenailles; 4) moats; 5) covered walkways and 6) glacis.

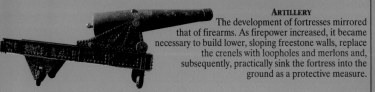

ARTILLERY

The development of fortresses mirrored that of firearms. As firepower increased, it became necessary to build lower, sloping freestone walls, replace the crenels with loopholes and merlons and, subsequently, practically sink the fortress into the ground as a protective measure.

THIRD DEFENSE SYSTEM

Fortress N° 1 in Habana del Este is the most representative of the fortresses constructed in Cuba during the 19th century. Completed in 1897, it was built to a modern architectural design. This defense system, the last to be built, comprised a large number of elements including military fortifications constructed during the wars for independence ● *39*.

SECOND DEFENSE SYSTEM, FROM 1763
9 Fortress of San Carlos de la Cabaña, 1763–74.
10 Castillo de Santo Domingo de Atarés, 1767.
11 Castillo del Príncipe, 1767–79.
12 Horn-work at San Diego, c. 1770.
13 Battery of Santa Clara, end of 18th century.
14 Battery of La Reina, 19th century.
15 Battery N° 2, 19th century.
16 Battery N° 3, 19th century.
17 Battery of La Chorrera, 19th century.

THIRD DEFENSE SYSTEM, FROM 1896
18 Fort N° 1 of Habana del Este, 1897.

1

From the beginning, Cuban cities featured religious buildings which, although initially austere, soon became lavishly ornamented. Like the fortresses, church towers functioned as visual landmarks on the cityscape. Religious architecture was also largely responsible for introducing the influences of Mudéjar art. These Moorish-style structures became increasingly complex and their façades boasted ornate baroque decoration.

CHURCHES AND CONVENTS (Nuestra Señora de Belén ▲ 131)

Convents, which usually extended over several blocks (sometimes as many as four), were an integral part of the city. The church and convent of Nuestra Señora de Belén (Bethlehem), built between 1712 and 1720, then enlarged and remodeled over the next two centuries, form the largest surviving religious complex in Old Havana. This complex comprises six cloistered courtyards; a striking vaulted arch, dating from 1775, stands over Calle Acosta.

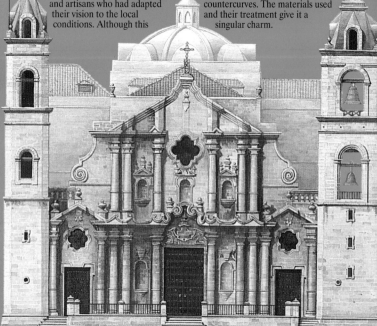

CUBAN BAROQUE (Havana Cathedral ▲ 126)

Often more restrained than the Spanish buildings they were modeled on, 18th-century Cuban baroque was the work of artists and artisans who had adapted their vision to the local conditions. Although this cathedral is inspired by Toledo cathedral, the façade is a rare example in Cuba of the interplay between baroque curves and countercurves. The materials used and their treatment give it a singular charm.

1 Espíritu Santo, Havana, 1638 (tower 1707).
2 Santa María del Rosario, 1766.
3 San Pedro, Versalles, Matanzas, 1857–70 (Daniel dalli Aglio).

STYLES DURING THE COLONIAL PERIOD

Although rebuilt in 1760 and 1847, the church of Espíritu Santo ▲ *131* is representative of an architectural typology that originated in the 17th century and continued to be popular, characterized by an adjoining tower and an almost complete lack of decoration. In the 18th century, the baroque influence found expression in lavishly ornamented portals. 'Retable-style' portals stretched the full height of the façade and were crowned by curvilinear scalloped motifs; side aisles made an appearance but some churches (Santa María del Rosario ▲ *147*) only had one. The neo-classical trends of the 19th century placed the emphasis on a restrained style which radiated a sense of majesty. The triangular pediment over the main portal became a common feature.

Portal of the Sagrado Corazón de Jesús, Havana, 1914–22

NEO-GOTHIC STYLE
Of all the styles that exerted an influence on the architecture during the first thirty years of the Republic, neo-gothic was favored by builders of churches. This was largely due to its highly symbolic character and its expressive soaring lines, which gave Cuban cities a sense of importance.

THE DECOR
(Altar in the chapel of the church of Nuestra Señora de los Dolores, Bayamo ▲ *204*)
Altars made of carved gilt wood were important decorative elements in baroque churches and were made in a wide variety of shapes and sizes. A product of the religious and creative ardor of local artisans which found expression in elaborate filigree work, these altars formed a striking contrast to the stark simplicity of the walls.

MODERNISM
Despite the country's genuine process of modernization, particularly after 1945, religious architecture developed slowly in the 20th century, with only a very few exceptions. Both in its overall design and its smaller details, it continued to show the influence of foreign models traditionally associated with religion. This can be seen clearly in the church of San Antonio de Padua, built in Havana in 1949 by Eloy Norman and Salvador Figueras.

THE COLONIAL HOUSE
DEVELOPMENT

NEOCLASSICAL GLAZED URN, TRINIDAD

The early dwellings, which had walls made of palm tree branches and roofs of palm fiber, evolved into sturdier examples with adobe walls and tiled wooden roofs. They also became structurally more complex: they occasionally had two stories, inner courtyards were added and they were decorated in a style that was inspired by Mudéjar art. During the baroque period, the main emphasis was placed on ornamentation in aristocratic homes, which later adopted the neoclassical style.

THE 17TH-CENTURY HOUSE
(House at the corner of Calles Obrapía and San Ignacio, Old Havana.) The 17th-century house was modeled on the Spanish house, built around a central patio. The upper story was reserved for the private apartments, while the first story was devoted to commerce. The austere façade featured a simple portal and balconies with turned wood railings.

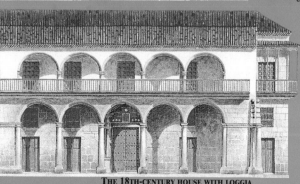

THE 18TH-CENTURY HOUSE WITH LOGGIA

(House at the corner of Calles Muralla, Nº 107 and San Ignacio, Havana.) Unlike the narrow streets, squares could accommodate houses whose façades boasted a portico and a loggia – often added later. The former provided shelter from sunshine and rain and the latter opened up the main story with a view over the city. The loggia, formerly open-sided, acquired slatted shutters in the 19th century. The space between the portal and the patio, the hall (*zaguán*), was open to the public. A typical Cuban baroque feature was the intricately carved and richly decorated archway ● 84 that led into the patio.

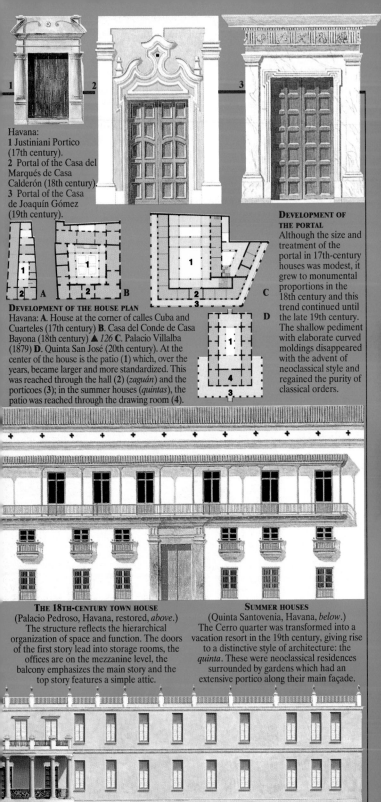

Havana:
1 Justiniani Portico
(17th century).
2 Portal of the Casa del
Marqués de Casa
Calderón (18th century).
3 Portal of the Casa
de Joaquín Gómez
(19th century).

DEVELOPMENT OF THE HOUSE PLAN
Havana: **A**. House at the corner of calles Cuba and
Cuarteles (17th century) **B**. Casa del Conde de Casa
Bayona (18th century) ▲ *126* **C**. Palacio Villalba
(1879) **D**. Quinta San José (20th century). At the
center of the house is the patio (**1**) which, over the
years, became larger and more standardized. This
was reached through the hall (**2**) (*zaguán*) and the
porticoes (**3**); in the summer houses (*quintas*), the
patio was reached through the drawing room (**4**).

**DEVELOPMENT OF
THE PORTAL**
Although the size and
treatment of the
portal in 17th-century
houses was modest, it
grew to monumental
proportions in the
18th century and this
trend continued until
the late 19th century.
The shallow pediment
with elaborate curved
moldings disappeared
with the advent of
neoclassical style and
regained the purity of
classical orders.

THE 18TH-CENTURY TOWN HOUSE
(Palacio Pedroso, Havana, restored, *above*.)
The structure reflects the hierarchical
organization of space and function. The doors
of the first story lead into storage rooms, the
offices are on the mezzanine level, the
balcony emphasizes the main story and the
top story features a simple attic.

SUMMER HOUSES
(Quinta Santovenia, Havana, *below*.)
The Cerro quarter was transformed into a
vacation resort in the 19th century, giving rise
to a distinctive style of architecture: the
quinta. These were neoclassical residences
surrounded by gardens which had an
extensive portico along their main façade.

The colonial house evolved from the traditional layout established in the 17th century. For four centuries, the patio remained at the center of the house, although its importance decreased in the 19th century when houses began to be surrounded by gardens. The window appears to be the only element to display any stylistic and technical development.

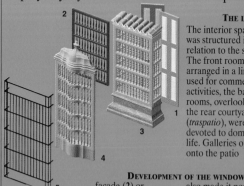

THE LAYOUT OF THE HOUSE

The interior space was structured in relation to the street. The front rooms were arranged in a line and used for commercial activities, the back rooms, overlooking the rear courtyard (*traspatio*), were devoted to domestic life. Galleries opening onto the patio enabled occupants to move around the house. The same layout was repeated on the main story: the reception rooms overlooked the street and the private rooms were at the rear.

DEVELOPMENT OF THE WINDOW

Protected by wooden panels (1) in the 17th century, windows later acquired wood balusters, either placed flush with the façade (2) or protruding (3) if the street was wide enough. The bars, which had the dual purpose of preventing intruders and ensuring ventilation, also made it possible to communicate with people outside. In the 18th century, the design of the grilles was often highly ornate (4) as in Trinidad ▲ 189 and Camagüey. In the 19th century, they were often replaced by metal grilles (5).

THE FIRST STORY

The patio (1) was where business deals were concluded, while the rooms around its perimeter were used as storehouses (2) and offices (3). The rooms opening onto the street, called *dependencias* (4), were rented out. The rear courtyard (*traspatio*) (5) was where the service areas and the stables (6) were located.

THE 19TH-CENTURY WINDOW

In addition to the metal grilles, glass began to be used in windows; a new development because it was such a scarce and costly commodity. Although glass did not replace wooden panels (1), multicolored and/or engraved panes (2) were inserted between the latter and the grille (3). Often there was a screen formed by a slatted eye-level shutter (4). Larger windows were protected by slatted shutters and, at the top, by *medios puntos* (5), stained-glass windows which filtered the sunlight.

Casa del Dominicano ▲ 188, 18th century, Trinidad.

THE ARCHWAY IN THE 'ZAGUÁN'

The opening that led from the hall into the other rooms was initially a semicircular arch, which became increasingly complex. The most common designs were multifoil and ogee arches (*left*).

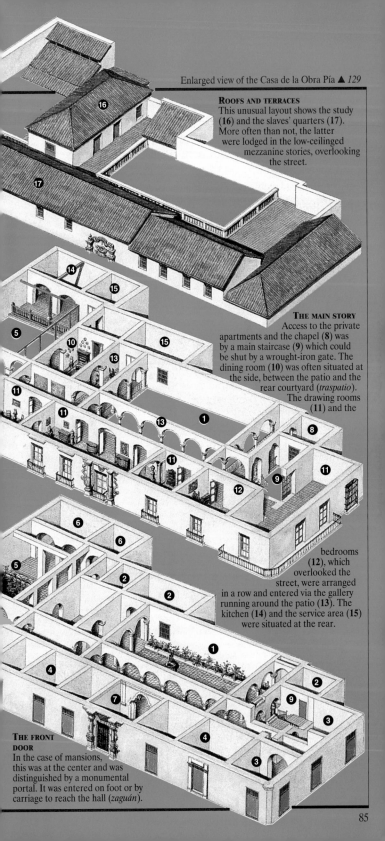

ROOFS AND TERRACES
This unusual layout shows the study
(**16**) and the slaves' quarters (**17**).
More often than not, the latter
were lodged in the low-ceilinged
mezzanine stories, overlooking
the street.

THE MAIN STORY
Access to the private
apartments and the chapel (**8**) was
by a main staircase (**9**) which could
be shut by a wrought-iron gate. The
dining room (**10**) was often situated at
the side, between the patio and the
rear courtyard (*traspatio*).
The drawing rooms
(**11**) and the

bedrooms
(**12**), which
overlooked the
street, were arranged
in a row and entered via the gallery
running around the patio (**13**). The
kitchen (**14**) and the service area (**15**)
were situated at the rear.

**THE FRONT
DOOR**
In the case of mansions,
this was at the center and was
distinguished by a monumental
portal. It was entered on foot or by
carriage to reach the hall (*zaguán*).

The guardavecino, *a grille separating one house from the next, prevented people climbing from balcony to balcony, but it became an extremely ornate decorative element.*

Neoclassicism made its appearance in Cuba as a result of the new cultural contacts that were now sanctioned by the government; the style soon became synonymous with artistic and economic progress. Bishop Juan José Díaz de Espada y Landa played a crucial role in this regard because he was responsible for the construction of the first building in this style, the Espada Cemetery (Havana, 1806; demolished). The flourishing economic climate led to a boom in the building sector.

EL TEMPLETE ▲ *123* (1828), Old Havana. This small temple, built by Antonio María de la Torre to commemorate the foundation of the city, promoted the spread of the neoclassical style because of its central position and its pleasing appearance. It contains three paintings by the artist Jean-Baptiste Vermay depicting events relating to the city's foundation.

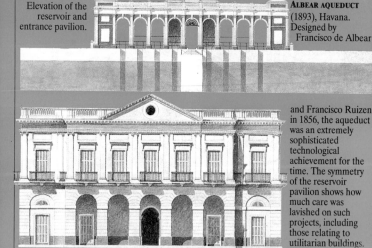

Elevation of the reservoir and entrance pavilion.

ALBEAR AQUEDUCT (1893), Havana. Designed by Francisco de Albear and Francisco Ruizen in 1856, the aqueduct was an extremely sophisticated technological achievement for the time. The symmetry of the reservoir pavilion shows how much care was lavished on such projects, including those relating to utilitarian buildings.

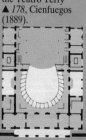

Above, Teatro Sauto ▲ *167*, Matanzas (1863); below, plan of the Teatro Terry ▲ *178*, Cienfuegos (1889).

THEATERS
Theaters, which provided a venue for a wide range of social activities, steadily increased in number, becoming an important feature of the city. Their façades usually sported arcades and the rectangular building housed a traditional horseshoe-shaped auditorium inside.

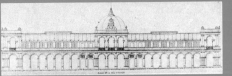

The Mercado Colón ▲ *136*, Havana (1884; demolished), Emilio Sánchez Osorio.

TOBACCO FACTORIES (Calixto López, 1886, Havana.)
The tobacco industry played a key economic role in the 19th century. The major factories were built in the city centers and their layout reproduced that of the houses: they had a first story, a mezzanine level and a main story.

MARKETS
These large buildings replaced the open-air stalls that had begun to spring up all over the city. Their façades were all very similar in appearance with arcades running round the outside of the building. In the Mercado Colón, the huge central space was covered by a metal structure imported all the way to Cuba from Belgium.

THE 'MAMPARA'
(Casa de los Sánchez-Iznaga ▲ *183*, Trinidad.)
This double door was used in conjunction with the front doors. When the latter were open, the inhabitants

left the mampara closed to avoid prying eyes; this also served to increase ventilation. The glass was usually either colored or frosted.

PLEASURE HOUSE
(Mansion of Félix G. Torres, 1867, Matanzas.)
Pleasure houses, with their portico, garden and terrace roof, were often built in the suburbs. These buildings, particularly in Matanzas, showed the influence of Palladianism, fashionable in Europe.

IRONWORK
(Grille of the Palacio Aldama, Havana.)
Wrought iron or cast iron, which replaced wood in the 19th century for the grilles and railings of houses, became a great favorite with craftsmen working with iron. Their works were as delicate as the finest lace.

THE PALACE
(Palacio de Aldama, ▲ *132*, 1844, Havana.)
Although the palace reproduced the layout of 18th-century houses, its design generally outshone them with its imposing dimensions, luxurious materials and lavish decoration.

Plan of the Ingenio Santa Rosa, Matanzas, 1875.

As a result of the sugar boom in the late 18th century, the sugar mill was replaced by the sugar mill (*ingenio*), an agro-industrial complex which benefited from periodic technological modernization. In addition, the number of coffee plantations had been steadily rising since the early 19th century, particularly in the eastern part of the island, as a result of mass immigration by Franco-Haitian landowners following the revolution in Haiti.

THE PLANTATION OWNER'S HOUSE
(Ingenio Manaca Iznaga, *above*; ingenio Buenavista ▲ *190, right*.) Standing at the center of the *batey* ● 35, this stone house was often surrounded by arcades and was the finest building on the plantation. Squat in shape, it sometimes had a patio and always stood in the midst of gardens.

THE SUGAR PLANTATION (INGENIO FLOR DE CUBA, COLÓN)
Like a village, the *batey* ● 35 incorporated all the buildings comprising the sugar refinery: the house, mill, heating and refining installations, distillery, *barracón* ● 36, where the slaves were kept, infirmary, animal pens, gardens, vegetable plots and orchards, stables and storehouses. Around the *batey*, the extensive fields of sugarcane stretched out far into the distance.

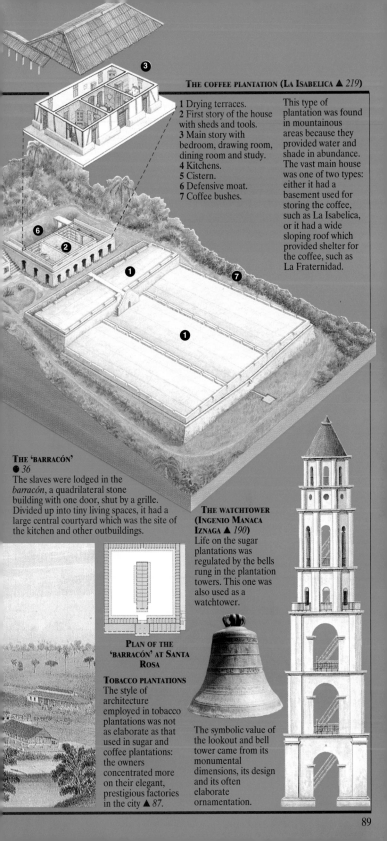

1 Drying terraces.
2 First story of the house with sheds and tools.
3 Main story with bedroom, drawing room, dining room and study.
4 Kitchens.
5 Cistern.
6 Defensive moat.
7 Coffee bushes.

This type of plantation was found in mountainous areas because they provided water and shade in abundance. The vast main house was one of two types: either it had a basement used for storing the coffee, such as La Isabelica, or it had a wide sloping roof which provided shelter for the coffee, such as La Fraternidad.

THE 'BARRACÓN'
● 36
The slaves were lodged in the *barracón*, a quadrilateral stone building with one door, shut by a grille. Divided up into tiny living spaces, it had a large central courtyard which was the site of the kitchen and other outbuildings.

PLAN OF THE 'BARRACÓN' AT SANTA ROSA

TOBACCO PLANTATIONS
The style of architecture employed in tobacco plantations was not as elaborate as that used in sugar and coffee plantations: the owners concentrated more on their elegant, prestigious factories in the city ▲ 87.

THE WATCHTOWER (INGENIO MANACA IZNAGA ▲ 190)
Life on the sugar plantations was regulated by the bells rung in the plantation towers. This one was also used as a watchtower.

The symbolic value of the lookout and bell tower came from its monumental dimensions, its design and its often elaborate ornamentation.

Ceramic detail from the Masía La Ampurdá (1919), Havana, Mario Rotllant.

With the start of the 20th century and the establishment of the Republic (1902) came a desire for modernity that found its best expression in the field of art. In addition to this, the latest developments in transportation and communication boosted cultural exchange: a wide variety of artistic styles, most of them originating in Europe and occasionally arriving via the United States, flourished throughout the island, even if Havana remained the true hub of artistic innovation.

ART NOUVEAU
(Casa Gutiérrez, 1913, Mario Rotllant.)
Art Nouveau, which developed in Cuba between about 1905 and 1920, varied stylistically depending on its place of origin: France, Belgium, Vienna or Catalonia. The large number of Spanish immigrants, particularly Catalans, played a decisive role in introducing Art Nouveau to the island. These new, essentially decorative forms were combined with traditional details.

ECLECTIC STYLE
(Cuban Telephone Company, 1927, Leonardo Morales.) This style gave Havana something of a facelift, diversifying its appearance and enhancing its individuality. This building's façades represented a milestone in the city's history. Their ornamentation showed the influence of the Plateresque style of the Spanish Renaissance.

BEAUX-ARTS STYLE
(Casa de José Gómez Mena ▲ *143*, 1927, Havana.)
The concepts taught by the Ecole des Beaux-Arts in Paris had a considerable impact on Cuba when introduced by the American architect Thomas M. Newton and Cuban architect Emilio Heredia. This style showed a classicism in its central plan, symmetry and purity of line.

Detail of the central panel from the lobby of the López Serrano apartment building of 1932, Mira and Rosich.

ART DECO

(Edificio Bacardí, 1930, Esteban Rodríguez.) Art Deco made its appearance in Cuba in 1928, two years after the Paris International Exhibition of Decorative Arts, and soon flourished. It promoted the use of veneer in decoration and employed linear designs, geometric motifs, polychromy and expensive materials.

LAVISH DECOR

The concept of recurrent modernity in the decorative arts found its expression in progress and speed: Hermes, the symbol of diligent and creative intelligence, is associated with three airplanes, thereby creating a modern myth.

THE MODERNIST MOVEMENT

(Cabaret Tropicana, *right*, 1951, Marianao, Max Borges, Jr.) European rationalism arrived in Cuba in the late 1920s. Over the following decades, it diversified, incorporating different trends. The esthetic of Max Borges, Jr., one of the leading architects of the time, combines a distinctive tropical sensuality with complex structural designs.

MODERNITY AND TRADITION

In the 1950s, a modern style of architecture tailored to suit the Cuban environment came to the fore. The Farfantes apartment building, designed by F. Martínez, combines Le Corbusier's esthetic of a rectangular prism, a building built on stilts and an open floor plan with large canopies, windows with slatted shutters and the suggestion of a patio using local materials.

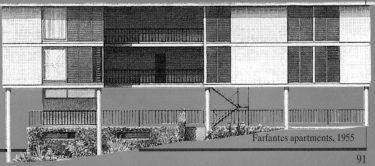

Farfantes apartments, 1955

91

The 'triumph of the Revolution' in 1959 influenced people's perception of architecture. The new government initially launched some large-scale building projects to prove their capacity for change. Although these programs were subsequently scaled down, they did not replace architecture in the country's cultural context.

1 Cross section of the *Coppelia* ice-cream parlor.

A STYLE OF ARCHITECTURE IN HARMONY WITH HISTORY AND THE ENVIRONMENT
The best modern works incorporate elements of local culture.
1 and 3 THE COPPELIA ICE-CREAM PARLOR, HAVANA (1966, M. Girona) Beneath a ribbed roof, the main rooms are separated by slatted blinds and colored glass.
2 LAS RUINAS RESTAURANT, HAVANA (1972, J. Galbán) This modern structure provides an effective showcase for lush vegetation and colonial ruins.
4 SCHOOL OF MEDICINE, SANTIAGO (1964, R. Tascón) The repetitive structural design of this building revolves around the traditional central patio.
5 THE LENIN SCHOOL, HAVANA (1974, A. Garrudo) Built of prefabricated elements, this type of school can be found throughout Cuba.
6 THE NATIONAL SCHOOL OF MODERN DANCE, HAVANA (1961–5, R. Porro) With traditional and symbolic references, this building is part of a complex comprising five schools devoted to the arts.

Cuba as seen by painters

Marie-Thérèse Richard Hernandez

In *El Triunfo de la Rumba* (Triumph of the Rumba, **1**), Eduardo Abela (1889–1965) portrays a group of people locked in a spiral composition. The woman, who has sprung from the shadows in an eddy of light, faces the viewer while, behind her, men twist, writhe and thrash about. She is the prize they are dancing for, the reason for all their feverish activity. They will do anything to win her and she will do everything to evade their bold moves. Abela's painting is a representation of the primitive and sensual law of the *rumba*. With his *Mujeres Junto al Río* (Women by the River, **4**), Antonio Gattorno (1904–80) presents a very different image of tropical sensuality.

In this painting, the gentle curves and undulations of the countryside imbue the work with a sense of tranquillity. Two women are relaxing by the water in the shade of a banana tree in this idyllic image of West Indian life, devoted to the simple, arcadian pleasures. The

'Far off, beyond the sugar fields, when the fireflies glow, the nights in certain villages are peopled by drums, maracas and song.'

Alejo Carpentier

harmonious blend of ochers and greens heightens the impression of well-being radiating from the painting; the masses, outlined in black in the manner of Gauguin, envelop the women's figures in the torpor of a day spent idly sun-worshipping. The restraint of Gattorno's language forms a striking contrast with Ramón Alejandro's violently subjective vocabulary. The rapturous use of color and the sensuality of the sun-ripened fruit, sliced open and offered up to the palate, make Alejandro's *Earthly Desires* (**3**) a paean to tropical life. The papaya, at the center of the artist's visual world, takes on an Edenic value. Using a similar chromatic range of colors, *Naturaleza Muerta en Amarillo*, (Still Life in Yellow, 2), by Amelia Peláez (1896–1968), recalls the *medio punto* ● *84,* a stained-glass window that is peculiar to Havana, in the geometry of its black outlined design and its bright colors. The decorative element here becomes a stylistic device, the hallmark of a work dedicated to the exploration of light and the flamboyant colors of tropical nature.

THE FIGURE OF THE *GUAJIRO*

In search of the 'human face of the nation', the avant-garde painters who were introduced at the exhibition of new art in Havana in 1927 naturally directed their gaze toward the emblematic figure of the peasant. With *Guajiros* (**3**), Eduardo Abela creates a picturesque and idyllic image. His painting depicts a village scene that exudes an unruffled happiness; men with cheerful faces seem to be making the most of a minute's rest to enjoy a chat. *Guajiros* has a certain naivety, is easy on the eye, boasts a classical and perfectly balanced composition and deploys a harmonious palette of warm colors; yet the painting continually surprises the spectator: both by adopting a stylistic approach inspired by Douanier Rousseau and by offering an idealized interpretation of reality. In this work,

Abela has produced one of the most powerful images of Cuban art. Mariano Rodríguez (born in 1912), on the other hand, gives a strange urban interpretation of the peasant. His *Guajiros* (**1**) are unusually depicted in a cityscape. Frequently subdued, occasionally emphatic, the line remains low profile while the light effaces volume, reinstates or breaks down colors depending on their respective values. Some thirty years separate Abela's peasants from the *Milicias Campesinas* (**2**) of Cabrera Moreno (1923–84). Living in a modern world, these peasant militiamen now have nothing left but the traditional straw hat of the *guajiro*. Profoundly tormented, closely connected with historic reality in this painting, they strenuously defend the revolutionary ideology.

'The artist must drink at the inexhaustible fount of the emotions which constitute the life of the people.'

Jorge Ibarra

'I am a Yoruba and I go on my way singing […]
I am a Yoruba from Cuba…'

Nicolás Guillén

Renowned healer and sorceress, Mantonica Wilson, the godmother of Wifredo Lam (1902–82), initiated the artist into African culture at a very early age. It was at her instigation that Lam (*below*) explored the invisible world. She told him the myths and legends of the Yoruba ● 58, and he

translated their poetry into line and color. The design and subtle blues of *The White Bird* (**1**) do not symbolize the human soul as in Catholicism, but the *orisha*, one of the deities in the *santería* ● 58. Heightened by the pulsing energy of the lines, the white prevails as an evocation of the divine. In *Santa Bárbara* (**2**), René Portocarrero (1912–85) highlights the ambivalent nature of Saint Barbara: in *santería*, she is the equivalent of Changó, the Yoruba god of

thunder and war, fire, lightning and masculine beauty. The painting by Manuel Mendive (born in 1944) is also inspired by the realm of the marvelous; the

deities, schematized in *El Malecón* (**3**), appear in a framework of symbolic colors, intended to summon the presence of certain *orishas*.

The graphic style of Raúl Martínez, inspired by pop art, found its most potent expression in the 1970s. *Sin título* (Untitled, **1**) depicts portraits of famous men, most of them heroes of the Cuban Revolution and Cuban historical figures. These recurrent images are placed against a vivid chromatic background, devoid of subtle shading. In *Masas y Vedado*, (Masses and Vedado, **2**), from the *Masas* series (c. 1980), Mariano Rodríguez (born in 1912) depicts a rally in Havana. In this picture, the crowd is gathered in the Vedado ▲ *141*, not the Plaza de la Revolución ▲ *145*, as if to listen to Castro's speeches. The ungainly shapes of modern buildings, in the background, obstruct the horizon.

CUBA
AS SEEN BY WRITERS

To present a vision of Cuba as it appears to its writers in just a few pages is not a task to be envied; to include in this the perspectives and insights of those that have come here from overseas merely compounds the problem. But Cuba is a powerful place that draws writers to it as much as it has cast others out, and each has added different depths and dimensions to what ultimately amounts to an intriguing overview of this complex and compelling island. That is why in the following pages you will find extracts from works written not only by resident Cubans but also those in exile, by those who have come and gone, and by those who have come and stayed. Whoever and wherever they are, they have drawn upon the same source of inspiration: 'the long green lizard' that is Cuba. All the works by Cuban writers included here are currently available in English translation, as are the titles in the Bibliography. The number of translated works now becoming available serves as a welcome indication that the richness of Cuba's literary heritage is at last becoming more widely recognized in the English-speaking world.

SLAVERY AND REPRESSION

The writer and orator José Martí (1853–95), who in the latter years of the 19th century did much to spark the flames that swept across Cuba, is today the most revered Cuban patriot. Deported when he was only seventeen for criticizing the Spanish military, he spent his life in exile, writing passionate poems and prose in the cause of Cuban independence.

❝ Look, look!

Here it comes, laughing – a wide Negro mouth laughing. The world depends upon it. Memory folded the wings in its brain and flew father. The curly wool is already white. It laughs and laughs.

'Master, why am I living?'

'Master, master, how ugly it sounds!' And he shakes the leg irons and laughs and laughs.

God is weeping
And how the people weep when they make God weep!

Look, look!

Here comes the quarry. It is an immense mass. Many arms covered with gold braid are pushing it. And it rolls, rolls along, and at every revolution a mother's despairing eyes shine forth within a black disc and disappear. And the men with the arms keep laughing and pushing, and the mass keeps rolling, and at every revolution a body is crushed and the chains clang together and a tear wells out of the stone and alights upon the neck of one of the laughing, pushing men. And the eyes shine and the bones break and the tears weigh heavily upon the necks, and the mass rolls along. *Ay!* When the mass finishes rolling, such a gross body will weigh upon your heads that you never will be able to lift them again. Never!

In the name of compassion, in the name of honor, in the name of God, stop that mass; stop it, lest it turn toward you men and drag you down with its horrible weight. Stop it, for it is scattering many tears upon the earth, and the tears of the martyrs are ascending to the sky in the mists, and then condensing; and if you fail to stop it, the sky will tumble down upon you.

The terrible cholera, the snowy head, the frightful smallpox, the wide Negro mouth, the mass of stone. And everything – like the corpse looming out of the coffin, like the white face looming out of the black robe – everything passes by enveloped in a heavy, spreading, reddish, suffocating atmosphere. Blood, always blood!

Oh, look, look!
Spain cannot be free.
Spain still has too much blood upon her head. **❞**

JOSÉ MARTI, 'POLITICAL PRISON IN CUBA',
OUR AMERICA
MONTHLY REVIEW PRESS, 1977

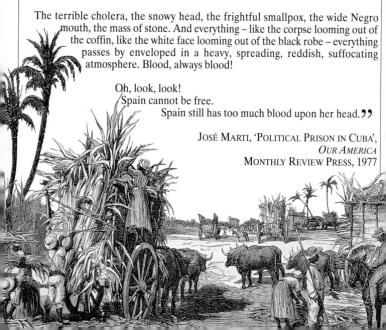

SWEAT AND THE LASH

Mulatto Cuban poet Nicolás Guillén (1902–89) was not only the leading figure of the Afro-Cuban movement, he was the pre-eminent exponent of black poetry in the Spanish-speaking world. His verse, of great lyrical beauty, became increasingly suffused with a dark and satirical potency, passionately championing human rights.

❝ Lash,
sweat and the lash.

The sun was up early
and found the Black barefoot,
his scarred body naked,
in the field.

Lash,
sweat and the lash.

The wind went screaming by:
'Your hands are two black blossoms!'
His blood said to him: 'Do it!'
He said to his blood: 'I'll do it!'

He left, barefoot, in his blood.
The canefield, trembling,
let him pass.

Afterward, the silent sky,
and beneath the sky, the slave
stained with the master's blood.

Lash,
sweat and the lash,
stained with the master's blood.
Lash,
sweat and the lash,
stained with the master's blood,
stained with the master's blood. ❞

NICOLAS GUILLÉN,
*PATRIA O MUERTE! THE GREAT ZOO
AND OTHER POEMS,*
TRANS. ROBERT MARQUEZ
MONTHLY REVIEW PRESS, 1972

THE HAVANA UNDERWORLD

SECRET AGENTS

The life and travels of novelist and playwright Graham Greene (1904–91) were often dominated by the allure of danger, and his preference for 'seedy' locations became characteristic of much of his work. His secret service comedy Our Man in Havana, *often thought his best book, conjures up the atmosphere of Havana before the Revolution. The tribulations of an unlikely spy are related with wry humour.*

❝ For some reason that morning he had no wish to meet Dr Hasselbacher for his morning daiquiri. There were times when Dr Hasselbacher was a little too carefree, as he looked in at Sloppy Joe's instead of at the Wonder Bar. No Havana resident ever went to Sloppy Joe's because it was the rendezvous of tourists; but tourists were sadly reduced nowadays in number, for the President's regime was creaking dangerously towards its end. There had always been unpleasant doings out of sight, in the inner rooms of the Jefatura, which had not disturbed the tourists in the Nacional and the Seville-Biltmore, but one tourist had recently been killed by a stray bullet while he was taking a photograph of a picturesque beggar under a balcony near the palace, and the death had sounded the knell of the all-in tour 'including a trip to Varadero beach and the night-life of Havana'. The victim's Leica had been smashed as well, and that had impressed his companions more than anything with the destructive power of a bullet. Wormold had heard them talking afterwards in the bar of the Nacional. 'Ripped right through the camera,' one of them said. 'Five hundred dollars gone just like that.'

'Was he killed at once?'

'Sure. And the lens – you could pick up bits for fifty yards around. I'm taking a piece home to show Mr Humpelnicker.'

The long bar that morning was empty except for the elegant stranger at one end and a stout member of the tourist police who was smoking a cigar at the other. The Englishman was absorbed in the sight of so many bottles and it was quite a while before he spotted Wormold. 'Well I never,' he said, 'Mr Wormold, isn't it?' Wormold wondered how he knew his name, for he had forgotten to give him a trade-card....

'...I want to talk to you about Lopez.'

The explanation that seemed more probable to Wormold was that the stranger was an eccentric inspector from headquarters, but surely he had reached the limit of eccentricity when he added in a low voice, 'You go to the Gents and I'll follow you.'

'The Gents? Why should I?'

'Because I don't know the way.'

In a mad world it always seems simpler to obey. Wormold led the stranger through a door at the back, down a short passage, and indicated the toilet. 'It's in there.'

'After you, old man.'

'But I don't need it.'

'Don't be difficult,' the stranger said. He put a hand on Wormold's shoulder and pushed him through the door. Inside there were two wash-basins, a chair with a broken back, and the usual cabinet and pissoirs. 'Take a pew, old man,' the stranger said, 'while I turn on a tap.' But when the water ran, he made no attempt to wash. 'Looks more natural,' he explained (the word 'natural' seemed a favourite adjective of his), 'if someone barges in. And of course it confuses a mike.'

'A mike?'

'You're right to question that. Quite right. There probably wouldn't be a mike in a place like this, but it's the drill, you know, that counts. You'll find it always pays in the end to follow the drill. It's lucky they don't run to waste-plugs in Havana. We can just keep the water running.'

'Please will you explain...?'

'Can't be too careful even in a Gents, when I come to think of it. A chap of ours in Denmark in 1940 saw from his own window the German fleet coming down the Kattegat.'

'What gut?'

'Kattegat. Of course he knew then the balloon had gone up. Started burning his papers. Put the ashes down the lav. and pulled the chain. Trouble was – late frost. Pipes frozen. All the ashes floated up into the bath down below. Flat belonged to an old maiden lady – Baronin someone or other. She was just going to have a bath. Most embarrassing for our chap.' **"**

GRAHAM GREENE, *OUR MAN IN HAVANA*
HEINEMANN, 1958

GUNS AND ONE-ARMED *BANDIDOS*

*G*uillermo Cabrera Infante *was born in 1929 in Gibara, but in 1941 his family moved to Havana where he worked in film. Although he was persecuted in the pre-Castro days, he quarrelled with Castro early on, and finally left Cuba in 1965.* Three Trapped Tigers *is a powerful black comedy about Havana before the revolution, acclaimed for its vicious parodies and intense interior monologue depicting a troubled and restless society populated by strange people.*

"I think of going back home and wonder if there would be anyone still there and when I'm passing the Hotel Saint John I can't resist the temptation, not of the *traganíqueles*, the coin-slot machines, the one-armed *bandidos* in the lobby which I would never put a dime in because I wouldn't ever get one out, but of the other Helen, of Elena Burke who sings in the bar and I sit at the bar to hear her sing and stay on after she's finished because there's a jazz quintet from Miami, cool but good with a saxophonist who looks like the son of Van Heflin's father and Gerry Mulligan's mother and I settle down to listening to them play 'Tonight at Noon' and to drinking and concentrating on nothing more than the sounds and I like sitting there at Elena's table and ordering her a drink and telling her how much I dislike unaccompanied singers and how much I like her, not just her voice but also her accompaniment, and when I think that it's Frank Domínguez who's at the piano I don't say a thing because this is an island of double and triple entendres told by a drunk idiot signifying everything, and I go on listening to 'Straight No Chaser' which could very well be the title of how one should take life if it wasn't so obvious that that's how it is, and at that moment the manager of the hotel is having an argument with someone who just a few moments ago was gambling and losing consistently and to top it off the guy is drunk and pulls out a gun pointing it at the head of the manager who doesn't even wince and before he could say bouncer two enormous fellows appear and tackle the drunk and grab his gun and give him two punches and flatten him against the wall and the manager takes the bullets out and slides back the bolt and returns the empty gun to the drunk who still doesn't know what's hit him and tells them to frisk him and they shove him to the door and shove him out and he must be some big shot as they haven't made mincemeat of him yet and Elena and the people from the bar turn up (the music has stopped) and she asks me what's happened and I'm just going to tell her

I don't know when the manager waves them back saying *Aquí no ha pasado nada* and then with a flick of his hand orders the jazz-men back to their music, something the quintet more asleep than awake do like a five-man pianola.

I'm already on the point of leaving when there's another uproar in the entrance and it's Colonel Ventura arriving, as he does every night, to eat at the Sky Club and listen to poetess Minerva Eros, the alleged mistress of this assassin in uniform, she who bleats happily (for her and myself) in the roof garden, and after greeting the manager Ventura goes into the elevator followed by four gunmen, while another ten or twelve remain scattered around the lobby, and as I'm sure I'm not dreaming and add up all the disagreeable things that have happened to me tonight and see that they were three in a row, I decide it's just the right moment to try my luck at the crooked slot machines.**"**

GUILLERMO CABRERA INFANTE,
THREE TRAPPED TIGERS, TRANS.
DONALD GARDNER AND
SUZANNE JILL LEVINE
PICADOR, 1980

ADDICTED TO RHYTHM

'RUNNING THROUGH MY VEINS WAS MUSIC'

M iguel Barnet, born in Havana in 1940, was one of the pioneers of the documentary novel. In Rachel's Song, *an incisive portrayal of pre-Castro Cuba, he uses newspaper accounts and personal testimonies to depict the many facets of his cabaret dancer heroine. Rachel tells of the superficialities and excesses all around her while remaining ironically unaware that in doing so she is revealing the racism and injustice of the society around her.*

❝ This city traps you. A Cuban woman seems to walk on air, not on the pavement. A Cuban man the same. We are gifted with a fleeting happiness. We don't expect a death or an accident either. That's why people are so emotional and cry and shout and stamp their feet if something happens that isn't part of the daily routine.

The people in this country amaze me. They are what has come to be known as a happy people, who live in a paradise and forget hell is the other part. People like that are admirable. Few of us have that gift. We all carry around a type of vain optimist. The birdie singing in the storm. The worst things here are fixed up with drums and beers.

Yesterday and today. That is a destiny. A grand destiny because if not, my poor people would be wasted, faithless.

I became enthusiastic again encountering this flowering place, the rowdy streets, the crowded parks, music halls, the barrio atmosphere itself, and since things had gotten ugly for my old lady, I began to look for work.

Also because what was running through my veins was music, like with Schubert.

A person addicted to rhythm, with a good ear, a figure and a desire to please, had already won half the battle. I fought like a fiend. I hit the street. I wouldn't go back to that place in Palatino, not even for a treasure. I aspired to acting. Dancing, singing a little and above all, acting. I found a little friend who went with me to theaters at night. We'd make the rounds all over Havana: the Moulin Rouge, the Albizu, the Comedia, all of them. My little friend, so he could go out with me, bought my tickets and meals. Afterward we would sit in the Prado to share our business. I was mostly silent, he was the one who had a head full of weird ideas, but he was knowledgeable and I was in the dutiful position of listening. Not a single detail escaped me. In a few matters I even dared to given him advice.

The poor guy was having a love affair that wasn't working out. One of those affairs that's not a true romance or a pastime either, because one side worships and the other gets worshipped. Well, my friend was very naive. He fell in love at first sight, without taking into account the quality of the individual, his origin, his behavior. I told him to think things through but it was like talking to the wall. Every day was tears and comedy. Unhappy creature. That kind of angel still exists.

Adolfo did my makeup, he taught me to bring out my eyebrows, to comb myself, to speak English... I came to feel affection for him and he for me, truth be told. Thanks to that friendship I met many dancers, chorus girls, impresarios. I never dared go into a theater alone.

Adolfo gave me something every month. Handkerchiefs, lipsticks, stockings. He was the one who made me see how much a woman, how attractive I was.

'Take a good look at yourself, you're wasting your time, silly.'

But he had a flaw, he was terribly jealous. The man who approached me was the man he found fault with. One day we went to a small costume party. He dressed as a Dutch Girl, he looked really cute, and I as a noble Andalusian.

We had the best costumes of the night. The place was in an uproar. I learned a few phrases and the Andalusian came out just right. Later in the Alhambra I did the Andalusian many times, remembering that party. Adolfo himself took me by the hand to the studio of El Sevillano, a great dance teacher in Havana.

It was there that I studied systematically for the first time, hours on end, holding on to the bar, lifting my leg. I'd leave a little puddle of sweat on the floor the size of a fry pan when I was done.

El Sevillano had no hope for me, as a chorus girl I mean. He told me I was a natural rumbera. But not a ballerina. I paid no attention. I answered:

'Stick to teaching me technique, I'll do the rest myself.' ❞

MIGUEL BARNET, *RACHEL'S SONG*,
TRANS. W. NICK HILL
CURBSTONE PRESS, 1991

AN ETHNIC MIX

THE CHINA GIRL

*N*ovelist and poet Severo
Sarduy (1937–93) was one of
the few writers to oppose Batista,
and at an early age was made
publisher of the Lunes de Revolución.
He left for Paris in 1960. His writing
searches for authentic ways to represent truth in
Cuba, given that the very medium of the printed word was
itself so mistrusted there. From Cuba with a Song *was Sarduy's first truly experimental
work. Its sections correspond to Cuba's ethnic groups (Spanish, African and Chinese)
and explores the disparate elements at work in Latin American culture.*

❝ *In the forest of Havana
A Chinee lost her way
and I, a poor lost goner
this fair maid did waylay*
– Homage to the 'Shanghai', Havana burlesque.

The moon, the partridge, the fading ferns, the four animals, the wine of the wind, the water of the Almendares: all was set for the rendezvous.

There, among the trunks of violet-striped sugar cane, licking reeds, following the crease of leaves like knives, silvery drivel, the snake jiggled its rattles along with the river's.

And nearby, the red turtle, the one that runs fastest: saddle of the immortals.

Further away, eyes of fire among the black leaves of the royal poinciana, the unicorn, with its hemplike mane. And next to him, the forever-on-one-foot, the pink heron.

The earth's murmur was like the clashing of sticks in The Capture of an Enemy Fort, so it wasn't at all strange to see Rose Ashes there. Sewn into that landscape,

exercising her Yin right smack in the forest of Havana, she was a white bird behind bamboo, a motionless prisoner among lances. She was reciting the Five Books, singing with her little whistle voice; she looked as if she'd burst like a salty toad; she'd gaze at the moon in silence and recite them over again.

So did the sweet smoke of the Romeo and Juliet, Havana's finest cigar, and clanking medals surprise her.

She did not turn pale; she already was, from so much rice and tea. [...]

Honoris Causa in pool and in the sack – those were her battlefields – the Condecorated, the Glorious One, did thus surprise her. Cushioned by a quilt of moss he crushed sleeping scorpions and orange snails, his step was the Invincible's: pectoral golds, its punctuation. He was the hood master of Seville's processions, the majesty of synagogues, the Galician *aîdos* in forward march. Not a general, but a long-shanked gladiator, yes.

The yellow one shrieked. And with good reason. He kept coming, parting branches, dealing blows, his arms, a double machete, his air one of combat as he fought his way through the bramble. A Peeping Tom, the licentious rake, and another mystic. But you must admit, the gymnastic arts sure come in handy! Lotus Flower leaps up, and, like the fish that jumping out of water becomes a hummingbird, she flies among lianas. Now she's the white mask striped by shadows of sugar canes, now the flight of a dove, the streak of a rabbit. Try and see her. You can't. Yes! her eyes, two golden slits, snake charmer eyes, betray her. A puckery *caimito* among clusters of *caimitos*. She's mimicry. She's a texture – the white plaques on the trunk of a God tree – a wilted flower beneath a palm, a butterfly embossed with pupils, she is pure symmetry. Where is she? I don't see her. She scarcely breathes. Now, with eyebrow pencil she draws faces on her hands and wiggles them far from her own, to bewilder Mr. Belicose. He, dividing the air with his sword, curses her in alphabetical order.

Rose Ashes becomes a cloud, a baby fawn, the murmur of the river among its pebbles. So they go around in circles, searching each other out with a stare, like two fighting cocks. And so recitation time passes.

The China maid attacks. Changes disguise, throws stones, appears and disappears in the same place, runs zigzag so that no weapon can reach her, erects a stone barrier to make the river run in the other direction and mislead the Enemy; she scats centipedes, squirrels, chameleons, so that they'll bite him as he passes; she imitates the clanking medals, the very voice of her pursuer, or appears as another lecherous general to drive him crazy. One by one she exhausts her scenic resources.

The Butcher is ready to fight. For him, her escapes are like the carriages of gold they give an invader to stop him. Around and around his prisoner he goes: it's no longer one but two swords he carries. With the second knife, the one that bends but never breaks, he opens the underbrush. A Pyrrhic little flute that one!

The finer the Yellow One becomes, the more liquid it gets, the sword you all know, the more fiery; why it's almost two-tongued!

Naturally, with an ally like that, it doesn't take long for Mr. Lecherous to attempt checkmate.

The Forest of Havana is the Summer Palace's forest, and the waters of the Almendares, the Yangtze; Rose Ashes weaves her own figure with lianas and flees, leaving her adversary with that intangible double, that unraveling and moving image.

He subtly approaches from behind; but abandoned by Chola Angüengue, the conga queen of weapons, he gets caught in her loom.

Faraway, the China maid shrieks, and dances the Canton mambo. And he, stuck, here. Still. **"**

SEVERO SARDUY, *FROM CUBA WITH A SONG*,
TRANS. SUZANNE JILL LEVINE
PICADOR, 1980

THE TEETERING STATE

The Franco-Russian writer Alejo Carpentier (1904–80) was born and raised in Cuba before he fled to Paris in 1928 following his arrest for his opposition to Machado. Reasons of State *is the satirical tale of a president of a minor Latin American country to which he is forced to return regularly from a life of ease in Paris to suppress the latest uprising.*

❝ The Head of State had learned from letters received that same morning that events which at first he had viewed with a certain irony were really happening: 'Utopian vegetarian notions,' he had said. Yet now, in Nueva Córdoba – between meetings, rallies, proclamations and factions – intensive military instruction for students and workers was going on, under the leadership of an obscure Captain Becerra – a spare-time entomologist – who had been named Military Chief of the town. And, observing that the movement was gaining strength, with signs of syndicalism inspired by foreign, antipatriotic doctrines, inadmissible in our country, the United States Ambassador offered a speedy intervention by North American troops, to safeguard democratic institutions. Some battleships happened to be manoeuvring in the Caribbean.

'It would be humiliating for our sovereignty,' observed the Head of State. 'This operation won't be difficult. And we must show these filthy gringos that we can manage our own problems by ourselves. Besides which, they are the sort who come for three weeks and stay two years, carrying out huge business deals. They arrive dressed in khaki and go away laden with gold. Look what General Wood did in Cuba.'

Three days passed in inspecting and preparing the East Railway, and after a grand campaigning Mass, at which they begged the Divine Shepherdess to grant triumph to the national forces, several convoys set off towards the new front, with a great noise of cheering and laughter under their regimental flags. […]

Night lay behind them, and frogs croaked in the black marshes of Surgidero, now restored to the peace of its slow provincial activities, with gatherings in the barbers' shops, a huddle of old women in the doorways, and – for the young – lotteries and games of forfeits, after telling their beads among the family with their minds focused on the fifteen mysteries of the Virgin Mary. ❞

ALEJO CARPENTIER, *REASONS OF STATE*,
TRANS. FRANCES PARTRIDGE, VICTOR GOLLANCZ LTD, 1976

THE SEA

'THE SEA SWALLOWS A MAN EVERY DAY…'

Reinaldo Arenas (1943–90) was one of Cuba's great 20th-century writers. Born into a poor rural Cuban family, he joined Castro's guerrillas against Batista's regime at the age of fifteen, only to witness monumental repression under Castro. He finally left Cuba for Paris in 1980. Before Night Falls *is his autobiography, begun while he was still in Cuba and completed shortly before he died of AIDS. It is both raw and fierce, tender and lyrical, particularly about the Cuban landscape.*

❝ My grandmother was also the one who first took me to the ocean. One of her daughters had managed to get a permanent husband, and he worked in Gibara, the seaport closest to our hometown. For the first time, I took a bus. I think that for my grandmother, who was already sixty, it was also the first time. We went to Gibara. My grandmother, and the rest of my family, had never seen the ocean, although it was only twenty or thirty miles from where we lived. I remember that once my aunt Carolina came to my grandmother's house crying and saying: 'Do you realize what it means that I am forty years old and have never seen the ocean? I will soon die of old age without ever having seen it.' From then on, I thought of nothing else but the sea. 'The sea swallows a man every day,' my grandmother would say. And I felt then an irresistible urge to see the ocean.

How could I explain what I felt the first time that I saw the sea! It would be impossible to describe that moment. There is only one word that does it any justice: the Sea. **99**

REINALDO ARENAS, *BEFORE NIGHT FALLS*,
TRANS. DOLORES M. KOCH, VIKING PENGUIN, 1993

DEEP-SEA FISHING

In his latter years, American writer and novelist Ernest Hemingway left the expatriate literary community in Paris to live in Cuba. His growing disillusionment with modern culture manifested itself in his interest in the primitive and brutal. His passion for deep-sea fishing inspired The Old Man and the Sea, *about man's struggle against nature.*

66 The old man drank his coffee slowly. It was all he would have all day and he knew that he should take it. For a long time now eating had bored him and he never carried a lunch. He had a bottle of water in the bow of the skiff and that was all he needed for the day.

The boy was back now with the sardines and the two baits wrapped in a newspaper and they went down the trail to the skiff, feeling the pebbled sand under their feet, and lifted the skiff and slid her into the water.

'Good luck old man.'

'Good luck,' the old man said. He fitted the rope lashings of the oars on to the thole pins and, leaning forward against the thrust of the blades in the water, he began to row out of the harbour in the dark. There were other boats from the other beaches going out to sea and the old man heard the dip and push of their oars even though he could not see them now the moon was below the hills.

Sometimes someone would speak in a boat. But most of the boats were silent except for the dip of the oars. They spread apart after they were out of the harbour and each one headed for the part of the ocean where he hoped to find fish. The old man knew he was going far out and he left the smell of the land behind and rowed out into the ocean. He saw the phosphorescence of the Gulf weed in the water as he rowed over the part of the ocean that the fishermen called the great well because there was a sudden deep of seven hundred fathoms where all sorts of fish congregated because of the swirl the current made against the steep walls of the floor of the ocean. Here there were concentrations of shrimp and bait fish and sometimes schools of squid in the deepest holes and these rose close to the surface at night where all the wandering fish fed on them.

In the dark the old man could feel the morning coming and as he rowed he heard the trembling sound as flying fish left the water and the hissing that their stiff set wings made as they soared away in the darkness. He was very fond of flying fish as they were his principal friends on the ocean. He was sorry for the birds, especially the small delicate dark terns that were always flying and looking and almost never finding, and he thought, 'The birds have a harder life than we do except for the robber birds and the heavy strong ones. Why did they make birds so delicate and fine as those sea swallows when the ocean can be so cruel? She is kind and very beautiful. But she can be so cruel and it comes so suddenly and such birds that fly, dipping and hunting, with their small sad voices are made too delicately for the sea.'

He always thought of the sea as *la mar* which is what people call her in Spanish when they love her. Sometimes those who love her say bad things of her but they are always said as though she were a woman. Some of the younger fishermen, those who used buoys as floats for their lines and had motor-boats, bought when the shark livers had brought much money, spoke of her as *el mar* which is masculine. They spoke of her as a contestant or a place or even an enemy. But the old man always thought of her as feminine and as something that gave or withheld great favours, and if she did wild or wicked things it was because she could not help them. The moon affects her as it does a woman, he thought. **99**

ERNEST HEMINGWAY, *THE OLD MAN AND THE SEA*
JONATHAN CAPE LTD, 1952

BEHIND CLOSED DOORS

In the early years of his career, José Lezama Lima (1912–76) was a keen exponent of the avant-garde. His greatest achievement as a writer is his complex and poetical novel Paradiso, *first published in Castro's Cuba in 1966. Autobiographical in inspiration, it interweaves intimate pictures of family life with a penetrating insight into his growth as a poet and his awareness of his own homosexuality. Since the book contained no mention of the revolution and included frank discussions of homosexuality (taboo in Cuba) Lezama, once director of the Department of Literature and Publications of the National Cultural Council, fell foul of the Castro regime.*

❝'Your mother must have regained consciousness now,' Dr. Santurce told him, cutting into the withdrawal into which Cemí had fallen. 'It was a long operation, it lasted more than three hours, but there was no risk at any time. Dr. Nogueira says that your mother has the makeup of a jiquí tree, an organism with prodigious resistance. Still, to diminish the risk of ventricular hypertrophy, he gave her a small dose of digitalis. That's why you may find your mother a little nervous now, with her breathing a little difficult.' [...]

When he went into the room, he saw how his mother's eyes fell on his face. Those tender, watery, waiting eyes which always bathed him in their distance and in their closeness. They had that surprising and unique faculty: they brought distance close to him, they made closeness distant. They erased the immediate and the distant for him to attain tender attachment, omnicomprehensive company. That glance, even if it were buried, seemed always to keep looking at him, as if his arrival gave her an endless joy, as if forgiving his departures. Only mothers possess that glance which contains a sad and noble wisdom, something unknowable, something that requires the regal accompaniment of the mother's look. Only mothers know how to look, have the wisdom of the look, they don't look to follow the vicissitudes of a figure, they look to see the birth and the death, something which is the unity of a great suffering with the epiphany of the creature. That look gave him the impression of reading an ancient prescription for curing asthma: the height of the damaged person is marked on a bejucubí tree, then it is cut down and sent to a distant place in another city. His mother's look seemed to him to occupy a distant place attained only by sleep in a city abandoned by its inhabitants. Yet he looked at her and met his mother's look as it came out of that burned or sunken city to receive him.

On the night table he noticed a bouquet of cream-colored flowers with tigery tips held by a green base with purple-rimmed white clouds. Next to her, a box similar to the shield of Harun al-Rashid, gilded and with a heraldic branch in its center. The open box displayed an English fruitcake. The mass of an old-ounce yellow showed red and green candies with an interpolation of dates and almonds from Reus. At the bottom of the box there was a card. Cemí went over to read it: 'Your grateful friends, Maria Theresa Sunster and Ricardo Fronesis.' He smiled; when he raised his eyes he met his mother's look again. That was the form of wisdom that he wanted to have with him always.❞

JOSÉ LEZAMA LIMA, *PARADISO*,
TRANS. GREGORY RABASSA,
UNIVERSITY OF TEXAS PRESS, 1988

THE LOCOMOTIVE

Virgilio Piñera (1912–79) is revered as one of Cuba's best writers. Most of the stories contained in Cold Tales *bear the hallmark of Pinera's prose: sceptical while strangely innocent, shocking and often absurd. 'The tales are cold because they limit themselves to hard facts,' Pinera commented. '...life neither rewards nor punishes, neither condemns nor saves...he is not obliged to judge his own acts, to give them any significance whatsoever...Soon the words, the letters run together, become confused; in the end, we understand nothing, we revert to infancy, we are like children, their mouths stuffed with candy. And then, mysterious babbling, spontaneous and noisy, bursts forth.'*

❝A locomotive – the biggest in the world – advances on a very narrow embankment. It's the biggest locomotive in the world because it has surpassed the previous model, which – until the appearance of this one that runs on a narrow embankment – used to be the biggest in the world. It's so big that you wouldn't even see the other one next to it because it is the biggest in the world. But it's all rather difficult to understand. For example, in relation to the place it hasn't yet occupied in its travels, it isn't the biggest in the world. I mean if it's as long as from here to here, and the volume it displaces is from there to there, as long as it hasn't yet occupied that space, one can't say that it's the biggest in the world. If it's moving at the incredible speed with which it eats up the track, you must know that it's the biggest in the world, because if you don't, you will be threatened by knowing that it exists, yet not knowing that it's the biggest in the world. The same holds true when you set your eyes on it: be careful how you look at it. Perhaps you will look at it and not see it as the biggest in the world, and will become greatly disappointed and even sad. I warn you, if you remain long in your contemplation with the complete understanding that it's the biggest in the world, be very careful, for it will grow so big that it will occupy the whole earth and beyond. After all, what does it mean to say that it's the biggest in the world? The world is very big, but it too is the biggest in the world. But you will tell me that before it was built the other one was the biggest in the world and that it's in relation to this one and not to the world itself that it's the biggest in the world. I'm not telling you that, but rather that the one that used to be the biggest in the world was, in its turn, the biggest in a world that was also very big. All right then, you will say, are there two locomotives that are the biggest in the world and two worlds that are the biggest in the world? And what about the locomotives built before the biggest in the world and before the biggest of the biggest in the world? And the worlds that have corresponded to those locomotives from long before the biggest in the world? Yes, where is the world prior to the biggest locomotive in the world, and the locomotive itself that used to be the biggest before the one that is now the biggest in the world? And so too, all those that were the biggest in the world before the one that now runs on the embankment and is the biggest in the world – were they thought the biggest in the world before the biggest in the world? Do you realize that there are many factors, that the whole question is surrounded by danger, that you could sink into an eternal night, that it's possible to repeat the words and concepts without arriving at their meaning? Do you clearly understand the perils of the adventure that lies in knowing that the locomotive advancing along the narrow embankment is the biggest in the world?❞

VIRGILIO PIÑERA, *COLD TALES*, TRANS. MARK SCHAFER
VIKING PENGUIN, 1993

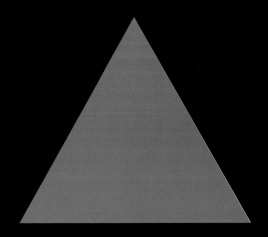

Cuban itineraries

▲ Viñales valley

▲ Archipiélago de Sabana, east of Varadero

▼ Valle de los Ingenios

▲ Domino players in Santiago de Cuba

▲ Traditional dances in the Plaza de la Catedral   ▼ *Pelota* (baseball) players in Trinidad

▲ Young residents of Havana

▲ Woman smoking a Havana cigar

▼ *Rumberos* (*rumba* players) in Havana

▲ The Casa de la Trova in Trinidad

▼ The Prado in Havana

Havana

THE CITY OF COLUMNS
This short story about the Havanese column was written by Alejo Carpentier ● *109*, ▲ *128, 144* in his work *The City of Columns*: initially a 'graceful internal column, born in shady courtyards', its slender silhouette typified this 'city where the streets were intentionally narrow, conducive to shade, and where neither twilight nor dawn blinded passersby by casting too much light in their eyes'. But, in the 19th century, the column was promoted to the façade of houses, it grew, blossomed and became intrusive. Havana turned into 'a Mecca of columns, a forest of columns, an infinite colonnade, the last city to have such a vast number of columns'.

A sprawling, eclectic and disorganized city, Havana exerts a powerful magic; despite continually being pulled down and rebuilt, it boasts many architectural treasures that make it one of the most picturesque capitals in the New World. In 1982, UNESCO named Havana's historical center a World Heritage Site. There is something both captivating and disturbing about its prevailing atmosphere of neglect, the stately splendor of its buildings coupled with the bleached colors of its dilapidated façades, the striking contrast between its past glory and its still exuberant lifestyle. For half a century, Havana has suffered the indignities of poor maintenance; overcrowded public transport, water shortages, blackouts and the black market are routine evils with which the residents of Havan have to contend, but they do so with a sense of humor. Our itinerary will take in the following districts: Habana Vieja (Old Havana), the historic heart of the city, between the bay of Havana to the east and the old city walls to the west; a stroll from east to west along the Malecón, the famous seafront promenade, into Centro Habana and the Vedado, flanked in the south by the more modern districts of the Plaza de la Revolución and Nuevo Vedado. The residential districts of Miramar and Cubanacán (the former Country Club) extend further west of the Vedado. Finally, in the east, on the other side of the bay, Habana del Este boasts two of the city's fortresses ● *78* as well as the beaches of Playa del Este ▲ *165*.

THE CITY'S HISTORY

FOUNDATION AND EARLY DANGERS. San Cristóbal de la Habana was founded in 1515 on the south coast of Cuba, in the kingdom of an Indian chief, Habaguanex, who gave the city its name. In 1519, the city moved to its current site on the north coast, around the Puerto de Carenas, whose sheltered bay was the last stopover for Spanish ships on their way home from the Indies. In 1553, the island's governor, formerly based in Santiago, took up residence in Havana. The city became the capital in 1607 ● *33* due to its strategic location. However, the

city's growth was stunted by the threat from pirates. Between the 16th and 18th centuries, it acquired a defense system, building many fortresses and a city wall, erected in 1674.

EXPANSION. In 1697, the Peace of Ryswick ● *33* put an end to piracy: trade and agriculture, revolving around the production of sugarcane, tobacco and rum, allowed Havana to expand. The city was governed by the Spanish captain generals, who ruled the wealthy settlers with a rod of iron but, in 1762, the English seized control and, for eleven months, the city enjoyed the benefits of free trade. On their return to power in 1763, the Spanish relaxed their monopoly. A Creole bourgeoisie emerged, building lavish palaces within the city walls. An ornamental style of architecture was gradually adopted, streets were paved, public baths built and, in 1846, a gas lighting system was installed. By the end of the 19th century, Havana had 250,000 inhabitants and the island had begun its fight for independence.

CONTEMPORARY CHANGES. In the early 20th century the United States was the city's inspiration, but although a few streets in Old Havana, the economic center, assumed the appearance of a 'little Wall Street', most of them deteriorated, leading to a housing crisis that worsened after the Revolution ● *44*: Castro, not wanting to neglect the nation in favor of a capital which had become synonymous with vice, concentrated his financial resources on agriculture. With its 2.5 million inhabitants, Havana is now the largest city in the Caribbean and the political, economic, cultural and scientific capital of the island.

AN OVERCROWDED CITY
From 1900 to 1950 Havana's population increased sixfold, swelled by a large influx of peasants and Spanish immigrants. The western part of the city became so crowded that a tunnel was built under the bay in 1957 to develop the unoccupied land to the east. The old houses in the center, abandoned since the mid-19th century by the wealthy, were converted into rental apartment blocks, the notorious *solares*, which were very quickly filled to overflowing.

⊒ c. 6 miles

PLAZA DE ARMAS ★

This is the oldest and finest square in the city. A simple parade ground in the 16th century, by the end of the 18th century it had been enlarged to become the administrative and political center of Havana, lined with the baroque façades of stylish palaces. The square was redesigned in 1934, reflecting the Romantic spirit of the 19th century. Kapok trees, royal palms and fountains break up the geometry of avenues that meet at the foot of the STATUE OF CARLOS MANUEL DE CÉSPEDES, sculpted in 1955 by Sergio López Mesa (*bottom right*). Like the Havana citizens of days gone by, who used to come here in their famous *volantas* (carriages) to listen to musical concerts, you can take a leisurely stroll in this square while enjoying the music that is still performed under the arcades.

CASTILLO DE LA REAL FUERZA ● *78*. In 1538, as part of the program to fortify the city, the governor Hernando de Soto ordered the construction of the first defense works, opposite the narrow pass marking the entrance to the bay. Completed in 1540 but destroyed in 1555 by the French pirate Jacques de Sores ● *33*, ▲ *206*, the original fortress was replaced by the existing building between 1558 and 1577. Constructed to a square plan and flanked at each corner by four bastions, its symmetrical design was the work of military engineer Bartolomé Sánchez who was the first designer to adopt Italian Renaissance principles in the Americas. The city's governors occupied the top story of the fortress from 1590 until their move to the Palacio de los Capitanes Generales ▲ *124*. The first story now houses the MUSEO DE LA CERÁMICA. From the top, there is a picturesque view over the two fortresses which guard the other bank of the canal ▲ *146*.

THE GIRALDILLA ★, EMBLEM OF THE CITY
The statue on top of the west tower of the Castillo de la Real Fuerza, the work of Jerónimo Martínez Pinzón, is the oldest on the island (1632). The original statue, toppled by a hurricane in 1926, is in the Museo de la Ciudad ▲ *124*.

This 18th-century house prefigured the neoclassical style of the 19th century. Once a residence of the Count of Santovenia, in 1867 it became the city's first hotel, the *Santa Isabel*, now lavishly restored and reopened. Its façade, punctuated by the columns of the portico, is graced by a first-story balcony with large openings. The polychromatic windows and the beautiful wrought-iron railings around the windows and the balconies add a graceful touch.

PALACIO DEL SEGUNDO CABO. Together with the Palacio de los Capitanes Generales, this palace forms the finest architectural complex on the square, a symbol of colonial power at the end of the 18th century. It was built by royal order between 1770 and 1791 to house the Casa de Correos (post office). It subsequently became the treasury and the home of the vice-governor in 1854, hence its name (Palace of the Second Lieutenant), then the seat of the Senate and the justice courts. It now houses the Instituto Cubano del Libro. Designed by J. A. de Armona, built by Antonio Fernández de Trevejos and refurbished in 1829 by Govantes and Cabarrocas, the building is a remarkable illustration of what is known as 'Cuban baroque' ● *82*, a more restrained style than its European

counterpart. The delicate outline of the windows and the intricate work on the pilasters of the portico enliven an austere façade. The narrow COURTYARD enclosed by a blind arcade on the first story with blue windows and huge white louvered shutters, is definitely worth a look.

EL TEMPLETE ● *86*. This small Greco-Roman style temple was inaugurated on March 19, 1828, to commemorate the first mass celebrated on the site when the hamlet of San Cristóbal de la Habana was transferred here in 1519. The Doric portico supports a pediment engraved with an inscription instructing the Cuban people to preserve the memory of this place. Inside, three paintings by the French artist Jean-Baptiste Vermay (c. 1786–1833) also illustrate these events. A *ceiba* (kapok tree) marks the spot where the original ceremony took place. Beside it stands a column, erected in 1754, topped by the Virgen del Pilar, patron saint of Spanish sailors.

OLD HAVANA: UNESCO WORLD HERITAGE SITE ✪
Try to visit Old Havana between 8am and 2pm to avoid the heat and the crowd of tourists. For an introduction to the historic and artistic heart of the capital, you should visit the Museo de la Cindad, Plaza de Armas, and the Museo de Arte Colonial, Plaza de la Cathedral.

THE PALACIO DE LOS CAPITANES GENERALES AND THE MUSEO DE LA CIUDAD

Havana's first parish church was destroyed in the 18th century when the warship *Invincible* exploded. Eighteen years later, the most remarkable baroque building in Cuba was built on its site. The work of Antonio Fernández de Trebejos y Zaldívar, the palace was finished in 1791. The seat of the captains-general – the Spanish government – and the city council until 1841, it also housed a prison until 1834, the US governor during the American occupation (1899–1902), the presidency of the Republic (1902–20) and the city hall (1921–67). The Palacio currently houses the office of the city's official historian and the Museo de la Ciudad (Museum of the City). The latter's original furniture and collections conjure up the lavish lifestyle enjoyed by the dignitaries of yesteryear and chart the history of Cuba's formative years.

A JOURNEY IN TIME
The museum has the oldest colonial relic in Cuba: a funerary bas-relief (*below*) which once adorned Havana's first parish church. It was placed on the very spot where, in 1557, young Doña María de Cepero y Nieto was accidentally killed by a bullet from an arquebus (handgun). Other rooms lead visitors into the very heart of 20th-century Cuba. The museum also has on display the bronze eagle that topped the monument to the victims of the *Maine* explosion ● *39* until the 1960s.

THE CENTRAL COURTYARD

Its size and splendor are unequaled in Cuba.
It serves as a fine setting for one of the first
sculptures of Christopher Columbus, the work
of the Italian artist Cucchiari. It was
inaugurated in 1862, several months before
the one by Cárdenas ▲ 170.

PAST GLORY
The luxurious
bathroom (*above*)
with its marble
bathtubs stands
monument to a
bygone lifestyle, as do
the Salones del Café y
del Ambientado
(coffee room and
period drawing room)
with their colonial
furniture dating from
the end of the 19th
century.

A SENSE OF HISTORY
The palace has some
fine private
apartments and
majestic ceremonial
rooms, such as the
Salón del Trono
(throne room) and
the Salón de los
Espejos (hall of
mirrors, *right*). It was
in the latter room
that two key events
took place in the
history of Cuba: the
transfer of power
from Spain to the
United States on
January 1, 1899
● *39* and, on May 20,
1902 ● *42*, the
appointment and
inauguration of the
first Cuban president,
Tomás Estrada
Palma, in the
presence of the North
American governor.

THE SALA DE LAS BANDERAS
(THE HALL OF FLAGS)
This room contains three emblems of the
Republic: flags belonging to Narciso López,
Máximo Gómez and Céspedes. However its
crowning glory is the 1908 painting *The Death
of Antonio Maceo* ● *39*, ▲ *215* (*below*) by the
Cuban artist Menocal. The work remains
controversial: it is said that some of the figures
depicted at the side of the 'bronze Titan' would
not have been present at his death.

PLAZA DE LA CATEDRAL ★

The best time to explore the Plaza de la Catedral is early morning, when the square is still deserted and quiet. Façades with harmonious porticos and long wrought-iron balconies make this square an architectural gem of the colonial era. Despite its imposing appearance, the Plaza radiates a feeling of intimacy because it is so small and enclosed. In the 16th century, it was a muddy piece of land that used to flood during the rainy season, and was thus called Plaza de la Ciénaga ('Square of the Swamp'). It was not until 1789, after the church here was consecrated as a cathedral, that it was given its existing name.

CATEDRAL DE SAN CRISTÓBAL ● 80. Dedicated to the Immaculate Conception, this cathedral is better known as San Cristóbal. It was begun by the Jesuits in 1748, but its construction was interrupted in 1767 when the order was expelled from the Americas by the Spanish Crown. It was finally completed in 1777. The church is built to the traditional Jesuit plan of three naves with side aisles; the design of the FAÇADE ★, inspired by the work of Francesco Borromini at St Agnese in Rome but freer in style, is pure baroque. The building, flanked by two asymmetrical towers with smooth, undressed walls, opens into a simple nave. Restored in 1814, it combines various styles with success. Its vault, made of wood, then stone, still has the original baroque cupola. The HIGH ALTAR, carved in the 19th century by Bianchini and surmounted by three frescos by Giuseppe Perovani, is alone worth the visit. The baroque altars were replaced in 1820 by neoclassical ones.

CASA DEL CONDE DE CASA LOMBILLO AND PALACIO DEL MARQUÉS DE ARCOS. These two buildings (*below, left*), whose porticos and balconies form one continuous line, were completed around the mid-18th century, a period that saw the rise of a new Creole aristocracy. Magnificent portals, elaborate cornices and Doric porticos marked the new status enjoyed by these wealthy families. The Marquis de Arcos, who gave the palace its name, inherited it from his father, Diego Peñalver, the Royal Treasurer, who bought it in 1796. The palace housed the Main Post Office in the mid-19th century. The two buildings are currently being restored.

CASA DEL CONDE DE CASA BAYONA. This is the oldest house on the square. Rebuilt in 1720 for J. Bayona y Chacón, it has retained the purity of line characteristic of 17th-century buildings. Its elegant, symmetrical proportions, tiled roof, patio surrounded by Tuscan pilasters supporting surbased arches, and stained-glass windows with shutters clinch its

PORTICOS AND BALCONIES
The new authority enjoyed by the Creole aristocracy found expression in the changing architecture of their homes. They discarded the model of the low-roofed, narrow refuge, popular in the 17th century, in favor of a style of house that was more spacious and airy, with interconnecting internal and external areas. The portico and balcony on the façade reproduced the inner structure of the patio. The intricate ones adorning the Palacio del Marqués de Arcos are worth a look.

appeal. The nephew of Bayona y Chacón, the count of Bayona, inherited the building, which has since been home to a college for clerks of the court, the newspaper *La Discusión* and the offices of the famous Arrechabala distillery. It now houses the MUSEO DE ARTE COLONIAL ★.

CASA DE LOS MARQUESES DE AGUAS CLARAS. Built between 1751 and 1775, this is the most recent building on the square (*below, second left*). Its portico boasts an original and attractive design: four semicircular arches flank a basket-handle arch which surrounds the portal. The *El Patio* restaurant occupies the inner courtyard which provides a delightful setting with its palm trees and fountain.

CALLEJÓN DEL CHORRO. In 1587, a cistern was built on the boggy square to supply the ships in the harbor with water. A small canal, the *chorro*, linked it, in 1592, to the Royal Aqueduct. The CASA DE BAÑOS (former public bathhouse) was then built in place of this cistern.

CENTRO WIFREDO LAM. Although Wifredo Lam (1902–82) ● 99 gave his name to this gallery (Calle San Ignacio, No. 22), it mainly exhibits the works of artists taking part in Havana's Art Biennale, which provides a renowned and respected forum for Third World artists.

CASA DE LA CONDESA DE LA REUNIÓN ★. This house (Calle Empedrado, 213–5), was built in 1809 to a plan typical of the homes of wealthy Creole families: commodities were stored on the ground floor, domestic servants

THE MUSEO DE ARTE COLONIAL ★
This museum reproduces the lavish interiors of an aristocratic house from the colonial period: furniture made of precious wood, Limoges porcelain, crystal chandeliers made by Baccarat, mirrors imported from Europe, plinths covered with frescos of plant motifs, in line with Cuban tradition. Other distinctive features are wrought-iron railings typical of 19th-century art, *medios puntos* ● 84 (stained-glass windows with wooden struts), *lucetas* (tall windows with panes of stained glass that filtered the light) and *mamparas* ● 87 (doors or screens used in spacious rooms to create a feeling of intimacy).

lived on the mid-story and the owners on the top story. Alejo Carpentier was captivated by the trefoil arch that led into a vast hall (*zaguán* ● *84*), the carved wood balcony with intricately worked corners enclosing the patio below, its walls decorated with flowered *azulejos* (painted tiles). The writer ● *109*, ▲ *120* set the first chapters of his novel *The Enlightenment* in this building, which now houses the Alejo-Carpentier Foundation.

Calle Tacón. Facing the bay, this is one of the oldest streets in the capital. It has retained its simple low-roofed houses from the beginning of the 17th century. There is also an 18th-century building, the Seminario San Carlos y San Antonio, a spiritual melting-pot which produced the intellectuals who were to lead the island to independence ● *38*.

Calle Obispo
This is Havana's main street. It is the site of two picturesque old pharmacies: the Farmacia y Droguería Taquechel (No 155) and the Droguería Johnson (No 260).

From the Plaza de Armas to the Plaza de San Francisco

Casa de la Calle Obispo ★. This small white and blue house with its tiled roof (*above*) at No 117, is the oldest in the capital (1648). The elegant turned wood balconies on its façade are worth looking out for. Nearby, on the left, on the corner of Calle Mercaderes, is the hotel *Ambos Mundos*

> '[…] The adolescent boy contemplated the city, which bore a strange similarity, at this hour filled with reflections and long shadows, to a huge baroque street lamp […]'

Alejo Carpentier

where Hemingway ▲ *150* used to stay. CALLE MERCADERES (Street of Merchants) and CALLE OFICIOS (Street of Craftsmen) are full of character: the buildings on these streets represent some of the city's most successful architectural achievements.

CASA DE LA OBRA PÍA ★ ● *85*. This 17th-century mansion, rebuilt in 1665 and in 1793, was created by two adjacent houses being combined. It is a highly original example of Cuban architecture owing to its size, character and cool patio surrounded by arches and galleries paved with terracotta slabs. Its majestic portal, brought back from Cádiz in 1686, forms a contrast with the austerity of its façade. The interior boasts surprisingly large drawing rooms, colored plinths and a wide variety of different arches adorning doors and windows. The house has been converted into a MUSEUM, which exhibits objects and personal effects belonging to Alejo Carpentier.

CASA DE ÁFRICA ★. This 17th-century building has a first story which has been used variously for storing wool and cars, as a stable and as accommodation for slaves. The top story was used exclusively by the owners. It holds many presents given to Fidel Castro during his travels to Africa and a collection of cult objects bequeathed by ethnologist Fernando Ortíz ● *42*.

CASA SIMÓN BOLÍVAR. Restored in 1993, this house is devoted to the hero of the independence movement and to the Venezuelan culture. A STATUE OF BOLÍVAR, a copy of the one in Santa Fe de Bogotá, stands nearby.

CASA DEL OBISPO. This former Episcopal palace dating from the 17th century, not to be confused with the Casa on Obispo street, was converted in 1858 into a pawnshop after being extensively restored. Currently it houses the MUSEO NUMISMÁTICO, which possesses a fine collection of Cuban currency as well as rare coins and notes, such as a banknote from the Cuban Republic in arms, printed in New York in 1869 and bearing the signature of Céspedes ● *39* and banknotes signed by Che ▲ *192*.

PLAZA DE SAN FRANCISCO. This vast square is a hive of activity owing to the presence of the Customs House (1914) and the commodities market. The Fountain of the Lions was sculpted in 1836 by Giuseppe Gaggini and symbolizes the power of the Spanish empire. The IGLESIA Y CONVENTO DE SAN FRANCISCO DE ASÍS ★ was built between 1580 and 1591, and modified between 1720 and 1737. This is one of the finest churches from the colonial period ● *80*. Its massive 140-foot-high bell tower looms over the city. The adjoining convent was built in 1739. The church has been converted into a concert hall and an art gallery.

CASA DE LOS ÁRABES

This simple building, with its vine-covered patio, sturdy wooden balustrades and large stained-glass windows, dates from the 17th century. In this recent incarnation, it combines two old houses on Calle Oficios and focuses on Arab culture in Cuba, the result of a large influx of immigrants from the Lebanon, Syria and Palestine. It also houses an Oriental restaurant, *Al Medina*, and the only mosque in Cuba. It was originally home to the Colegio San Ambrosio before the construction of the Seminario on Calle Tacón.

LA LONJA DEL COMERCIO

Built in 1909, this commodities market was restored in the 1990s with the help of foreign capital, a first for Cuba since the Revolution. Its dome is surmounted by a bronze of Mercury.

▲ HAVANA
HABANA VIEJA

1. CASA DE LAS HERMANAS CÁRDENAS
2. CASA DE LOS CONDE DE JARUCO
3. IGLESIA Y CONVENTO DE SANTA CLARA
4. IGLESIA Y CONVENTO DE NUESTRA SEÑORA DE BELEN
5. IGLESIA DEL ESPÍRITU SANTO
6. IGLESIA Y CONVENTO DE NUESTRA SEÑORA DE LA MERCED
7. CASA NATAL DE JOSÉ MARTÍ
8. CENTRAL STATION
9. FRAGMENT OF CITY WALL

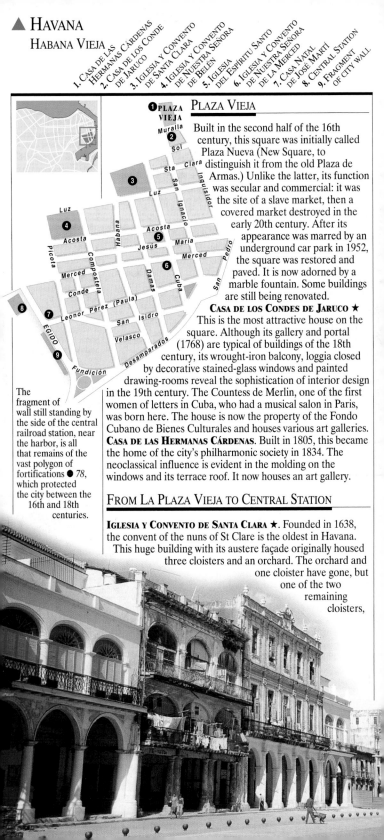

PLAZA VIEJA

Built in the second half of the 16th century, this square was initially called Plaza Nueva (New Square, to distinguish it from the old Plaza de Armas.) Unlike the latter, its function was secular and commercial: it was the site of a slave market, then a covered market destroyed in the early 20th century. After its appearance was marred by an underground car park in 1952, the square was restored and paved. It is now adorned by a marble fountain. Some buildings are still being renovated.

CASA DE LOS CONDES DE JARUCO ★
This is the most attractive house on the square. Although its gallery and portal (1768) are typical of buildings of the 18th century, its wrought-iron balcony, loggia closed by decorative stained-glass windows and painted drawing-rooms reveal the sophistication of interior design in the 19th century. The Countess de Merlin, one of the first women of letters in Cuba, who had a musical salon in Paris, was born here. The house is now the property of the Fondo Cubano de Bienes Culturales and houses various art galleries.

CASA DE LAS HERMANAS CÁRDENAS. Built in 1805, this became the home of the city's philharmonic society in 1834. The neoclassical influence is evident in the molding on the windows and its terrace roof. It now houses an art gallery.

FROM LA PLAZA VIEJA TO CENTRAL STATION

IGLESIA Y CONVENTO DE SANTA CLARA ★. Founded in 1638, the convent of the nuns of St Clare is the oldest in Havana. This huge building with its austere façade originally housed three cloisters and an orchard. The orchard and one cloister have gone, but one of the two remaining cloisters,

The fragment of wall still standing by the side of the central railroad station, near the harbor, is all that remains of the vast polygon of fortifications ● 78, which protected the city between the 16th and 18th centuries.

> 'It was a city that eternally welcomed the wind which would penetrate it, avid for breezes off sea and land; shutters, slatted blinds, flaps, arms opened wide to the first passing gust of cool air.'
>
> Alejo Carpentier

peaceful and cool under the shade of the palms and kapoks with its pretty fountain of a Samaritan woman (17th century), seems imbued with the contemplative mood created by the five nuns from Cartagena de Indias who took up residence here in 1643. It is now the head office of the Centro Nacional de Conservación, de Restauración y de Museología. The other cloister is a hotel.

IGLESIA Y CONVENTO DE NUESTRA SEÑORA DE BELÉN ★ ● *80*. Built between 1712 and 1720, this is the largest religious complex in the old city, with six cloisters and a baroque church. It was occupied by the congregation of Bethlehem until 1842, and was then the seat of the Spanish governors before being handed over to the Jesuits in 1854. After their departure, in 1925, the building housed the Academy of Science, the Ministry of Internal Affairs and then a hospice. The attractive BAROQUE FAÇADE of its church, with its ornamental cornices and pilasters, is set back slightly from the street, behind a small atrium. THE ARCH OF BELÉN ★, erected in 1775 by Pedro de Medina, connects the convent to the neighboring houses and marks the entrance to the old Jewish quarter, which is clustered around Calle Acosta. The arch and convent are currently being restored.

IGLESIA DEL ESPÍRITU SANTO ● *81*. Built in 1638 by a group of free Afro-Cubans, it was modified several times throughout the 18th and 19th centuries. It has some fine 17th-century carved wooden ceilings in the Mudéjar style, and a vaulted stone choir. The crypt, which contains the CATACOMBS, dates from the same period (1638). The only church in the city able to provide sanctuary to people hunted by the authorities, one of its most famous priests was Father Gaztelu who, with José Lezama Lima ● *111*, belonged to the literary group formed around the review *Orígenes*, active between 1944 and 1957.

AROUND THE CENTRAL RAILROAD STATION. Calle Leonor Pérez, formerly Calle Paula, was renamed in honor of the mother of José Martí ● *40*, who was born in a HOUSE ★ now converted into a museum, close to the CENTRAL STATION (1905).

The Alameda de Paula, (*above*) the first promenade built in Havana in the 18th century.

NUESTRA SEÑORA DE LA MERCED (*top, right*) This church, started in 1755 and not finished until 1876, is well worth a visit for its lavishly decorated interior. Each of its three naves, separated by arches, end in a chapel. The dome above the transept and the vault of the nave are decorated with FRESCOS ★ by famous Cuban artists such as Esteban Chartrand (1823–84).

THE 'JUNTA' The Central Station displays the *Junta*, the locomotive that opened the railroad link between Havana and the sugar-producing region of Güines in 1837.

▲ HAVANA
CENTRO HABANA

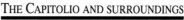

1. PALACIO DE ALDAMA
2. PARQUE CENTRAL
3. HOTEL INGLATERRA
4. TEATRO GARCÍA LORCA
5. CENTRO ASTURIANO
6. FOUNTAIN OF THE INDIAN QUEEN

'Morning in Havana. Buses, shouts, people continually crossing and recrossing the city from one side to another.'
Severo Sarduy

THE CAPITOLIO AND SURROUNDINGS

During the 19th century cramped Havana began to overstretch its city walls, which led to the creation of the Centro Habana district. In the late 19th century, the glacis or forward face of the ramparts ● 76 was covered with grand, flamboyantly decorated mansions. Theaters and parks were built; a wide avenue, the Prado (also called the Paseo de Martí) was remodeled; and the Capitolio was built, which became the center of political power on the island between 1929 and 1959. This lively district is still one of the most popular places for Cubans to take a stroll.

CAPITOLIO NACIONAL ▲ *139.* The outline of this building's 300-foot-high dome is highly reminiscent of the Capitol in Washington, DC. Begun in 1910, work was not completed until 1929, under the presidency of Gerardo Machado ● *42.* The Capitolio was the seat of Parliament, comprising the House of Representatives and the Senate, until the Revolution. Entrance to the building is through a monumental portal decorated with bas-reliefs representing scenes from Cuban history. The vast Hall of the Lost Steps, 394 feet long, with its central rotunda and polychromatic marble walls, is a breathtaking sight. It leads to the two chambers, as well as conference rooms, including the Martí room, which is decorated with frescos, and the library. Once home to the Academy of Sciences, the Capitolio currently houses the Ministry of Science, Technology and the Environment. The Natural Science museum recently moved to 61 Calle Obispo.

PARQUE DE LA FRATERNIDAD ★. The park was laid out in 1892 on the site of a former Spanish military parade ground to mark the fourth centenary of the discovery of America. Originally called Parque de Colón, its name was changed in 1928 when it was remodeled by Jean Claude Nicolas Forestier ● 77 for the sixth Pan-American Conference, held in Cuba. Since then, the bustling Parque de la Fraternidad Americana has become one of the capital's most animated places. Cubans linger in the shade of the royal palms, waiting for their bus, the famous *guagua*.

PALACIO DE ALDAMA ★. (Not open to the public.) Built by military engineer Manuel José Carrerá in 1844, this is one of the finest neoclassical palaces to be constructed in Havana in the 19th century. Two adjoining mansions had to be combined to produce a building of such vast proportions. The façade, decorated with a wide Doric portico, a wrought-iron balcony and an elaborate parapet on the roof, conceals luxurious rooms with sparkling chandeliers, large patios and colorful galleries adorned with marble and tiles. The palace was confiscated and partially destroyed in 1868 by the Spanish government, who suspected the Aldama family of supporting the independence movement in Oriente. Restored in 1948 and again in 1971, it is now home to the Institute of the History of the Communist Movement and the Socialist Revolution.

TREASURES OF THE CAPITOLIO
The lavish interior of the building forms a striking contrast to the sober façade. Visible from the entrance, a bronze statue representing the Cuban Republic, 56 feet tall and weighing 49 tons, is one of the tallest in the world. In the floor at the center of the rotunda, underneath a dome similar to that of the Pantheon in Paris, a diamond (probably a replica) marks zero point, from which all distances on the island are calculated.

132

PARQUE CENTRAL ★. (*left*) This park replaced three open squares opposite the city gates in 1877. It is a favorite meeting point for Cubans, who enjoy watching and commenting on the *pelota* (baseball) games, a national sport. Its walks are paved with pink slabs in Moorish style; the street lamps were designed in New York. At the center, the STATUE OF JOSÉ MARTÍ, sculpted in 1904 by Vilalta de Saavedra ▲ *144*, stands on the site of former effigies of Queen Isabella of Spain. This was one of the first statues to be erected in memory of the hero of the Cuban independence movement.

HOTEL INGLATERRA ★. Rebuilt in eclectic style between 1856 and 1915 and a listed national monument, this hotel is one of the best in the city, full of character and charm.

CENTRO GALLEGO AND TEATRO FEDERICO GARCÍA LORCA ★ ▲ *138*. The Galician Center was built around the former Teatro Tacón, a building constructed in 1834 and inaugurated, several years later, with a series of Verdi's operas. The theater was subsequently renamed the Teatro Federico García Lorca. The Galicians, who formed a large community, commissioned Paul Belau to build their center on its site. Between 1906 and 1915, the Belgian architect designed a neo-baroque building with a flamboyant façade incorporating the theater. The latter currently houses Cuba's National Ballet Company, directed by Alicia Alonso (*right*). It is possible to visit the auditorium and watch rehearsals during the week.

CENTRO ASTURIANO. This great rival of the Centro Gallego was rebuilt in 1927, after a fire, by the Spanish architect Manuel del Busto, who drew his inspiration from Madrid's Palacio de Comunicaciones (Post Office). The portal is topped by a wrought-iron canopy, and the Renaissance façade is decorated with neoclassical motifs. The stained-glass window above the main staircase represents Columbus' three sailing ships. The building, currently being restored, is due to exhibit some of the paintings from the Museo de Bellas Artes ▲ *136*.

A SYMBOLIC PARK
A kapok tree surrounded by a high railing grows at the center of the Parque de la Fraternidad. It was planted on February 24, 1928, to mark the start of the sixth Pan-American Conference. Soil from all the countries in North and South America taking part in the conference was placed at its foot. Southeast of the park stands the beautiful fountain ★ (*top*) sculpted in 1837 in Carrara marble by Gaggini. This symbolic figure depicts a native Indian queen, surrounded by four dolphins and holding a shield stamped with the city's coat of arms and a cornucopia.

The Catalan settler Jaime Partagás Ravelo was an ambitious businessman. The modest shop he opened in 1828 was succeeded, in 1845, by his own large cigar factory. Partagás drew a veil of mystery over the origin of the tobacco leaves and his manufacturing process and was one of the key architects of the 'legend of the Havana'. He was also one of the first to age the leaves in wooden casks to control the fermentation process and the development of the aroma. The Partagás factory was soon renowned for its workers' ability to recognize the taste and aroma of each of its sixty-seven cigars. Today, Partagás produces fifty-six brands of cigar.

THE SHOP
The shop sells only a limited selection of the factory's products, but the back-store, reserved for the initiated, sometimes allows access to its treasures. The best workers (*left*), who roll the larger brands, sit in the front of the workshop.

REAL FÁBRICA DE TABACOS

Partagás

FUNDADA EN 1845

Empresa: Francisco Pérez Germán

ATMOSPHERE...

In the stifling heat, about ten workers prepare the tobacco leaves ● *68* on the first story of the factory. Although the muggy air is almost unfit to breathe, several aromas can be distinguished from the intermingled smells: apple, gingerbread, dark undergrowth with ice-cold moss, reminiscent of amber and truffle. This is the world of aromas, a bouquet of gunflint combined with sensual, alkaline plant fragrances. Fermented tobacco gives off a very primitive smell.

GOOD ROLLERS

In theory, the rollers make one single brand per day and do not know which type they are producing, except in the case of the rollers of Cohibas.

THE FAÇADE

The neoclassical façade is a fine example of the style of industrial architecture popular in Havana in the second half of the 19th century. The bicolored front is decorated by pilasters, moldings and string-courses. Characteristic wrought iron is used around the balconies. The prominent pediments are the only baroque features.

HISTORY

The Partagás label was a rapid success, but its creator, Jaime Partagás, was not satisfied: he wanted to control the entire chain of production from start to finish by buying a tobacco plantation in Pinar del Río Province. His tragic death, on June 17, 1868 – he was mysteriously murdered – put an end to these plans. The factory was then sold to Ramón Cifuentes Llano, who proved to be as shrewd a businessman as his predecessor; he purchased many brands of Havana cigars, including Ramón Allones, which is still made in the factory.

THE TRADITION OF READING

On the rostrum, in front of portraits of heroes of the Revolution – with the exception of Fidel Castro – stands the lector, who helps to relieve boredom. The practice of reading was instituted in 1865 at the Fábrica El Fígaro and the idea was taken up by Jaime Partagás in 1866. In this way, laborers received a form of intellectual or political education. The reading is now broadcast by loudspeaker throughout the building and is alternated every half hour with music and information played on the radio.

135

FROM THE PARQUE CENTRAL

TO THE BAY VIA THE PRADO

THE PRADO ★. Called Alameda de Isabella II or Calle Ancha (Wide Street), Havana's long boulevard was christened the Paseo del Prado, then Paseo de Martí in 1904, but is more commonly known by its former name. It was initially built in 1772 for carriages going to the seafront, allowing them to bypass the busy roads of the old city. In 1834, the boulevard was paved, decorated with wrought-iron street lamps and, later, lined with elegant mansions. Fencing establishments and dance halls abounded while noblewomen came here to be seen in their carriages. In 1929, the French landscape artist Forestier ● 77, assisted by the Cuban Raúl Otero, again transformed the boulevard. Widened, shaded by laurels (*below*), flanked by marble benches and eight bronze lions, it has become a paradise for children playing *pelota* and a beautiful place for a leisurely stroll.

ARCHITECTURAL PROMENADE. At the beginning of the 20th century, many of the houses that were built on the Prado and on nearby streets set a new trend architecturally. The PALACIO DE LOS MATRIMONIOS (where weddings are performed) ★, at No 302, the former seat of the Association of Spanish Immigrants, was built in 1914 by Luis Dediot and has an exuberant neo-baroque façade. The same is true of the HOTEL SEVILLA, with its Moorish decor, dating from 1908. In 1923, the American architectural firm Schultze & Weaver added a ten-story tower whose height provoked an outcry. The restaurant on the top story, with its neoclassical decor and panoramic views, is a perfect place to savor the famous cocktail, the Mary Pickford (rum, pineapple juice, grenadine), that was invented here. The house at No 120, CASA DE PEDRO ESTÉVEZ ★, was built in 1905 by the Frenchman Charles B. Brun, pioneer of the use of reinforced concrete.

PALACIO VELASCO ★
This imposing building, an example of Spanish eclectic architecture (1912), houses the Spanish Embassy.

MUSEO NACIONAL DE BELLAS ARTES. This museum, currently being refurbished, stands on the site of the former, legendary Mercado Colón ● 87, a vast building erected at the end of the 19th century. It was destroyed after 1945 to make room for the present building. The museum, whose collections have had to be divided between several sites ▲ 133, is due to reopen in 2001.

GRANMA MEMORIAL. (Entrance through the Museo de la Revolución). Opened in 1976, this celebrates the high points of the Revolution. An immense glass structure contains the *Granma*, the 66-foot-long yacht on board which Castro, Guevara and their seventy-nine companions left Tuspán, in Mexico, to land at Playa Las Coloradas in 1956 ● 44. At its side are the truck used in the

assault on the Presidential Palace and a plane used in the Bay of Pigs invasion ▲ *176*.

MUSEO DE LA REVOLUCIÓN ★. The former Presidential Palace ▲ *139* (*below*) has been converted into a museum devoted to the Revolution. The palace was built between 1913 and 1920 on the site of the city ramparts (a small sentry box still stands there) and enlarged between 1940 and 1950. From the terraces overlooking the bay, orators used to harangue the crowd gathered on the esplanade of the Plaza de Marzo during the great post-Revolution rallies. The museum, which retraces the history of the island from the colonial period, is focussed on the history of the Cuban uprisings, particularly the events of 1959 and it contains an exceptional collection of old documents and photos.

EDIFICIO BACARDÍ
The headquarters of the Bacardí firm ● *51* were built around 1930 on the outskirts

CASA DE PÉREZ DE LA RIVA. Since 1981, this house (1906) with its neo-Renaissance façade has housed the MUSEO NACIONAL DE LA MÚSICA ★. The vast number of instruments on display gives some idea of the extraordinary richness of Cuban music. The collection once belonged to the Cuban ethnologist Fernando Ortíz ● *42*. Of great historical and cultural value, they are not restricted to the music of the archipelago: in addition to the many Cuban instruments, there are original scores and instruments from all over the world.

OPPOSITE THE WATERFRONT. The promenade ends at the PARQUE DE LOS MÁRTIRES. The STATUE OF GENERAL MÁXIMO GÓMEZ, dating from 1935, stands in the center. A plaque on the MONUMENT TO THE MEDICAL STUDENTS, a fragment of wall encased in marble, commemorates the eight students shot here on November 27, 1871: the colonial government had accused them of desecrating the tomb of a Spanish officer to impress young Cubans sympathetic to the idea of independence. The CASTILLO DE SAN SALVADOR DE LA PUNTA, designed between 1589 and 1600 by Juan Bautista Antonelli ● *78*, ▲ *217*, Juan de Tejeda and Cristóbal de Roda, was the island's first defense, with the Castillo del Morro ▲ *146* erected at the same time on the other side of the bay. It is not at present open to the public but it is soon to house the MUSEO NAVAL.

of the old city. The building's geometric façade, with soaring lines in colored brick and pyramidal roof decorated with ceramics, recalls buildings constructed in New York during the heyday of Art Deco. The bat, the firm's emblem, recalls a more modern hero: Batman.

Central Station, 1912,
Habana Vieja, K. M. Murchison.

A city is defined by its public buildings. From the very beginning of the 20th century, a period of rapid, radical change in architecture and urbanization, the importance of modifying the public image of the country's official and social institutions was understood. There were two distinct approaches: certain architects rejected the Hispanic heritage while others, on the contrary, drew their inspiration from it.

ASSOCIATIONS
(Spanish Casino, 1914, Habana Vieja, Luis Dediot)
Certain trades in Havana had their own social and mutual-aid organizations: when these associations had accumulated enough money, they then constructed a building to house their headquarters. Other national groups constructed buildings which were reminiscent of their country of origin. A particularly fine example of this is the Spanish Casino, recognizable by its Plateresque-style façade. The ceiling of the ballroom is decorated with the escutcheons of all the Spanish provinces.

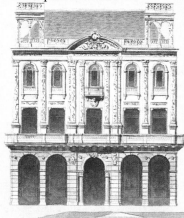

THE INFRASTRUCTURES
As part of the city's modernization program, the new railroad station was designed as a 'monumental gateway' graced by two high towers overlooking the country. The façades, which combine Spanish and Italian Renaissance elements, are reminiscent of both the Giralda in Seville and the Villa Medici in Rome. They are a compelling invitation to travel.

RIVALRY AND HERITAGE
(Centro Gallego ▲ 133, 1915, Habana Vieja, Paul Belau)
Various Spanish communities, which also founded groups based on their province of origin, vied with one another to build increasingly lavish palaces. The two most remarkable buildings are the Centro Asturiano ▲ 133 and the Centro Gallego, which stand opposite each other and were designed respectively in neoclassical and neo-baroque style.

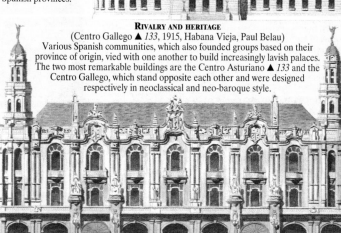

Presidential Palace, 1919,
Paul Belau and Carlos Maruri

CENTERS OF POWER
Despite its highly
sophisticated interior
decoration by Tiffany,
the Presidential
Palace was built very
much in the image of
the new republic:
there is an air òf
uncertainty about its
proportions and
stylistic motifs. It
was later surpassed by
the magnificent
Capitolio.

THE CAPITOLIO ▲ *132*
(1929, Raúl Otero and *alii*)
This building draws
its inspiration from
an established and
internationally accepted
model, even if it was clearly
influenced by its counterpart
in the United States.
Exceptional in its design,
materials and execution, it
stands on the site of the
former railroad station
and the ancient ramparts.
Despite its size, its
neoclassical sobriety blends
with its surroundings
without being too
overpowering.

PUBLIC BUILDINGS STATUARY
(*The Tutelary Virtue*, left,
Capitolio, Angelo Zanelli)
After the republic was
established, many public
buildings incorporated
sculpture in their structures
following a Beaux-Arts
model. These symbolic
statues were all designed to
convey a message. The
sculptures in the Capitolio
are particularly
noteworthy, especially
the *Republic* ▲ *132*, also
by Zanelli, in the
central rotunda.

THE GREAT HOTELS
(Hotel *Nacional* ▲ *140*, 1930, McKim, Mead & White)

The rapid growth of
tourism led to the
construction of
several large
hotels in the
capital. Their
cosmopolitan
clientele required
a blend of luxury

and exoticism. The Hotel *Nacional,* built on
the site of a former battery, takes full
advantage of the panoramic view.
Neo-Renaissance style is
complemented by such
flamboyant touches as the
Seville-style decor of the great
hall or the carved lobsters on
the arches in the garden.

Lobster (detail)

'The rain had just washed the city.
From the open windows came the sound of
voices and music, here a nostalgic *bolero*,
there a *rumba caliente*...' Eduardo Manet

HOTEL 'NACIONAL' ★
This hotel (*below*) occupies one of the best sites in Havana, on the battery of Santa Clara, overlooking the Malecón. It was built in 1930 by the firm of McKim, Mead & White in neo-Renaissance style. The hotel has become legendary: it was once a favorite haunt for Americans fleeing Prohibition, movie stars and several Mafia bosses. Batista settled some scores here during his *coup d'état* of 1933. A palm-lined walk leads to a Palladian porch, opening onto a Seville-style vestibule decorated with tiles; the garden contains several cannons. A waterfall has been created at the end of a promontory.

THE MALECÓN ★

This wide boulevard runs along the seafront for five miles from Old Havana to Miramar ▲ *146*, on the other side of the Río Almendares. It evolved in several stages: a short sea wall was built by the American troops in 1902 to protect the city from tidal waves caused by hurricanes; the Cubans continued to extend it until 1958. Twilight is a good time to take a walk along the strip: fishermen are gathering their nets, children are playing on the rocks and lovers are taking a stroll. However, the *jineteros*, men and women who target tourists and are often prostitutes, are also out in force, although Cuban authorities have recently cracked down on these activities. In August 1994, this boulevard was also the place from which many Cubans fled on *balsas* (rafts) in an attempt to reach Florida ● *46*. Many old MANSIONS WITH PASTEL FAÇADES, superb remains of houses built at the beginning of the 20th century by the city's merchants and industrialists, now faded by sun and spray, line the boulevard in the section that runs through the Centro Habana district. Further on, along the Vedado, the Malecón is lined with modern apartment blocks and luxury hotels.

THE MONUMENTS. Walking east to west up the avenue, you will see many monuments celebrating the saga of Cuban independence, such as the EQUESTRIAN STATUE OF ANTONIO MACEO (1916) ▲ *215*. Close by, a small fortified tower, the 17th-century TORREÓN DE SAN LÁZARO ● *78*, recalls the early days of Spanish domination. Beyond the Hotel *Nacional*, stands the imposing MONUMENTO A LAS VÍCTIMAS DEL *MAINE* (the work of Cubans Govantes and Cabarrocas), erected in 1925 by the Americans in homage to their soldiers killed when the battleship *Maine* exploded in the island's waters ● *39*. Further on you will come to the six-story building which houses the US Interests Office (the former American embassy), followed, at the corner of Calle G, by the MONUMENTO A CALIXTO GARCÍA ▲ *200*, erected in 1959 in

memory of the hero of the independence movement. The Malecón ends at the fort of LA CHORRERA ● 78, ▲ 146, built in 1645 to defend the river mouth against pirates.

THE VEDADO ★

Vedado means 'forest reserve'. In the colonial period, this vast open space, which extended between Centro Habana and the right bank of the Río Almendares, served as a buffer zone in case of an attack on the city: no construction or traffic was allowed. But, in the 19th century, the city overstretched its walls and its population doubled. In 1859, engineer Luis Yboleón Bosque drew up plans for a new district in keeping with the grid system used in modern town-planning programs: wide avenues, tall houses and a harmonious balance between natural sites and built-up areas.

The Vedado initially appealed to the wealthy residents of Havana, who built houses in eclectic styles, then the Americans, who opted for New-England-style cottages.

LA RAMPA. This is the name given to the part of Calle 23 linking Calle L to the Malecón and the area bounded by these streets. Lined with travel agencies, jazz clubs, cinemas, restaurants and hotels, it is the urban heart of the Vedado. Under Batista, the area was known for its gambling and other pleasures; its hotels were used as meeting places for the Mafia big shots. The good times ended in 1959 when Castro set up headquarters on the 22nd story of the *Habana Hilton* (corner of Calle L), a 27-story hotel completed in April 1958. It was then nationalized and renamed the *Habana Libre* in 1960.

'COPPELIA'
At the corner of Calle 23 and Calle L, the most famous ice-cream parlor in Havana occupies a bizarre contemporary building ● 92 in the center of a large square at the heart of the Vedado. Two scenes from the film *Fresa y Chocolate* (Strawberries and Chocolate, 1994) by Tomás Gutiérrez Alea, were filmed here. Its design of six circular rooms beneath a ribbed vault, the inspiration of Mario Girona (1966), with chairs inspired by the American designer Harry Bertoia, and its attractive gardens, give this ice-cream parlor a sense of style.

FAMOUS HOTELS
The *Capri*, Calle 21, George Raft's domain, has rococo mirrors on all stories (the view over the bay from its top-story swimming pool is superb); the *Riviera* (1957) ★, is on the corner of Paseo and the Malecón, with monumental fountains.

Assembled crowd at the foot of the wide staircase leading to the university (*above*).

Quinta de los Molinos
The railings of this magnificent property line Avenue Carlos III, at the foot of the Castillo del Príncipe. The house, built between 1837 and 1840, was used as a summer palace by the captains-general and, in 1899, became the home of General Máximo Gómez ● *39*, commander-in-chief of the liberation army. A museum is currently devoted to him. This white house is modeled on the wealthy *quintas* (villas) built by the nobility of Havana in the 19th century in the Cerro and Vedado districts. Its extensive grounds liberally scattered with statues, fountains, summer-houses and grottos were transformed into a botanical garden for the university in the early 20th century.

The Vedado: The University District

Universidad de la Habana ★. Founded in 1728 by Dominican friars, the university was originally in the old city. Secularized in 1842, it was moved in 1902 to a small hill in the Vedado. It now stands on Plaza Ignacio Agramonte, which is reached by a wide staircase leading up from Calle L. At the foot of the steps, viewed from the other side of the street, is the bust of Julio Antonio Mella, founder of the University Students' Federation and the first Cuban Communist Party, and, on a landing, there is a bronze statue of the Alma Mater, sculpted in 1919 by Mario Korbel. The students have access to a luxuriant garden. The Great Hall (Aula Magna) boasts a Mural Painting (1910) by Armando Menocal and a marble urn containing the ashes of Father Félix Varela ● *38*. In the university grounds, the Museo Antropológico Montané, dating from 1903, exhibits the largest collection of pre-Columbian art on the island. Worthy of note are the wooden and stone idols dating from the 10th century and skulls of Arawak Indians ● *32*.

Museo Napoleónico ★. Below the university, on Calle San Miguel (No 1159), a large attractive house built in Florentine Renaissance style in 1928 now houses one of the largest collections in the world devoted to Napoleon Bonaparte. It was amassed by Julio Lobo, a Cuban millionaire who was passionately interested in the emperor. Exhibits include a bronze funeral mask of Napoleon and a painting by Jean Vibert showing Bonaparte preparing for his coronation. The rooms are furnished with Empire-style furniture and Sèvres porcelain. The architecture of the building is also an attractive sight in itself with its asymmetrical yet graceful stone façade, pierced by loggias and arches.

Castillo del Príncipe ● *79*. (Not open to the public.) Calzada Zapata and Avenue Carlos III converge on this imposing pentagon, erected on the Aróstegui hill between 1767 and 1779 to complete the city's defense system. The fortress was modeled on the Spanish plan fashionable at the beginning of the 18th century, but broke new ground with its

bastions and the tunnel surrounding it, which enabled men to move around the fortress safely. The castle was linked to the ramparts by the continuation of Avenues Carlos III (the modern Salvador Allende) and de la Reina. Once it was put out of commission, the fortress was used as the city's central prison. A military zone, closed to the public, it is currently undergoing restoration.

VEDADO: RESIDENTIAL DISTRICT

AVENIDA DE LOS PRESIDENTES ★. From the Castillo del Príncipe, this attractive avenue, also called Calle G, gently slopes down toward the northwest to join the Malecón, crossing a district which boasts some splendid villas. Busts were put up here of the first president of the Cuban republic, Tomás Estrada Palma ● *42* in 1921, then of his successor, José Miguel Gómez ● *42* in 1936. After 1959, the revolutionaries accused these presidents of being American 'puppets' and their statues were taken down (the one of Gómez has recently been reerected). Both the CASA DE LOS ALCALDES (Mayors' House, 1921, by Leonardo Morales; *above*) on Calle 23, with its Moorish-style green glazed roof tiles and the HOTEL PRESIDENTE (1927), popular with artists and celebrities, are definitely worth a look.

ARCHITECTURAL PROMENADE ★. The architecture of the Vedado is dominated by the Beaux-Arts style ▲ *139*, introduced to Cuba in the early 20th century. Attracted by its prestigious reputation in the New World, prospective Cuban architects attended the École des Beaux-Arts in Paris, where they studied European monuments. On their return, they drew their inspiration from Renaissance, classical, baroque and neoclassical architecture for their designs. The Beaux-Arts style was their interpretation of one of these styles. This trend lasted until the 1930s and has left its stamp on several buildings in the area. Most notable are the house of the architect T.L. Hustons (1909), which shows a marked mudéjar influence, the CHINESE EMBASSY (1916; *third photo above right*), Calle 13, Nº 551, surrounded by extensive landscaped gardens and the house of José Gómez Mena (1927), which is today home to the MUSEO DE ARTES DECORATIVAS (Calle 17, Nº 502; *first photo above right*).

CALLE 17 ★
The house of Juan Gelats (Nº 351, 1920; *fourth photo above*), now the seat of the National Union of Writers and Artists of Cuba (UNEAC), belongs to the famous 'row of magnificent mansions' described by Alejo Carpentier. Its appeal lies in the sinuous curve of its façade and the white marble spiral staircase, illuminated by six Art Deco windows. The seat of the Institute of Cuban Friendship between Nations, the Casa de los Marqueses de Avilés (Nº 301, 1915; *second photo above*) is in Beaux-Arts style. Its portico gives it the appearance of a Greek temple.

143

THE MILAGROSA
This tomb is regarded as miraculous and is always covered in flowers. A woman who died in childbirth was buried here with her still-born baby at her feet. When the grave was opened, the baby was discovered at its mother's breast. Supplicants come here to pray for children.

COLLECTIVE PANTHEONS
This is one of the most striking features of the cemetery. Most of the funerary monuments belong to various communities: Asturians, Galicians, French settlers, the Abakuá secret society ● *61*, theater and circus performers, film and radio stars each have their own monument. Some house the remains of martyrs or great Cuban historical figures such as the Pantheon of the Medical Students ▲ *137*, the Veterans' Tomb (1944), the final resting place for soldiers who fought in the wars for independence ● *39*, the Mausoleum of the Revolutionary Armed Forces, for those who took part in the Revolution and who died after 1959, and for the students who were killed in the attack on the Presidential Palace ● *44*.

CEMENTERIO DE CRISTÓBAL COLÓN ★

The Cementerio de Cristóbal Colón is reached by walking along Calzada Zapata to Calle 12. The entrance is marked by a large neo-Roman porch, topped by a Carrara marble sculture representing Faith, Hope and Charity, the work of José Vilalta de Saavedra ▲ *133*. No ordinary cemetery, this is an impressive necropolis, filled with flamboyant tombs, Greek and Assyrian temples, and magnificent mausoleums; a huge open-air museum of almost every artistic style from the 19th and 20th centuries. Spanish architect Calixto de Loira drew up the plans for the majestic entrance gate in 1870. One landmark is the OCTAGONAL CHAPEL in neo-Byzantine style (*above*) at the intersection of two avenues, which contains fine frescos by Miguel Ángel Melero. Many famous people and national heroes are buried in the capital's main cemetery: the writer ALEJO CARPENTIER ● *109*, ▲ *120*, *128* (immediately to the left of the entrance, Avenue A), the novelist CIRILO VILLAVERDE (Avenue G, east of the central chapel) and GENERAL GÓMEZ ● *39* (to the right of the central avenue near the entrance).

TOBÍAS GALLERY. Calixto de Loira is buried in this 312-foot-long underground structure, to the left of the entrance. With numerous recesses for coffins, it was the cemetery's first tomb and was in use until 1875.

THE 'MININT'
This is a must for any visitor to the area. Since 1995, the facade of the Ministry of the Interior (*below*) has displayed a giant portrait of Ernesto 'Che' Guevara ▲ 192. The image, cast in bronze, replaced the frescos that were first

PLAZA DE LA REVOLUCIÓN

In 1925, the French town-planner Forestier ● 77 devised a large-scale project to make the Loma de los Catalanes (Hill of the Catalans) the new administrative center of Havana. After many competitions, the plan developed by architect Aquiles Maza, assisted by sculptor Juan José Sicre, was chosen in 1952 to construct the José Martí

displayed on the guerrilla's death, in 1967. The artwork reproduces Korda's universally known photo ▲ 192.

memorial at the center of the square. The rest of the buildings were erected throughout the 1950s, without any definite plan. However, they demonstrate a monumental style with hints of Le Corbusier, favored by Batista ● 43. New buildings, more modern in design, appeared after the Revolution, but many areas are still under construction. First called Plaza Cívica, then Plaza de la República, it was finally given its current name by Fidel Castro. The square is a vast eleven-acre esplanade which can hold a million people. It is packed during the great Communist Party rallies held on January 1, May 1 and July 26. The rest of the time, it is kept under close surveillance; do not linger here too long.

JOSÉ MARTÍ MEMORIAL ★ ● 40. This architectural edifice was renovated and opened to the public in 1996. The museum built at the foot of the obelisk is devoted to the great hero of Cuban independence. It contains original archive material, engravings, documents, recordings and films. Its ultra-modern design distinguishes it from other Cuban museums.

OFFICIAL BUILDINGS. Opposite the memorial stand the MINISTRY OF THE INTERIOR, colloquially known as the 'Minint', and the MINISTRY OF COMMUNICATIONS, recognizable from the slogan '*Venceremos*' ('We will overcome') that graces its roof. The MUSEO POSTAL CUBANO holds a fascinating collection of stamps from all over the world. To the right of the memorial are the headquarters of the Revolutionary Armed Forces (RAF) or Ministry of Defense, and the BIBLIOTECA NACIONAL J. MARTÍ. On the other side of the square, to the left of the memorial and opposite the library, is the TEATRO NACIONAL (1958), with its modernist façade. It possesses several auditoriums and a nightclub, the *Café Cantante*. The main national newspapers, particularly *Granma* and the *Review Bohemia*, almost a hundred years old, also have head offices near this square. Finally, behind the memorial, the imposing PALACIO DE LA REVOLUCIÓN, the former Ministry of Justice (1958), is home to the highest state authorities and the Party's Central Committee. Fidel Castro has his office here.

HOMAGE TO JOSÉ MARTÍ ▲ *40*
The top of the 454-foot obelisk, which surmounts the memorial, is the highest point in the city. The soaring structure, shaped like a five-pointed star and designed by the architect Enrique Luis Varela, was not completed until 1958. This monolithic stepped tower is reminiscent of the massive bulk of Art Deco buildings. From its summit, on a clear day, you can see for thirty miles. The 59-foot-tall white marble statue sculpted by Juan José Sicre, at the foot of the obelisk, shows Martí seated in a priest-like pose.

MIRAMAR ★

THE SHRINE OF SAN LÁZARO
The Santuario de San Lázaro at El Rincón is one of the main centers of pilgrimage on the island. Extremely popular, Saint Lazarus has a counterpart in the Afro-Cuban religion: Babalú Ayé ● 58, the god of healing. During the night of December 16, believers flock to this shrine to exorcise evil spirits.

CANNON FIRING CEREMONY ★
Every day, at 9pm, the cannon at La Cabaña is fired. This custom dates back to the colonial period: it was the signal that the harbor was closed (a long chain was stretched between San Salvador de la Punta and El Morro) and that the city gates were shut.

On the left bank of the Río Almendares stretches the *municipio* of Playa, an oasis of lush greenery and magnificent houses to which the district of Miramar belongs. Its shady avenues are lined with embassies and private mansions. It is well worth taking a stroll down the grandiose QUINTA AVENIDA, the continuation of the Malecón. Interesting sights to see in Miramar include the MUSEO DEL MINISTRO DEL INTERIOR, devoted to foiled plots against the island, the CITY MODEL ★ at No 113 Calle 28 and the CHAPEL OF SANTA RITA, at the junction of Quinta Avenida and Calle 26, which boasts a Virgin sculpture by Rita Longa. The westernmost part of the district is the site of former sports clubs dating from the early 20th century and the National Art schools dating from 1961–5 ● 92. Their original architecture deploys vaulted brick areas, covered in terracotta, in the midst of dense vegetation.

THE FORTRESSES OF HABANA DEL ESTE ● 78

When promoting Havana to the rank of city in 1592, Philip II instructed Havana to be the 'key to the New World' and the 'rampart of the West Indies'. This defensive role grew during the 17th and 18th centuries, when clashes between the great powers gave way to piracy and trade wars. Along a seven-mile front, from Cojímar ▲ 164 in the east to La Chorrera ▲ 141 in the west, a series of formidable fortresses were built. The two largest are in the Morro-Cabaña Historical Military Park in Habana del Este. The entrance is through a long tunnel dug beneath the bay in 1957.

CASTILLO DE LOS TRES REYES DEL MORRO ★. This fortress (*below*) was built in 1589 by Juan Bautista Antonelli ▲ 217. Situated at the entrance to the harbor, on top of a bluff which gave the watch an unimpeded view over the ocean, this stronghold was the city's main defense until it fell, in 1762, to the English army. After the Treaty of Paris in 1763, which

gave Havana back to Spain, the fortress was restored and a lighthouse constructed. This beacon remained the highest structure in the capital for many decades.

FORTALEZA DE SAN CARLOS DE LA CABAÑA ★. After the defeat in 1762 which revealed the weaknesses in the bay's defenses, the residents of Havana began, in 1763, the construction of one of the largest fortresses in Latin America (*above*). Completed in 1774, it was used as a military prison under Machado and Batista and at the beginning of the Revolution. Che ▲ *192* set up his headquarters here after January 1959. It is now home to the MUSEO DE LAS ARMAS and the MUSEO DE LA COMANDANCIA DE CHE GUEVARA, where visitors can see personal objects belonging to the guerrilla (rucksack, radio, rifle, etc) as well as a reconstruction of his ministerial office.

OTHER MUNICIPALITIES OF HAVANA

REGLA ★. This small harbor village on the other side of the bay can be reached by the *lanchita* (ferry) from the landing stage of Muelle de Luz, in Old Havana. A militant, working-class municipality since 1812, it was the first to elect a socialist mayor. Regla's history began in 1687 with the construction of the CHAPEL OF NUESTRA SEÑORA DE REGLA, primarily known as a center of *santería* ● *58*. The church, a small building with a neoclassical pediment, contains a black Virgin holding a white baby Jesus in her arms. On September 8, a pilgrimage combining Catholic and Afro-Cuban ceremonies is celebrated here. The statue is the incarnation of the patron saint of Havana Bay and fishermen and Yemayá, god of the sea.

GUANABACOA. Guanabacoa's history began in 1554 when the Indians living around San Cristóbal de la Habana were rounded up and moved to this area. Founded in 1607, the town played a key role in the defense of the capital against pirates and particularly in resisting the English invasion of 1762. In the 18th century, its climate and beneficial waters made it a popular holiday resort for the nobility. The HERMITAGE POTOSÍ ★, whose church (1644) is one of the oldest in Cuba, and the CONVENTO DE SAN FRANCISCO (18th century) are reminders of this prestigious past. The town has a rich musical tradition and was the birthplace of artists such as Ernesto Lecuona and Rita Montaner ● *53*. The practice of Afro-Cuban cults here ● *58* has earned this former center of the slave trade the nickname Pueblo Embrujado ('enchanted village').

GUANABACOA, QUEEN OF 'RUMBA'
There are many *rumberos* and players of the *batá* drums in Guanabacoa, the birthplace of some of the great families of musicians such as the Aspirinas, percussionists and singers of *guaguancó*, and the Arangos. Every year, the finest musicians in the region flock to Guanabacoa.

SANTA MARIA DEL ROSARIO ● *81*
Modern town-planning programs have spared this former colonial town. Its gem is the 18th-century church of Nuestra Señora del Rosario. Baroque in style, it was financed by a local landowner, the Count of Casa Bayona ▲ *126*, infamous for the cruelty with which he suppressed the revolt of his slaves. On the hill where the ringleaders were executed, three crosses are reminiscent of Calvary. The first was erected at the time, as a warning; the other two in 1959, during the Revolution.

In 1939, Hemingway completely changed his life: he left Key West in southern Florida and made his home eighty miles away in a hotel in Havana.

The writer and his new wife, Martha Gellhorn, soon began looking for their own home on the island. Nine miles from the capital, they discovered a large Spanish colonial-style house in *Finca Vigía*, which Hemingway rented, then bought in 1940. Perched on a hill in San Francisco de Paula, this peaceful haven 'untouched by war or revolution' is surrounded by palms, mango trees and hibiscus. Hemingway left the house and Havana in 1960 to return to the United States, and he committed suicide one year later.

> 'Today is an absolute perfect, cool day; but with fine sun and high clouds and everything looks fresh and new and lovely.'
> Letter from Ernest Hemingway to Mary Welsh

'LOOK-OUT FARM'

From his house, Hemingway could see the bright lights of Havana. The property was made up of a one-story villa, the Little House for friends, a swimming pool and a two-story tower, the first story reserved for the couple's fifty-seven cats and the second story converted into a study. The author left his typewriter, hunting trophies, paintings by Klee, Gris, Masson and Miró and 8000 books at the *Finca* when he left the house.

THE STUDY

Hemingway preferred this study to the one in the tower, which was too isolated. On a wall hangs a buffalo head, a souvenir from his first safari. The writer rarely used the desk: he got up at dawn and worked until 1pm, standing in front of his portable Royal placed on a shelf.

The room also contained a bed where he piled his mail. It has been kept as he left it, as has the rest of the house. Only the gardens are open to the public.

THE OLD MAN AND THE SEA

Hemingway loved fishing for marlin and swordfish. At Cojímar ▲ *164*, 'Papa' Hemingway had his boat, *El Pilar*, his restaurant, *La Terraza* and his friends, including the sailor Gregorio Fuentes, who is said to have inspired the character of Santiago in the novel *The Old Man and the Sea*. In 1954, the author dedicated his Nobel Prize for Literature to his adoptive island, declaring that it belonged to Cuba, because his work had been written and conceived in Cuba, with the people of Cojímar, who were his fellow citizens. After his death, the village erected a memorial to him. Although Marina Hemingway ▲ *162*, a tourist center situated twenty minutes from Havana, pays homage to the writer, the latter never set foot here.

THE DRAWING ROOM

Mary Welsh, Hemingway's last wife, designed the furniture for this room. Near the author's armchair is the bar, which he designed himself, with the original bottles. At the back are his record collection and a hunting trophy: the head of a deer killed in 1930 in Wyoming.

THE DINING ROOM

Hemingway dined here with his friends, the rich and famous, ordinary people or passing celebrities such as Ava Gardner, Gary Cooper, Ingrid Bergman, and the bullfighters Ordóñez and Dominguín. A painting by Miró, *The Farm*, graced one of the walls for twenty-two years. The door is flanked by two heads of pronghorns, American antelopes, killed in Idaho.

> 'People ask you why you live in Cuba and you [...] tell them the biggest reason you live is Cuba is the great, deep blue river [...] that you can reach in thirty minutes from the door of your farmhouse, riding through beautiful country to get to it, that has, when the river is right, the finest fishing I have ever known.' (*The Great Blue River*)

Hemingway loved literature, good company and drinking, three passions which he indulged freely within the enchanted surroundings of Old Havana.

The capital honors the memory of his many jaunts: the spots he frequented have been lovingly preserved and his favorite stroll, from his hotel to his preferred bars, is regarded as a historical itinerary in its own right. All 'Papa's' friends are featured there: movie stars, boxers, bullfighters, politicians and ordinary folk who accompanied him on his travels have all become part of the legend of Havana.

THE 'FLORIDITA'

Journalist Fernando Campoamor was Ernest Hemingway's guide through Havana's nightlife, a service that 'Papa' repaid by giving him scoops on his Hollywood friends. It was with Fernando Campoamor that he discovered *El Floridita*, a bar-restaurant near the Capitolio ▲ *132*. The establishment has retained its original red and black decor, but a chain prevents anyone from sitting on the writer's stool at the far end of the bar. Ernest Hemingway refused to have anything to do with the place when it installed air conditioning, then forgave this sacrilegious act and immortalized the 'best joint in the Caribbean' in print in his book *Islands in the Stream*.

THE 'AMBOS MUNDOS' HOTEL

This was Hemingway's first pied-à-terre, a stone's throw from *La Bodeguita del Medio* and the *Floridita*. He stayed here regularly from 1932 to 1939 and wrote *A Farewell to Arms* and part of *For Whom the Bell Tolls* here. His room on the fifth story has remained as he left it, but the typewriter is not his and the view of the cathedral, the Morro fort and the Casablanca peninsula is spoiled by modern buildings.

THE 'DAIQUIRI' ● 66

As legend has it, the *daiquiri*, made with white rum, refined sugar, lime juice and crushed ice, was invented by Hemingway and Constante Ribalaigua, the owner of the *Floridita*. Hemingway drank double daiquiris, without sugar, a version which he called 'Papa's Special'. It was at the *Floridita* bar that he set his own impressive record: fifteen cocktails in one evening.

LA BODEGUITA DEL MEDIO

Casa Martínez was originally a grocery shop near the cathedral. In April 1950, it was renamed the *Bodeguita del Medio* and became a restaurant serving what the Americans called Creole food. Hemingway hardly ever visited what was soon to become one of the most stylish places in Cuba. The sentence attributed to him, which appears prominently on the wall: 'My mojito at the *Bodeguita*, my daiquiri at the *Floridita*' is apparently apocryphal.

Western Cuba:
Pinar del Río province

Andrés Escobar and Maryse Roux

▲ Western Cuba: Pinar del Río province

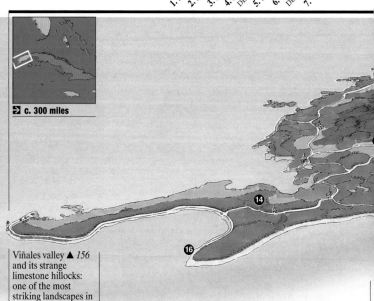

→ c. 300 miles

Viñales valley ▲ *156* and its strange limestone hillocks: one of the most striking landscapes in the province.

The 'Punto Guajiro'
This kind of singing ● *54* first emerged on the tobacco plantations of Western Cuba, then in those of Central Cuba, owing to the *guateques* (folk festivals, *right*) in the 19th century.

Pinar del Río Province (4220 square miles) is the westernmost region in Cuba. Devoted to tobacco farming, it also boasts a wide variety of natural riches. The mountain chain of the Guaniguanico, divided into two ranges, the Sierra del Rosario and the Sierra de los Órganos, and their respective hills, the Alturas de Pizarra, occupy much of the territory. The climate is cooler here than in the rest of the country. In the sierras, which are fairly low (the Pan de Guajaibón reaches an altitude of 2289 feet) and receive more rain, the forest vegetation is much denser than in the southern plains, which are covered by a typical savanna, dotted with big belly palms (*Colpotrinax wrightii*), an ancient native species. The province has two designated UNESCO Biosphere Reserves, containing animals and plants that are found nowhere else in the world but Cuba: the Sierra del Rosario and the Guanahacabibes Peninsula at the westernmost tip of the island. The province's other main claim to fame is the Vuelta Abajo region which produces probably the finest tobacco in the world.

152

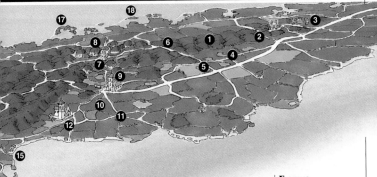

THE LAND OF THE GUANAJATABEY. Archeological excavations have revealed that in 6000 BC this region was populated by the Guanajatabey people ● *34*. Columbus, who came into contact with them on his first voyage, noted that they were less civilized than the inhabitants of Oriental lands whom he had met on his previous expeditions.

A PROVINCE THAT OWES ITS BIRTH TO TOBACCO. In the 16th and 17th centuries, poor Spanish settlers, generally from the Canary Islands, cultivated tobacco farming ● *68* in this region. The growing importance of the tobacco trade led to the creation of the province then known as the New Philippines by the Spanish governor Felipe de Fondesvila, Marquis de la Torre. In 1800, Pinar del Río, situated at the heart of the great tobacco-producing region, became capital of Pinar del Río province.

THE INTRODUCTION OF COFFEE. In the first half of the 19th century, coffee was introduced into the Sierra del Rosario by French settlers, most of whom came from Louisiana. Many of these settlers also played a vital role in the growth of large-scale sugar production and, within several decades, the lucrative sugar industry was one of the causes for the decline of the coffee plantations. The ruins of some fifty plantations offer an insight into the once sophisticated French-influenced lifestyle of their owners, wealthy planters from the plain of Havana, who had traveled west for the country air. The Cuban coffee industry is not entirely dead, however: the towns of San Cristóbal, Candelaria, Bahía Honda and Viñales still have some small coffee plantations.

THE WEST: A CAMPAIGN OBJECTIVE. The westward advance led by Antonio Maceo ● *39* from the eastern provinces was a key phase in the war for independence at the end of the 19th century. The Pinar del Río province was the scene of bitter clashes with the Spanish at the time. In 1958, on Castro's orders, another guerrilla front led by Commander Dermidio Escalona was opened.

FISHING
In addition to tourism, tobacco and sugar, the economy of this region, which has around 700,000 inhabitants, relies on fishing. Crayfish, albacore (similar to tuna), striped grouper and bonito sustain several small ports, La Coloma, on the south coast, being the largest.

BIRTH OF ECOTOURISM
From the 19th century, the proximity and balmy climate of the region has attracted people living in the capital. They go on vacation in the verdant mountain valleys and take the waters at San Diego de los Baños or San Vicente. Activities include hiking, nature-watching, fishing, hunting and even speleology.

153

TOWARD SIERRA DEL ROSARIO

THE CARRETERA CENTRAL. More picturesque than the highway (*autopista*) that gets you from Havana to Pinar del Río in two hours, the two-lane Carretera Central winds its way through fields, sugar plantations and small towns in the hinterland outside Havana. This area supplies the capital's vegetables, pork, poultry and milk.

FINCA ANGERONA. In 1828, Reverend Abiel Abbot visited this coffee plantation (now in ruins) ten miles west of Artemisa. Cornelius Sausse, who ordered its construction in 1813, made it the richest plantation in the region. According to Abbot, it numbered around 750,000 coffee trees tended by 450 slaves: 'His *batey* […] is approached by a broad and superb avenue, adorned in the usual manner, except that at the foot of the hill, on an elevated pedestal, stands his sylvan deity, the Goddess of Silence […] The next apartment is an elegant hall, floored with wood, an unusual thing in this country […] In one of the windows was an Aeolian harp of great power and sweetness, resounding at the touch of the norther. The next apartment is a breakfast room and library; through which we passed into a spacious bedchamber.' (*Letters written in the Interior of Cuba*).

FOR THE LOVE OF A MULATTO WOMAN
In 1809 Cornelius Sausse, a Franco-Prussian from Baltimore, met Ursule Lambert in Havana, a wealthy, cultivated woman from Haiti. Their love affair was condemned at the time, so they lived quietly at the Finca Angerona. When Sausse died in 1837, Ursule returned to the city without accepting her legacy of an annual pension.

San Juan river at Las Terrazas.

THE SIERRA DEL ROSARIO ★

The first wooded slopes of the Sierra del Rosario rise less than thirty-one miles from Havana. The two highest peaks of this mountain range soar to an altitude of more than 1640 feet. In 1985, UNESCO designated it a Biosphere Reserve – the first in Cuba – because of its well-conserved ecosystems and the completed reforestation. The sierra, which is covered by mixed forest vegetation – tropical rainforest and semi-deciduous – is home to a remarkable variety of fauna: 90 species of birds, 50 percent of which are native, 16 species of amphibians, including the smallest frog in the world (*Smithilus limbatus*) and 33 species of non-venomous reptiles. There are 608 species of higher plants, 11 percent of which are indigenous,

Orquídeas Cubanas · *Orquídeas Cubanas* · *Orquídeas Cubanas* · *Orquídeas Cubanas*

including the copaiva tree whose resin is used in the production of varnish. The inhabitants of the Sierra, who once lived in scattered groups, now live for the most part in communities.

LAS TERRAZAS. This village is thirty-one miles from Havana and there is a charge for admission. The architecture has been designed to blend in with its natural setting: the cluster of small buildings and prefabricated houses follows the gradual slope of the hillside down to the central lake. The village was part of a program that developed new rural communities in the 1970s. Its 900 inhabitants work on restoring forest areas damaged by erosion. As well as cattle breeding, ecotourism is one of the main sources of income for the village, which has seen the arrival of several craftsmen and the construction of the HOTEL MOKA, whose original design incorporates trees and vegetation inside the building. This is the point of departure for walks in the Sierra del Rosario which lead to several picturesque destinations such as the old Buena Vista coffee plantation or riverside conservation areas: the Baños de San Juan and the Cañada del Infierno Trail.

SOROA. This tourist village (1960) is nicknamed 'the Rainbow of Cuba' because its 72-foot-high waterfall assumes all the colors of the rainbow at certain times of day. It also has one of the few swimming pools in the region. The view from the terrace of the *Castillo de las Nubes* restaurant, which looks out over the valley, takes in the entire forest of Soroa with its ferns, begonias,

arum lilies and springs. At the heart of this lush paradise is the ORQUIDEARIO, one of the most beautiful gardens in Cuba, with 700 varieties of orchids, 250 of them indigenous (*top*, four varieties), which flower from November to February. It is thought to have been created in 1943 by T. F. Camacho, a wealthy landowner from the Canary Islands, in memory of his daughter who died in childbirth and who loved orchids.

SAN DIEGO DE LOS BAÑOS AND ENVIRONS

The Río San Diego, which runs through the little town of the same name, forms a natural frontier between the Sierra del Rosario and the Sierra de los Órganos.

SAN DIEGO DE LOS BAÑOS. Some seventy-five miles from Havana, this spa has been renowned since the 18th century and has recently been restored. Its waters are recommended for respiratory and skin problems.

CUEVA DE LOS PORTALES. Judging from the remains found here, this cave, discovered in 1800, was once used as a refuge by aborigines on the run. In 1947, the landowner Manuel Cortina annexed it to his estate, adapting it for his family's use. It is now famous for being used by Che as his headquarters during the Cuban Missile Crisis. Items belonging to Che and rustic furniture are exhibited here.

THE RIVER LIZARD
The Cuban stream anole (*Anolis vermiculatus*) is one of two native reptiles that are found in the Sierra del Rosario. It can often be sighted near moving water, hence its name.

PARQUE LA GÜIRA
Hacienda Cortina, the former estate of the wealthy landowner Manuel Cortina (*below*), is three miles to the west of San Diego de los Baños, on the road leading to the Cueva de los Portales. It was one of the first estates to be

nationalized during the First Agrarian Reform ● *44*; Manuel Cortina, however, left the country after 1959. The trail goes past the ruins of the former medieval-style mansion (*above left*), as well as some charming remains, scattered around a formal English garden, a Chinese pavilion, statues of Venuses, sphinxes and satyrs. Visitors who want to play at being the Swiss Family Robinson can rent a lofty tree house.

▲ VIÑALES VALLEY

URANIA
Primarily diurnal, this large butterfly occasionally flies at night, attracted by electric lights.

A phantasmagoric landscape, the symbol of Pinar del Río province, lies about ninety-three miles from Havana: giant knolls tower over a serene vista of red soil patterned by the greens and browns of *bohíos* and tobacco and corn fields. Viñales is one of the valleys in the Sierra de los Órganos, so named by sailors who glimpsed, from a distance, the organ-pipes of its hummocks. In reality, these strange hills or *mogotes* form a vast karst terrain which is the result of millions of years of erosion by underground streams. The water has hollowed out countless caves (Cueva del Indio) in Cuba's oldest rocks. The town of Viñales, built on land devoted to cattle breeding since 1607, was founded in the 19th century as a result of the rapid expansion of tobacco farming.

FLORA ON THE 'MOGOTES'
The *mogotes* are covered in dense vegetation, more characteristic on the slopes than on top of the hills: sierra palms, kapoks and caïman oaks, mountain species that have adapted themselves to tough conditions over hundreds of years, grow in cracks in the rock.

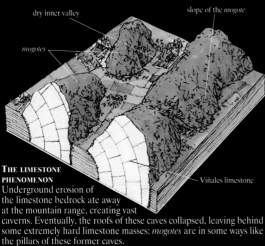

dry inner valley

slope of the *mogote*

mogotes

THE LIMESTONE PHENOMENON
Underground erosion of the limestone bedrock ate away at the mountain range, creating vast caverns. Eventually, the roofs of these caves collapsed, leaving behind some extremely hard limestone masses: *mogotes* are in some ways like the pillars of these former caves.

Viñales limestone

THE WALL OF PREHISTORY
This fresco, painted in 1961 by Leovigildo
González Morillo on the side of the *mogote*
Dos Hermanas, charts the evolution of the
Sierra de los Órganos. An ammonite from the
Cretaceous period and a megalocerus, a
mammal from the Pleistocene Epoch, are shown.

A NATURAL WONDER ✪
A breathtaking sight
at any time of day,
whether you go on
foot or horseback:
you should plan to
spend the night here.
The village of Viñales
is a good place to
stop: have lunch at
the Casa de Don
Tomás.

In Calle José Martí, the main road in Pinar del Río, this house in eclectic style dates from the turn of the 20th century, with elaborately carved portico and railings.

PINAR DEL RÍO

This small town, which was to give its name to the region and become a provincial capital of 100,000 inhabitants, was founded in 1774 in the shade of a pine forest on the banks of the Río Guamá. Pinar del Río has retained the laid-back rustic charm of its colonial origins with its brightly painted, flamboyantly decorated houses. Situated 109 miles from Havana, the city was for many years a large, wealthy agricultural town devoted to tobacco production before most of the factories moved to the island's capital. Some vestiges of the town's past glory can still be seen on Calle José Martí.

PALACIO GUASCH
This building, home to the Sandalio de Noda Museum of Natural Sciences (Calle Martí, N⁰ 202), is a remarkably flamboyant mansion which combines Moorish arches, Gothic arrows and baroque elements. Built in 1909 by a wealthy doctor, its eclectic use of styles ● *90* reflects its owner's love of traveling.

TEATRO JOSÉ JACINTO MILANÉS. This Italianate Renaissance-style theater, modeled on the one in Matanzas ▲ *167*, was built in 1883. It is currently undergoing restoration.

MUSEO PROVINCIAL DE HISTORIA. Close to the Teatro Milanés, this museum traces the region's history from Indian times. Like many of the island's historical museums, its collection is extremely eclectic: furniture from the colonial period, paintings by local artists, rebel weapons and other exhibits.

CASA GARAY. All Cubans know and enjoy Guayabita, the local liquor from Pinar del Río. Distilled since 1892, it owes its name to a local variety of guava (*guayaba*) and is fermented with a blend of rum and spices. A tasting is available on a visit to the Casa Garay (Calle Isabel Rubio, N⁰ 189).

FÁBRICA DE TABACOS FRANCISCO DONATIÉN. A former hospital, this attractive house (Calle Maceo, N⁰ 157) has, since the 1960s, been home to a tobacco factory converted into a popular training center for *torcedores* ● *72*. Its products are distributed under the Veguero label. Every day, around forty *torcedores* display their considerable talent at rolling Cuban cigars, making this both an entertaining and educational visit.

THE VUELTA ABAJO ★

The Vuelta Abajo produces the finest tobacco in the world: the heart of this region, the largest tobacco-growing area on the island, forms a triangle roughly bounded by Pinar del Río in the northeast and San Juan y Martínez and San Luis in the south. The most famous *vegas* (plantations) are those of Hoyo de Monterrey, El Corojo near San Luis and Las Vegas de Robaina in the Cuchillas Barbacoa at San Juan y Martínez.

A MIRACULOUS LAND. The most renowned area in the Vuelta Abajo is in the plain south of Pinar del Río: the *vegas* are planted on fine reddish sandy loam, which is well drained, nutritious and rich in nitrogen. Sheltered in the lee of the Sierra del Rosario, which protects them from heavy rain, they grow a unique tobacco which provides wrapper and filler leaves for Havana cigars. Former plantation owners, who left the country in 1959, went on to plant seeds from this excellent tobacco in Santo Domingo, Honduras, Nicaragua and the United States. But the tobacco they produced was never as good as that of the Vuelta Abajo because it lacked the distinctive synthesis of climate and soil found in this region. At San Juan y Martínez, the TOBACCO RESEARCH INSTITUTE has nurtured these seeds since 1937.

SMALL FAMILY FARMS. The majority of plantations have been farmed by generations of *veguero* families since the colonial period. Often simple tenant farmers, they were forced to sell their products to the owners, merchants and then manufacturers at very low prices. But their farming techniques draw on ancestral expertise, which is why family-run farms (limited to an area of seventeen acres) are thriving, despite the growth of state-controlled farms and the cooperative sector. The state, which still owned forty percent of the land in 1990, redistributed 34,594 acres to 7000 families during the 'Special Period' ● *46*. In 1998, the state possessed less than 10 percent of the land. It remains, however, the only producer and distributor of Cuban cigars.

LAS VEGAS DE ROBAINA

Alejandro Robaina owns one of the most famous *vegas* in the Vuelta Abajo: each year, his 200,000 *corojo* plants produce magnificent wrapper leaves that have earned him recognition by the Cuban government: his name appears on a Havana label. Robaina's story illustrates the crucial importance of handing down family expertise from generation to generation: his grandfather, originally from the Canary Islands, started out as a *veguero* in 1845 on an estate in San Luis, and his son is being trained to take over the family business.

Havana cigar box labels ● 74.

LOS 'HOYOS'

In the enclosed flat-bottomed valleys of the Sierra del Rosario, tobacco is grown on what little arable land there is: these plantations are called *hoyos*. The Hoyo de Monterrey has given its name to a prestigious cigar label: Hoyo de

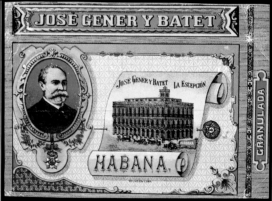

Monterrey. It was registered in 1867 by José Gener. Originally from Catalonia, he was the undisputed cigar king until his death in 1900. His daughter carried on the name which was sold, in 1931, to the Fernández y Palacio company. With cigars such as Hoyo des Dieux or Epicure № 2, José Gener's successors have achieved renewed success.

160

The Guanahacabibes Peninsula

This peninsula, with its aboriginal name, forms the westernmost tip of the province. The spur-shaped tongue of land at its end is rocky along the south coast and swampy along the north. Narrowing over sixty-two miles, barely four miles wide for less than half its length and twenty-one miles across at its maximum width, it was designated a UNESCO Nature Reserve in 1987.

The Cuban 'Finistère'. The region begins south of the Río Cuyaguateje, between the river mouth and Guane, where the *vegas* are still farmed between savanna and pine forest. It then becomes a narrow stretch of land, isolated by the line of lakes and swamps (drained for part of the year), between La Fe in the west and Cortés in the east. The peninsula is covered with rocks from the Bay of Corrientes to Cape San Antonio in the far west, which can be reached by a road running along the south coast.

Playa Bailén. Situated southeast of the village of Isabel Rubio, this long beach is very popular with Cubans who often come here for daytrips.

María la Gorda ★. The peninsula's only seaside resort, María la Gorda (Fat Mary) is ideal for keen scuba-divers and the International Dive Center is based here. Five miles of golden sand nestle in an inlet of the Bay of Corrientes with warm clear water throughout the year. Legend has it that pirates abducted a buxom young woman called María from the coast of Venezuela. Marooned in the creek of Resguardo, she was forced to sell her ample charms to passing pirates, giving the area its name.

Parque Nacional de Guanahacabibes. (Entrance tickets can be bought from the Hotel Villa María la Gorda). In this national park, the mangroves, sealife and the mixed forest of deciduous and coniferous trees form a protected reserve (250,806 acres). Hunting is prohibited. The area, relatively unexplored for many years, has been studied since 1985. It has 600 species of plants as well as many species of animals: deer, wild boar, bats, hutias (*below*) and various non-venomous reptiles. The myriad birds nesting here include green woodpeckers, parakeets, the Cuban trogon ■ *20*, two species of humming-bird ■ *20*, ▲ *175* and the spectacular great lizard cuckoo. The few people living in the reserve mainly work at the research center and in a local state forestry company. In the village of Valle San Juan, 1200 bee hives produce local honey. Several people here also earn their living from fishing and there is still a community of charcoal-burners who use the mangrove trees on the north coast as a source of plant charcoal and the small dolines (depressions) on the south coast to produce food crops.

Cabo de San Antonio. The lighthouse on the cape was built by slaves in 1849 under orders of the Spanish governor of the time, Federico Roncalli.

Block of tabular coral at María la Gorda.

THE BEACH OF CAYO JUTÍAS
The quietest beaches, such as this one, are often used as a stopover by small waders such as sandpipers migrating between North and South America. The shallow water also attracts terns in search of fish.

THE NORTH COAST OF PINAR DEL RÍO PROVINCE

On the way back from the Guanahacabibes peninsula, you will come to Guane, a large rural village at the opening of the Río Cuyaguateje valley. Intrepid visitors can walk up the river and cross the fissure in the Sierra de los Órganos ▲ *152*, passing through San Carlos and Sumidero to reach the famous copper mines at Matahambre. Those who like landscapes nestling between sea and mountains can take the fork from Guane toward Mantua in the west and follow the rudimentary road through the plain to Santa Lucía. The often swampy coastline is dotted with isolated cays ■ *28* belonging to the Archipiélago de Los Colorados, which provide fine fishing. Two or three of the islands are equipped for tourism

and provide the perfect opportunity to indulge in doing nothing.
CAYO JUTÍAS.
A recently built sea wall, branching off some two miles before Santa Lucía, leads to a pretty beach of white sand. The site is still relatively well-preserved and quiet.

PRIMITIVE LIFE
Sponges (*right*) and corals (*below*) form a brightly colored backdrop to life on

CAYO LEVISA. Unlike Cayo Jutías, this islet, linked to the jetty at Playa Rubia by a daily ferry, has been developed for tourists. Its two miles of white sandy beaches ringed with coral reefs make it an idyllic place to relax.
RETURNING TO HAVANA ALONG THE COAST. With the small Manuel Sanguily sugar mill, opposite Cayo Levisa, sugarcane returns to center stage on the coastal plain, indented by the characteristic 'flask-shaped' bays of Bahía Honda and Bahía Cabañas, small ports dedicated to fishing and inshore navigation. Because of its proximity to Havana (twenty-five miles) and its quarries, the port of MARIEL possesses one of the island's seven cement factories. The industrial town is also

the Caribbean seabed. Despite their static appearance, they are primitive animals. They feed on minute prey by constantly filtering the water.

famous as the site of the 'boatlift' of 1981 when thousands of Cubans left the island from this port following the events at the Peruvian Embassy ● *46*. Twelve miles from Havana, the luxurious yachting resort of the MARINA HEMINGWAY doubles as a popular tourist center. The annual marlin fishing competition in May, which pays homage to Hemingway ▲ *148*, attracts anglers from all over the world.

The north coast,
from Havana to Cárdenas
José Dos Santos López

➦ 90 miles

With such nicknames as the 'Cuban Riviera', the 'Coastal Road' and the 'Blue Circuit', the stretch of road running along the coast from Havana to Cárdenas is clearly dedicated to the heady pleasures of sun, sea and sand. The appropriately named Vía Blanca ('White Road') leads to the east coast beaches of Playas del Este and to Varadero ▲ *168*, the largest seaside resort on the island. While the former beaches, because of their proximity to the capital, are especially popular with the residents of Havana, the latter is completely oriented toward international tourism. Visitors who have come to Cuba to savor the charm of its colonial towns, however, can round off their trip by visiting Matanzas and Cárdenas, built with fortunes from the region's sugar industry.

COJIMAR ★

This fishing village (*left*), founded in the 17th century at the mouth of the River Cojímar, continues to cherish the memory of one of its guests, Ernest Hemingway

HOMAGE TO HEMINGWAY
This tribute takes the form of a bust of the writer, surrounded by a neoclassical peristyle. Only several feet from the Spanish fortress of Cojímar (1643, *above*), this work was built by the Cojímar fishermen in 1962, using propellers and other pieces from their boats. La Terraza ◆ *249*, an ultra-stylish restaurant overlooking the bay, displays numerous photos of fishing expeditions in which the novelist took part.

▲ *148*, the writer who loved deep-sea fishing. His boat, *El Pilar*, was moored here for many years.

PLAYAS DEL ESTE

PLAYA BACURANAO. This small beach, eleven miles from Havana, is the first possible stopping place along the six-mile-long ribbon of sand formed by Playas del Este. It is probably also the quietest in terms of hotel accommodation.

Yumurí Valley, one of the most impressive landscapes in Cuba.

PLAYA TARARÁ. The Marina Tarará has everything: it is a sailing resort with excellent facilities for fishing and deep-sea diving and there is a beach-side complex of fifty-six bungalows dating from the 1950s. There is an admission charge. The CIUDAD DE LOS PIONEROS JOSÉ MARTÍ sprawls between the Vía Blanca and Tarara Beach. This 'City of Pioneers', named after the national hero ● *40*, provides vacations for Cuban schoolchildren who have achieved the highest national marks.

PLAYA SANTA MARÍA DEL MAR ★. With several hotels, restaurants and excellent facilities, this beautiful beach lined with coconut palms is larger than the neighboring beaches and resembles a 'small Varadero'. It is very popular with tourists as well as the residents of Havana, who willingly cycle all the way here. The small beach between Playa Santa María del Mar and Playa Guanabo is a discreet rendezvous for homosexuals.

PLAYA GUANABO ★. This beach, seventeen miles from the capital, is a favorite with Cuban families, who picnic here on summer weekends. Many of the people who live in the village, which boasts a delightful fishing harbor, rent rooms in their homes, and the atmosphere is more family-oriented than in Santa María del Mar.

TOWARD MATANZAS

PLAYA JIBACOA. This other hub of national tourism, less luxurious than the east coast beaches, is popular with scuba-divers because of its fine coral formations.

VALLE DE YUMURÍ ★. The most breathtaking view of this beautiful natural amphitheater is from the viewpoint near BACUNAYAGUA BRIDGE, the highest in the country (361 feet). There are many health centers up here for the treatment of stress, asthma or high blood pressure.

THE 'RONERA SANTA CRUZ'
Situated on the outskirts of Santa Cruz del Norte, between Playas del Este and Matanzas, this is the largest Havana Club rum factory in Cuba (no visitors allowed). The current factory, rebuilt and enlarged between 1973 and 1975, has a dozen aging facilities for Gold Label rum. The distillery, which also produces other liquors and fruit juices, employs around 600 people.

Approaching from the west, the Vía Blanca gently slopes down to Matanzas (120,000 inhabitants). It provides a beautiful view of the 'city of rivers' nestling behind the wide bay and crossed by the Río Yumurí in the north and the Río San Juan in the south. The city was founded between these two rivers in October 1693, on the orders of the King of Spain. Its name remains enigmatic: *matanzas* means 'slaughter' or 'massacre' and probably relates to the drowning of the settlers by the Indians in Matanzas Bay, following the outbreak of a rebellion in 1509.

THE SUGAR CAPITAL OF 19TH-CENTURY CUBA. Known by the Indians as Guanima Bay, Matanzas was destined to become a great port. It made its fortune in the early 19th century with the construction of large sugar mills and the arrival of large numbers of slaves.

THE 'ATHENS OF CUBA'. The city flourished as a result of this prosperity, becoming, by 1830, a focal point for many writers, poets, artists and scholars. The first national newspaper was founded here. The former 'Athens of Cuba' is now the liveliest cultural center after the capital. Dancing is also very popular here: Matanzas, the birthplace of the Abakuá, is looked on as the 'queen of *rumba*' ● 55.

A MODERN INDUSTRIAL CITY AND PORT. Although Matanzas is still the fourth largest sugar port in the world, it has diversified widely, now producing paper, textiles, chemical products and fertilizers. Its port has a supertanker base, linked to inland cities by the 'Friendship Pipeline'. It also has the most powerful thermoelectric plant in Cuba and it was here, in the 1990s, that the government decided to accept the challenge of the 'smokeless fuel industry'.

THE BIRTHPLACE OF THE 'DANZÓN' ● 54 The *danzón*, the first dance for an entwined couple, was derived from the Creole version of the formal French quadrille. It was created in 1879 in Matanzas, where 'these dances could be heard on all sides coming from every house in the town' (Frederika Bremer, *Cartas desde Cuba*). On January 1, the composer Miguel Failde presented the first *danzón*, called *Las Alturas de Simpson*, named after one of the city's fashionable quarters at the time. Until the end of the 1920s the *danzón* remained the queen of popular Cuban dances. In 1929, in Matanzas, Aniceto Díaz invented the *danzonete*, a sung version of the *danzón*.

PLAZA DE LA VIGÍA

This lovely square, which seems suspended between the Calixto García bridge (1849) and the Concordia bridge, marks the original site of the city. A STATUE OF THE UNKNOWN SOLDIER has been erected in homage to the victims of the war for

independence ● *39*.
Close enough to compete with Havana, Matanzas was also its emulator, as can be seen by the buildings lining the square.

PALACIO DEL JUNCO.

This neocolonial building, easily recognizable by its blue walls and two stories of arcades, was built by a wealthy planter between 1835 and 1840. It now houses the MUSEO HISTÓRICO PROVINCIAL, which retraces the history of the region from the Pre-Columbian period to the Revolution. Points of interest include engravings by Edouard Laplante and a collection of instruments of torture that were used on slaves.

TEATRO SAUTO ★. The former Teatro Esteban (named after a former governor of the province; Sauto is the name of the patron who financed the building) was erected in 1862 by the Italian architect and set designer Daniele Delaglio. He was also responsible for the church of SAN PEDRO APOSTÓL (1870) in the Versailles *barrio* (quarter), perched atop one of the town's hills. The building was to be a source of inspiration for Cuba's two other neoclassical theaters, in Cienfuegos ▲ *178* and Pinar del Río ▲ *158*, and was to welcome some prestigious guest artists, including Sarah Bernhardt (in *La Dame aux Camélias*) in 1887 and the ballerina Anna Pavlova in 1915. The neoclassical FIRE STATION (1897–1900), on the side of the bay, is regarded as the finest on the island.

PARQUE LIBERTAD

The city's hub, this square was once the site of public executions, including the poet Gabriel de la Concepción Valdés. The former LICEO ARTÍSTICO Y LITERARIO (1860), the former SPANISH CASINO (early 20th century) and the PALACIO DE GOBIERNO, 'typical of the finest houses of its type' in the words of Abbé Abbott ▲ *154*, give some idea of the cultural and social life that once enlivened this town.

MUSEO FARMACÉUTICO ★. Adjoining the HOTEL EL LOUVRE, which has a beautiful patio, this pharmacy, formerly owned by Frenchman Ernesto Triolet (1882), is one of Matanzas' architectural gems. Everything has been left intact: the dispensary, which was converted into a museum in 1964; counters made of precious wood and faïence jars and flasks made of Bohemian crystal. The preparation table was awarded a bronze medal at the Universal Exhibition of 1900.

The banks of the Río San Juan (*top*); a street in Matanzas in 1908 (*above*).

THE CAVES OF BELLAMAR
'He who has not seen the caves of Bellamar has seen nothing of Cuba,' or so the saying goes. The oldest tourist site in the country (*below*), situated on the estaté of Finca La Alcancia, three miles southeast of Matanzas, was said to have been found by a slave on the estate looking for water with a divining rod. It is full of white crystal formations, stalactites, stalagmites and 26-million-year-old marine fossils. There are over two miles of galleries; one of them, thirty-one miles deep, is only visited by speleologists. Some areas of the caves are unexplored to this day.

167

The Hicacos Peninsula, an eleven-mile-long tongue of land eighty-seven miles east of Havana, suddenly changes direction from the main coastline and heads northward. The stretch of fine sand along the Atlantic coast has secured the success of its resort, Varadero, the largest tourist center in Cuba. The wealthy families of Cárdenas began building villas here at the turn of the century, and the residents of Havana soon followed suit. The first hotel was built in 1915, but the town's swift expansion dates from the late 1920s, as a result of the impetus given by American billionaire Irénée Du Pont de Nemours. Today, Varadero is covered with vast complexes and has a third of the total number of hotels in Cuba.

A HANDFUL OF WOODEN HOUSES

Some ancient houses, shrouded in coconut palm trees and hibiscus, can still be seen between Calles 1 and 54. Next to magnificent mansions built of canto, a porous stone indigenous to the region of Cárdenas, stand three or four wood-plank structures surrounded by verandas, painted in bright colors and weathered by the sea spray. The most attractive of these 'beach houses' is perhaps the one housing the Museo Municipal (*below*). It contains fragments of Pre-Columbian objects found in a cave in the vicinity, the *Cueva de Ambrosio*. But its greatest asset is its façade, painted in the traditional blue of the Caribbean Islands and decorated with openwork wood ornamentation inspired by Victorian wrought-ironwork. Constructions of this type were often prefabricated by American companies in the early 20th century and sold to the Cubans by mail-order.

A BEACH FOR FOREIGNERS

An insight into the Varadero of yesteryear can be gained by visiting the Du Pont de Nemours mansion, Josone Park, a fine estate dating from the 1940s, and the Hotels Kawama (1940–50) and Internacional (1955), all representative of their period. After the Revolution, Varadero became a socialist resort, but it is now given over to tourism. Foreigners are treated like royalty and the only Cubans you will meet are employees.

'From the other side of the magnificent [Du Pont de Nemours] mansion, a terrace overlooked the open sea. The rock formed a steep cliff from which it was possible to watch the sharks frolicking in the deep water […] Legend had it that they were in the habit of coming to the foot of the residence during the prosperous days when the employees of the extremely wealthy owner would daily throw them seafood and fish that would otherwise have gone to waste.' Jorge Luis Camacho, *The Monkey's Tail* (Actes Sud, 1997).

GOLFING TRADITION
The golf course built for the Du Pont de Nemours family is now surrounded by hotels. Renamed the Varadero Golf Club, it is very popular with tourists.

SOME LOCAL POINTS OF INTEREST
The dolphins at the Dolphinarium give three daily shows. Visitors are even permitted to swim with them. Nearby, on a site called Rincón Francés ('French Corner'), stands a giant 500-year-old cactus plant.

THE LARGEST SEASIDE RESORT IN CUBA ✪
After a day spent sunbathing on the beach, swimming and playing golf, enjoy a drink gazing out over the sea from the terrace of the *Las Américas* restaurant. Head into the city center for supper.

DU PONT DE NEMOURS MANSION
This magnate's mansion, in neo-Spanish style, was built in the 1930s by the Havana architects Govantes and Cabarrocas. It was named Xanadu after a poem by Samuel Taylor Coleridge: 'In Xanadu, did Kubla Khan/A stately pleasure dome decree.' It was highly expensive for the time, having cost a reputed $338,000.

'LAS AMÉRICAS'
The Du Pont de Nemours mansion houses the *Las Americas* restaurant. All five stories can be visited. The marble floors, ceilings, mahogany banisters, cellar with wine bar and automatic organ are all worth a look.

THE WONDERS OF VARADERO
There are twenty-three dive sites along this stretch of the north coast, but the seabed is even more exciting around the ten or so uninhabited islets just off the coast of the seaside resort. The waters are home to more than forty types of coral, more than seventy species of mollusks, shells, turtles and fish, as well as a superb coral reef, which can be reached by sailing toward Cayo Libertad.

169

CÁRDENAS

Founded in 1828 under the name of San Juan de Dios de Cárdenas, the city has a strict grid layout of streets which is regarded as the most perfect on the island. Cárdenas prospered as a result of the flourishing sugar trade throughout the 19th century and pioneered the use of street lighting (1889). Its industry began to decline in the 1930s, however, and now the majority of its inhabitants work in Varadero ▲ *168*, eleven miles away. Near the port is the FÁBRICA DE RON ARRECHABALA, the distillery that originally produced Havana Club rum ● *66*, founded by a Basque businessman in 1878. It is not open to the public.

THE FIRST STATUE OF COLUMBUS
In 1862, Cárdenas was privileged to provide a home for the first Cuban statue of the famous admiral. It was erected in the Parque Colón, opposite the cathedral, and inaugurated by the great Spanish-Cuban poetess, Gertrudis Gómez de Avellaneda (1814–73).

The layout and flat terrain of Cárdenas are ideal for horse-drawn carriages and bicycles, which have been in use here for many years – well before the 'Special Period' ● *46*.

PARQUE COLÓN. Near the CATEDRAL DE LA INMACULADA CONCEPCIÓN (1846), the HOTEL LA DOMINICA is a listed national monument. The Cuban flag was raised for the first time in 1850 from the top of this building, then the seat of the Spanish government. This symbolic act celebrated the defeat of the governor's troops by the rebel force led by Narciso López.

MOLACOFF COVERED MARKET. At the corner of Calle 12 and Avenida 3 stands an unusual metal building, crowned by a 52-foot-high dome. It is the last surviving example, in Cuba, of this type of structure.

PARQUE ECHEVARRÍA. This elegant square, the former Parque Estrada Palma, is dominated by a handsome neoclassical building with archways and balustrade (1862): the former town hall, which houses the MUSEO MUNICIPAL OSCAR MARÍA DE ROJAS (1900). This is the oldest museum on the island and contains an array of coins, medals, military decorations as well as devoting several display cases to a collection of shells, snails, butterflies and minerals. Also worth a visit is the house where JOSÉ ANTONIO ECHEVARRÍA was born in 1932. Echevarría became president of the University Students' Federation and lost his life in the attack on the Presidential Palace in Havana. His simply rendered statue stands opposite the entrance of the building. The house contains a museum illustrating the town's history: many of the objects on display date from the wars for independence and the Revolution.

Central Cuba

1. LA HAVANA
2. ZAPATA PENINSULA
3. BAY OF PIGS
4. CIENFUEGOS
5. CASTILLO DE JAGUA
6. JARDÍN BOTÁNICO DE LA SOLEDAD
7. TRINIDAD
8. PLAYA ANCÓN

⊇ c. 570 miles

AN OPEN-AIR MUSEUM
The fertile Valle
de los Ingenios
▲ 190, which

Central Cuba extends from Matanzas in the west to Camagüey in the east. Its provinces, Villa Clara, Cienfuegos, Sancti Spíritus, Ciego de Avila and Camagüey, can be reached via the *Carretera Central* (Central Road), perhaps in the company of *guajiros* (peasants) riding on horseback and wearing the baggy trousers and large straw hats inherited from their ancestors. The road passes through some flat open countryside that offers diverse scenery, including towering hills of unusual vegetation, and is fringed by beaches and mangroves. It is bordered, to the southwest, by the mysterious Zapata Peninsula.

CUBA'S RURAL PROVINCES

People moved into the area with the introduction of cattle breeding, tobacco and sugarcane: villages and parishes were founded during the 17th and 18th centuries, mainly in the western part of the region at first, then extending toward Sancti Spíritus during the 19th century. In the east, only Camagüey and a few ports grew rich from cattle breeding. The latter land remained sparsely populated and it was not until the 20th century that the area was truly colonized. The principal market towns flourished as a result of their strategic position along the communication routes and because they provided an outlet for agricultural produce. Later, industrialization benefited the two large inland towns of Santa Clara and Camagüey, as well as ports such as Nuevitas and Cienfuegos.

stretches for nineteen miles from Trinidad to Sancti Spíritus, boasts some of the island's most beautiful scenery as well as being a vast museum. This was where the Trinidadians amassed their sugar fortunes in the 18th century at the expense of their slaves. This erstwhile penal colony, now a museum, tells its story: the UNESCO Cultural Heritage Site contains no fewer than seventy-one archeological sites.

THE 'HEART' OF CENTRAL CUBA. This covers *grosso modo*, the former province of Las Villas, which now comprises the three provinces of Villa Clara, Cienfuegos and Sancti Spíritus. This region survives on food crops, sugarcane, cattle breeding and tobacco: Vuelta Arriba is the second largest producer of the filler leaves for

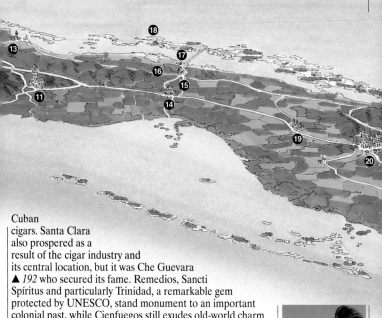

Cuban
cigars. Santa Clara
also prospered as a
result of the cigar industry and
its central location, but it was Che Guevara
▲ 192 who secured its fame. Remedios, Sancti
Spíritus and particularly Trinidad, a remarkable gem
protected by UNESCO, stand monument to an important
colonial past, while Cienfuegos still exudes old-world charm
despite its modernity. The city owes some of its activity to the
proximity of the southern sugarcane plantations and is one of
the island's main ports. The Guamuhaya mountain range,
colloquially called the Sierra del Escambray, dominated by
Pico San Juan (3740 feet), provides the city with a dramatic
backdrop. On the north face, its bare slopes are devoted to
cattle breeding. The sheer southern slopes have been
reclaimed for coffee farming and food crops are grown in the
narrow inland valleys.

THE PLAIN OF CAMAGÜEY. Only the low mountains of the
Sierra de Cubitas break the monotony of this flat fertile land,
a sparsely-populated region devoted to the production of
sugarcane, with the exception of the Trocha Plain, in Ciego de
Ávila Province, where citrus fruit and pineapples are also
grown. At the region's heart stretches the savanna given
over to cattle breeding, from which Camagüey, the
leading producer of milk and beef in Cuba, gets
most of its resources. The province has another
natural asset: the islets and beaches along its
northern shores.

**THE BEACHES ALONG
THE NORTH COAST**
Spectacular dive sites
can be found at Santa
Lucía (*above*), seventy
miles northeast of
Camagüey. Its waters
conceal more than
fifty different types of
coral formation.
Another place worth
exploring in the area
is the Camagüey
archipelago, close to
the second longest
coral reef in the
world. Its main
attraction is Cayo
Coco, one of Cuba's
largest islands (143
square miles), which
boasts a fourteen-
mile-long beach.

173

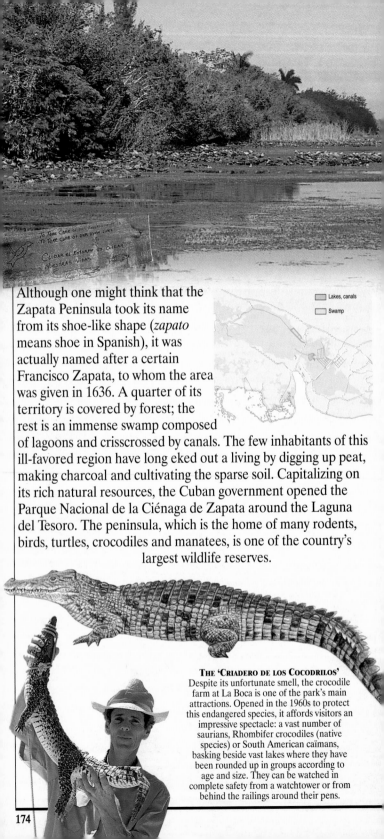

Although one might think that the Zapata Peninsula took its name from its shoe-like shape (*zapato* means shoe in Spanish), it was actually named after a certain Francisco Zapata, to whom the area was given in 1636. A quarter of its territory is covered by forest; the rest is an immense swamp composed of lagoons and crisscrossed by canals. The few inhabitants of this ill-favored region have long eked out a living by digging up peat, making charcoal and cultivating the sparse soil. Capitalizing on its rich natural resources, the Cuban government opened the Parque Nacional de la Ciénaga de Zapata around the Laguna del Tesoro. The peninsula, which is the home of many rodents, birds, turtles, crocodiles and manatees, is one of the country's largest wildlife reserves.

Lakes, canals
Swamp

THE 'CRIADERO DE LOS COCODRILOS'
Despite its unfortunate smell, the crocodile farm at La Boca is one of the park's main attractions. Opened in the 1960s to protect this endangered species, it affords visitors an impressive spectacle: a vast number of saurians, Rhombifer crocodiles (native species) or South American caïmans, basking beside vast lakes where they have been rounded up in groups according to age and size. They can be watched in complete safety from a watchtower or from behind the railings around their pens.

CUBAN PYGMY OWL
Not much bigger than a tennis ball, this tiny night hunter lays its eggs in a hollow tree.

ZAPATA'S RAIL
An extremely rare, almost mythical bird, it has only been glimpsed in the swamp by a lucky few.

BEE HUMMINGBIRD
(*zunzuncito*)
The male is the smallest bird in the world; the female lays eggs the size of peas.

The thirteen tiny islands of the Laguna del Tesoro are connected by hanging bridges. Straw huts on stilts form the hotel complex of Guamá. They are modeled on Taino Indian homes, traces of which have been discovered here and are on display in a small museum.

175

THE BAY OF PIGS

'Playa Girón: the First Defeat of Imperialism in Latin America.' A billboard with these words and depicting a raised submachine gun immediately plunges visitors into the historic event of the Bay of Pigs, known in Cuba by the name of one of two beaches where the counterrevolutionary forces landed in 1961 (group of American tourists in Playa Girón, April 1961, *above*). The long, narrow bay, like a stake driven into the Zapata Peninsula ▲ 174, also has some fine beaches.

THE INVASION. On April 14, 1961, a brigade of 1400 Cuban exiles trained by the CIA in Guatemala left Nicaragua for Cuba on board six ships. On April 15, six American B-26s, painted in Cuban air force colors, bombed the three air bases on the island, with the intention of wiping out the Cuban air force. The casualty toll was seven dead and fifty-three wounded. On April 16, the invasion fleet landed at Playa Girón and Playa Larga. The revolutionary troops, led by Fidel Castro, mounted a counteroffensive. On April 20, the brigade of exiles surrendered, outnumbered and out-gunned.

ANALYSIS OF DEFEAT. The invaders had been counting on an easy victory, underestimating the revolutionaries' solidarity and their defensive resources, strengthened by Soviet arms. Castro's intelligence services had also warned him about preparations for this operation. In addition to this, the landing site was poorly chosen: the coral reefs fringing the Bay of Pigs made it difficult to come ashore. Finally, fearing that American involvement in the affair might provoke an international outcry, President Kennedy had canceled an air strike intended to provide the invasion force with cover at the last minute (only the US Navy was authorized to escort the ships as far as Cuba). This decisive factor enabled the Cubans to defeat the enemy bombers and sink the ships that were to provide fresh supplies to the anti-Castroists.

MUSEO GIRÓN. In Playa Girón, a Sea Fury, a British fighter-aircraft used by the Castroist army, marks the entrance to this small museum dedicated to the Bay of Pigs invasion. The first room chronicles the drastic changes made in the Zapata Peninsula since the Revolution, since this region was originally one of the poorest in the country. Many of the documents and photos held in the museum relate to the literacy campaign ● *45*. There is a detailed exposé of the landing at the Bay of Pigs, from the initial preparations to the battles.

CALETA BUENA. A coastal road leads to this delightful cove, five miles from the Bay of Pigs, which provides excellent conditions for scuba-diving.

PLAYA LARGA
Very popular with Cubans, this is the most attractive beach in the Bay of Pigs. Lined with beautiful coral reefs, it provides excellent scuba-diving.

THE CAVE OF FISH ★
Halfway between Playa Larga and Playa Girón, just off the road lined at intervals with memorials to soldiers who died in the invasion, is the Cueva de los Peces. The cave owes its name to the myriad fish found in its natural 230-foot-deep swimming pool, a superb dive site. Another feature of this area is a bomb that was dropped during the invasion.

CIENFUEGOS ★

Capital of the province of the same name, Cienfuegos overlooks the magnificent and vast Bahía de Cienfuegos where Columbus landed in 1494. The town is a military and naval base and one of the country's major industrial centers: the largest cement factory on the island is based here, as well as an oil refinery, a sugar terminal and a shipyard. Construction of the only nuclear power plant in Cuba, financed by Moscow in the 1980s, was begun here but abandoned after the collapse of the Soviet bloc. The beauty of its historic center has earned Cienfuegos the name 'pearl of the south'.

A BORDEAUX COLONY. Fernandina de Jagua was founded in 1819 by Frenchman Louis de Clouet, with the help of fifty settlers from Bordeaux in France and New Orleans. The colony took the name of Cienfuegos in 1829, in honor of José Cienfuegos, then captain-general of Cuba. In order to counterbalance the huge presence of black slaves, Cienfuegos had offered free land to these French nationals who arrived from Louisiana in 1803.

A SUGAR PORT. The town flourished when businessmen turned away from Trinidad ▲ *180* to invest in local sugar refineries. Decline set in at the beginning of the 20th century. After 1959, Cienfuegos benefited from an industrial reorganization and, despite the adverse effects of the 'Special Period', it remains one of the world's leading sugar ports.

Punta Gorda (*above*), was once the most fashionable quarter of Cienfuegos; the Paseo del Prado (*below*) is still the city's busiest shopping street.

THE 'PEARL OF THE SOUTH' ✪
Spend an afternoon in Parque Martí. Remember that the sensational Teatro Tomás Terry closes at 4 pm. Walk or travel by carriage down the Paseo del Prado, then make for the Punta Gorda peninsula, which boasts some of the finest villas on the island.

Parque José Martí (1839) celebrates the foundation of the city on the spot marked by a rosette, and the establishment of the Republic ● 42 by a triumphal arch.

PARQUE JOSÉ MARTÍ ★

A statue of José Martí ● 40 guarded by two marble lions dominates the Parque Martí, a pleasant place to take a rest under the shady trees. This central square is lined with buildings dating from the 19th and 20th centuries, which represent the finest examples of the city's architecture.

CATEDRAL DE LA PURÍSIMA CONCEPCIÓN. The cathedral of the Immaculate Conception (1833–69), with its fine neoclassical façade, owes its fame to its French stained-glass windows of the twelve apostles.

TEATRO TOMÁS TERRY ★. A Parisian board commissioned Sánchez Marmol to build this elegant building on the north side of the square. The monument, the largest in Cienfuegos, is one of three provincial neo-classical theaters ● 86, along with Matanzas ▲ 166 and Pinar del Río ▲ 158. Built between 1887 and 1889, it owes its name to its builder, a sugar baron who had arrived from Venezuela in 1820. His statue adorns the lobby. The auditorium, typical of Italian-style theaters, with balconies lined with wrought-iron railings, can seat 850 people. With the floor raised and the rows of seats removed, the theater could be converted into a ballroom. Enrico Caruso and Sarah Bernhardt, who both performed here, would have been able to contemplate the delicate, witty ceiling frescos, surrounded by the seven muses and portraits of Cuban artists (including the poets Gertrudis Gómez de Avellaneda ▲ 170 and Gaspar Villate). An angel holds a clock showing the exact time – four o'clock in the afternoon – when the artist completed his work.

PALACIO FERRER. Built in the early 20th century by a sugar magnate, this building on the west side of the square looks like an enchanted palace and forms a striking contrast with the sober façades of neighboring houses. Painted a dazzling blue, the building, with its balconies and tower, combines baroque and neoclassical elements to form a delightfully

THE TOWER AT THE PALACIO FERRER ★
After climbing the fine spiral staircase, visible from the exterior of the building, to the top of the tower, visitors can enjoy a spectacular view over the tiled roofs of the city and Cienfuegos Bay.

> 'I am sitting by the bay in Cienfuegos [...] the light here is wonderful just before the sun goes down: a long trickle of gold.'
>
> Graham Greene, *Our Man in Havana*

antiquated ensemble. Visits to this labyrinthine building, which now houses the Casa de la Cultura Benjamin Duarte, involve some serious climbing for those who want to see the view from the top of the tower.

MUSEO PROVINCIAL. This museum – which is just before the magnificent Palacio del Gobierno, the seat of the Poder Popular Provincial – boasts a collection of furniture and objects illustrating the luxurious, sophisticated lifestyle of city nobility in the 19th century.

PUNTA GORDA ★

This former aristocratic quarter boasts a magnificent view over the bay. An evening stroll from the Hotel Jagua to the park at the far end of the peninsula will take you past some elegant villas, all remarkably well preserved. Most of them are made of brightly painted wood (*below, left*) and were prefabricated in the United States at the start of the 20th century.

CASTILLO DE JAGUA

Situated at the mouth of Cienfuegos Bay, this fortress, dedicated to Nuestra Señora de los Ángeles de Jagua, was built in 1745 to plans by Bruno Caballero in order to protect the region from Jamaican pirates. Legend has it that a mysterious woman in blue used to walk through the rooms of the citadel every night, terrorizing the soldiers. One morning, a guard was found lying senseless with fear on the floor, his sword held in a vice-like grip, surrounded by fragments of blue cloth. He ended his days in a lunatic asylum.

AROUND CIENFUEGOS

JARDÍN BOTÁNICO DE LA SOLEDAD ★. In 1912, plantation owner Edwin F. Atkins founded a garden on this site, nine miles from Cienfuegos, to study sugarcane varieties, but the collection of tropical trees he planted here soon gained the advantage. The place officially became a botanical garden when Harvard University acquired the estate in 1919 and turned it into a research center. The Soledad is now one of the most beautiful botanical gardens in Latin America, despite severe damage caused by Hurricane Lily in 1996: its 222 acres are home to more than 2000 plants, including nearly 300 species of palm and 200 varieties of cactus. Other sections are devoted to medicinal plants, orchids, bamboos and fruit trees.

PALACIO DE VALLE ★
The most remarkable building in Punta Gorda is the Palacio de Valle, opposite the Hotel Jagua. Built between 1912 and 1917 by wealthy businessman Aciclio Valle, this masterpiece of eclecticism ● *90* is a blithe mixture of Roman, Gothic, Venetian and Moorish styles, with the emphasis on the latter. It has been converted into a restaurant and its rooftop bar affords fabulous views over the bay, particularly at sunset.

THE ROYAL PALM
This indigenous species (*left*) is found throughout Cuba. The palm owes its name to its height, since it generally grows to 66 feet and can even reach an incredible 90 feet. It is easily recognizable by its slender light gray trunk which has a bulge in the middle. Each palm measures nearly 15 feet in diameter. Its oval fruit are purple when ripe.

In 1519, Hernán Cortés set sail for Mexico ● *33* from the banks of the Río Guaurabo (*Diego Velázquez Gives Hernán Cortés Command of the Army*, late 18th century, *below*). In his *Historia de Trinidad*, Francisco Marín Villafuerte writes: 'Hernán Cortés traveled from Santiago to Trinidad and bought a boat from Alonso Guillén, as well as three horses and 500 loads of grain. While he was there, he learned that

Juan Nuñez Sedeno was in the vicinity with a boat laden with supplies. He ordered Diego de Ordeas to attack the boat and bring it to Punta San Antón. Sedeno went to Trinidad, presenting his cargo record: 4000 *arrobas* [about 50 tons] of bread, 1500 hams and hundreds of chickens. Cortés gave him several trifles, some pieces of gold and a document officially acknowledging his participation in the conquest.'

Trinidad's buildings, painted in every shade of ocher, blue, green and pink, glow against the verdant backdrop of the Sierra del Escambray. This elegant city, which grew extremely prosperous in the 19th-century sugar boom but was then hit hard by competition from the sugar beet, offers a fascinating history tour for those visitors wanting to take a step back in time. Its fine palaces and family mansions, preserved during a gentle economic decline that lasted more than a century, still stand monument to the town's past glory and were designated a World Heritage Site by UNESCO in 1988.

HISTORY OF A 'MUSEUM TOWN'

FOUNDATION. On January 4, 1514 Diego Velázquez ● *32* founded the town of Santísima Trinidad at the point where the valley of San Luis ▲ *190* opens out. It had originally been planned that the colony's third town would be founded further east, in Cienfuegos Bay ▲ *177*, but the presence of a large settlement of Indians at the mouth of the Río Guaurabo and, more importantly, evidence of gold in the nearby mountains determined the town's new site.

IN CONQUEST OF MEXICO. By 1519, the gold was exhausted. Hernán Cortés set sail for Mexico ● *33* from the banks of the Río Guaurabo. Trinidad lost the majority of its population. Those who were left turned to cattle breeding and tobacco farming to survive.

PIRACY, TRADE WARS AND SMUGGLING. Confronted by the Spanish Crown's monopoly, an intensive smuggling operation developed in the area, centered around the ports of La Boca and Casilda. The era of trade wars and piracy had begun. Trinidad took measures to protect itself. However, in 1675, the Englishman John Springer sacked the town and, in 1702, his compatriot Carlos Gant stripped the town bare, even stealing the sacred urns from the parish church.

HISTORICAL TRINIDAD
The streets of the historic center are paved with cobbles with a central channel made of larger stones. This ill-assorted collection of granite, gypsum, coral and travertine from the 18th and 19th centuries was designed to prevent the soil being eroded by the heavy showers that regularly descend on the city. These cobbles would have disappeared beneath bitumen in the 1960s if Trinidadian lawyer Eduardo López had not fought to preserve them. Thanks to his efforts, they are still here to wear holes in walkers' soles.

THE SUGAR BOOM. From the second half of the 18th century, Trinidad threw itself heart and soul into the production of 'white gold': sugarcane. The region's small farmers benefited from the collapse of the Haitian sugar industry ● *38*. Cuba held itself aloof from the emancipation of slaves from Haiti; a new law even authorized plantation owners to make free use of those arriving from the island. *Ingenios* (sugar mills) ● *50* were built in the neighboring valley of San Luis ▲ *190* and the port of Casilda was equipped for international trade in 1818. In 1846, Trinidad had become the fourth largest commercial market in Cuba.

A LIVELY CULTURAL LIFE. Trinidad received a visit from Alexander von Humboldt ● *103* in 1801 and many foreigners flocked to the town, as can be seen from the census of 1827. Until 1868 and the outbreak of the Ten Years' War ● *39*, their strong cosmopolitan influence transformed the town's appearance: sugar magnates invested their fortunes in bricks and mortar and made Trinidad the wealthiest city in Latin America.

THE END OF THE GOLDEN AGE. In 1830, the first slave rebellions took place. Around 1840, the birth of the sugar beet industry in France and Germany threatened sugar cane's monopoly on the production of sugar. In the late 19th century, sugar prices plummeted; faced with competition from Cienfuegos ▲ *177*, Trinidad sank into a profound lethargy.

COUNTERREVOLUTIONARY TRINIDAD.
Sandwiched between sea and mountains, the town spent the first half of the 20th century completely isolated: an asphalt road linking it to the rest of the island was

THE CORPUS CHRISTI PROCESSIONS
These processions, which were first held in the late 18th century, inflamed the wildly enthusiastic Trinidadians, who would lead unruly parades through the city streets for a week or more. Because it was believed that the Christian liturgy was being tainted by its paganism, the festival was banned by royal decree on April 10, 1772. It reappeared in 1815 in the form of an annual carnival in June, associated with the festivals of San Pedro, San Pablo and San Juan.

REMARKABLE ARCHITECTURE ✪
Allow at least two hours to visit the Brunet and Cantero palaces then, wearing comfortable shoes, wander at will through the cobbled streets in the surrounding area, letting them weave their magic. Renting a room for the night in a family home near the city center is a must: some of the *casas particulares* are old colonial houses.

not built until 1952. From 1959, this isolation was increased by the fact that the government suspected the town of being resistant to new ideas. From 1960 to 1965, the counterrevolution, which had its base in the Sierra del Escambray, only heightened the central government's distrust with regard to the town. Trinidad's historic core, bounded by a polygon of cobbled streets that all lead to Plaza Mayor, is the main reason why UNESCO named the city a World Heritage Site. The central square is best visited in the late afternoon when the warm colors glow beneath the setting sun, showing off the magnificent buildings to their best advantage. The attractive ornamentation of the Parque Central, divided into four small gardens, enhances its charm: white wrought-iron railings, late 19th-century flame ornaments, two bronze greyhounds standing guard at the entrance of the main walkway and a central statue representing Terpsichore, the Muse of Dancing.

PLAZA MAYOR ★

IGLESIA PARROQUIAL DE LA SANTÍSIMA TRINIDAD. A familiar shape towering above Plaza Mayor, Trinidad's present five-naved parish church was rebuilt between 1814 and 1892. Its restrained splendor is breathtaking. The marble altar is dedicated to the Virgin of Mercy, but the church's crowning glory is without doubt the CRISTO DE LA VERA CRUZ (1731). Even the most inveterate atheists in Trinidad know all about 'their' *Señor de la Vera Cruz*. The statue, bound for one of the churches of the True Cross in Mexico, was transported by boat from Barcelona but never progressed any further than Trinidad: on three occasions, the ship, buffeted by storms, took refuge in Trinidad's port, Casilda ▲ *188*. The superstitious captain eventually went on his way, leaving part of his cargo on the quay, including a large chest containing

the Christ statue. After his departure, the villagers took an inventory and found the sacred object. Interpreting its stay in Trinidad as a sign from God, they refused to part with it.

Casa de los Sánchez-Iznaga. The long pale blue façade along the left-hand side of the square when you stand with your back to the church belongs to the two houses of D. Saturnino Sánchez Iznaga, dated 1738 and 1785 respectively. The buildings house the Museo de Arquitectura Colonial, which illustrates techniques of colonial construction in rooms decorated with heavy wooden beams.

Casa de Aldemán Ortiz ★. This fine mansion opposite the parish church is recognizable by the long wooden balcony that runs along its two façades (*above*). It was built in 1809 on the very spot where Hernán Cortés camped when preparing for his expedition to Mexico ● *33*. The opulent house stands monument to a period of expansion in Trinidad since it was built with the fortune amassed by its owner, a former slave trader who also became mayor of the town. At that time, the local sugar barons did not have an adequate workforce and were forced to pay very handsomely for slaves from Africa.

An ART GALLERY on the second story exhibits a collection of modern paintings. On the third story there is a display of handicraft objects and sculptures. The gallery is a must, if only for the views from the balcony of Plaza Mayor in all its glory.

Casa Padrón. Walking back toward the Palacio Brunet ▲ *184*, you will pass a small 18th-century building with railings reminiscent of those in Parque Central. The German naturalist Alexander von Humboldt (*right*) stayed here in 1801. The building, remodeled in the 19th century, now houses the Museo de Arqueología Guamuhaya, which has collections associated with the Indo-Cuban civilization prior to Spanish settlement. Some stuffed animals show the type of food eaten by the early Cubans. Visitors will also be able to take a look at the delightful patio.

The ways of the cross
The Holy Week processions in Trinidad were famous, particularly Thursday's, dedicated to the Cristo de la Vera Cruz. Banned in 1959, they were revived in 1997, a year before the Pope's visit ● *46*. (A photo from 1904 shows a station on the way of the cross on the left, *top*.)

'We passed the evening very agreeably at the residence of Don Antonio Padron, one of the most wealthy inhabitants, where we met nearly all the principal residents of Trinidad.'
A. von Humboldt, *Island of Cuba*, 1855.

▲ The Palacio Brunet and the Museo Romántico

The Palacio Brunet is the most eloquent expression of Trinidad's golden age. Its ocher façade, the benign serenity of its patio and its inner galleries give no hint of the battle once waged between three great families, the Borrels, the Iznagas and the Becquers, to prove which was the most prosperous. Mariano Borrel was the clear winner, to judge from his palace, which was built between 1740 and 1808 and which still has exactly the same appearance as it did at the time of construction. Since 1974, it has housed the Museo Romántico, whose lavish decor reveals the passion of the Cuban aristocracy for goods made in Europe or the United States.

THE PATIO

In 1807, an additional story was added above the palace's remarkably high first story (almost 23 feet). The galleries around the patio, which house the rooms of the museum, only have arches on two sides: the other two sides have lean-to roofs, a clever architectural device that made it possible to have a larger patio. The wooden balustrade around the galleries creates an impression of unity.

THE KITCHEN

The kitchen still has its beautiful original tiles, which provided an extremely hygienic cooking environment.

THE DRAWING ROOM

The luxurious decor of this spacious room reflects its owners' wealth: Carrara marble floors, coffered cedar ceiling, neoclassical paintings and moldings, de Sèvres vases and chandeliers made of Bohemian crystal. The furniture, made of precious wood, was imported from Europe and copied by local cabinet makers. English spittoons bear witness to a ritual that became popular in the 19th century: cigar smoking.

THE DINING ROOM

The decorative wooden *medio punto* arches (*above* and *below*) ● *84* and the slatted shutters closing the arcades leading onto the patio filtered the light and ensured that the room was ventilated.

Austrian secretaire (18th century) decorated with mythological scenes on enamel, *above.*

RISE AND FALL

The marriage of Mariano Borrel's daughter to Count Nicolas de la Cruz y Brunet – who gave his name to the palace – marked the beginning of the end for the wealthy Borrel family. The count embarked on the costly construction of a theater, more interested in a certain actress than the building dedicated to her. The couple divorced and went their separate ways, to Madrid and Cádiz. The palace was abandoned and pillaged in the early 20th century; it took years to reassemble its treasures.

THE COUNTESS' BEDROOM

Niece of Mariano Borrel, Doña Antonio María Domínguez de Guevara Borrel, Countess of San Antonio, married General Francisco Serrano, Duke de la Torre. He became Captain-General of Cuba, then served as regent to the Spanish crown after Isabella II was deposed during the Rebellion of September 1868.

PROMENADE BY 'QUITRÍN'

The *calesero* (coachman), who enjoyed special status among the slaves, drove the *quitrín*, a horse-drawn carriage with two wheels used by the wealthy families of Trinidad (early 20th century, *above*). The one exhibited in the *zaguán* ● *84* (lobby) of the Palacio Cantero looks as if it were still ready to parade through the

It was on the worn *parvis* of Nuestra Señora de la Candelaria that the French painter Edouard Laplante executed one of his famous engravings, a print of which can be found in the Museo de Arquitectura Colonial ▲ *183*.

AROUND PLAZA MAYOR

From the Palacio Brunet ▲ *184*, head down Calle Simón Bolívar past Casa Padrón and Casa Aldemán Ortíz.

PALACIO CANTERO ★. This palace, along with the Palacio Brunet, is the most eloquent testament to Trinidad's architectural glory. Although it was rebuilt between 1810 and 1812 by J. M. Borrel y Padrón, one of the four leading members of the local sugar aristocracy (Cantero, Brunet, Borrel and Bécquer), it owes its name to J. G. Cantero, a powerful plantation owner from the Valle de los Ingenios ▲ *190*. Cantero bought the building in 1841 and transformed it into one of the most lavish neo-classical mansions of its period. The palace, restored in 1996, has been home to the MUSEO MUNICIPAL DE HISTORIA since 1980. Visits to the museum begin in a vast room with walls decorated in vibrant colors and a floor paved with Italian marble. The dining room leads onto an immense patio, surrounded by open arcades which were originally closed. The thirty slaves of the palace were housed on the other side of the patio at the rear of the building, near the wonderfully preserved kitchen. The museum charts the history of Trinidad by exploring several themes: the Cantero family, piracy, the slave trade, the large plantations in the Valle de los Ingenios and the wars for Cuban independence.

PALACIO IZNAGA. On the other side of Calle Bolívar, on the corner of Calles Muñoz and Izquierdo, stands the home of Pedro Iznaga y Borrel, cousin and rival of Don Borrel y Padrón and owner of five sugar refineries. The height of the ceiling on the first story, 23 feet, is exceptional for Cuba. The tower and its façade cinched by a simple wrought-iron

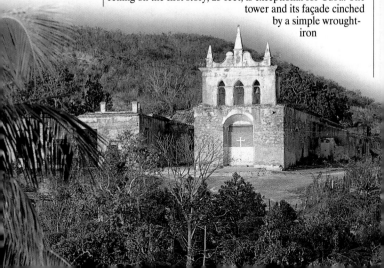

> '[…] and commands […] a magnificent view of the ocean, the two ports, Casilda and Guaurabo, a forest of palms, and the group of high hills of San Juan.'

Alexander von Humboldt, about La Popa

balcony lend the residence a stately air. In the early 1990s it was still inhabited by a descendent of the family, Leopoldina Iznaga. Once restored, it will accommodate one of the luxury hotels in the Rumbos chain. (On leaving the palace, walk back up Calle Izquierdo and turn right into Calle Piro Guinart.)

PLAZA DEL JIGÜE. This was where Father Bartolomé de Las Casas celebrated the first mass in Trinidad in 1514. The square is named after the acacia (*jigüe*) planted to honor the occasion. In the shade of its foliage, on Sunday mornings, birdsong contests are held. Players place bets on the birds and the winner of the stake is the one who backs the bird that sings the longest.

CONVENTO SAN FRANCISCO DE ASÍS. At the corner of Calles Piro Guinart and Echerri, the tall BELL TOWER ★ of the convent of Saint Francis of Assisi, completed in 1813, dominates the town. It contains a remarkable bell weighing 2645 pounds, made in 1853 by José Giroux, a French caster from the Jura and bought on a subscription basis. The former convent houses the MUSEO DE LA LUCHA CONTRA BANDIDOS, which retraces the fight against the *bandidos* (counterrevolutionary gangs) operating in the peaks of the Sierra del Escambray, starting in 1960. The patio, whose statues of saints have been replaced by armored vehicles and a tractor-drawn cannon, stands monument to the building's new calling. (Return to Plaza Mayor and walk back up Calle Bolívar.)

ERMITA DE NUESTRA SEÑORA DE LA CANDELARIA ★. This 18th-century hilltop hermitage bears the nickname of 'La Popa'. A narrow path links it to the Plaza Mayor. Not as highly frequented as the parish church and a little neglected due to its dilapidated appearance, its shrine still attracts the pious who relish its authenticity. It was once the scene of *romerías*, lively festivals which used to be part of Cuban religious life. As it falls within the historic center, it is included in UNESCO's restoration program. (Walk back down Calle Bolívar and turn left into Calle Mendoza.)

PLAZA DE SANTA ANA. Also scheduled to be restored under the UNESCO program is the church of Santa Ana, which dominates the square. The church was remodeled in 1800 and the tower and steeple were added in 1812. The imposing building on its right was once the ROYAL PRISON; built under the orders of the governor Don Pedro de la Pena, it was inaugurated in 1844. Now converted into a shopping mall which houses art stores and restaurants, the building still boasts its original structure and is one of Trinidad's most convivial places, despite its original calling.

TRINIDADIAN CRAFTSMANSHIP
The local craft market is held opposite the Casa de la Trova in Plaza Segarte. Here you can buy clothing, musical instruments, lace tablecloths and ornaments. The market also sells basketwork made of yarey, a local plant fiber, which is also used to make hats.

PALACIO CANTERO
This is a typical example of Trinidadian architecture (*top*). The reception rooms are delineated by arcades and not by solid walls, as was the case with houses in Havana.

TRINIDAD VIEWS ★
The tower of the Palacio Cantero, the hermitage of Nuestra Señora de la Candelaria ('La Popa') and the bell tower of the Convento San Francisco de Asís (*above*) afford the three most beautiful views over the tiled roofs of Trinidad.

187

HOUSE AT CALLE BOLIVAR, NO 518.
The drawing room in this house, known as the Casa del Domenicano (or 'the Crocodile House' because of the animal that adorns it), dates from the first half of the 18th century. It reveals the glittering lifestyle enjoyed by the grandparents of the current owner, Lidia Zerquera y Mauri. Antonio Mauri Seballs made his fortune with the La Nueva Era cigarette factory.

ARCHITECTURAL PROMENADE

The UNESCO restoration program also takes in several houses that still retain vestiges of their former glory. Some of them, occupied by descendants of the original owners, are open to the public. Most of the houses in the historic center were renovated at the end of the 19th century and their façades are identical. The wooden front door is carved into square panels or vertical lathes. It opens into the drawing room, furnished with the rocking chairs that provide Trinidadians with a place of refuge during the hottest hours of the day. On either side of the room, doors made of wood or decorated with frosted glass motifs lead into the bedrooms, of which there are usually four. On either side of the front door, halfway up the wall, are the house owner's 'lookout posts': two or three openings protected by wooden or wrought-iron grills and shut with wooden shutters on the inside.

CASA DE LA CALLE IZQUIERDO, NO 111. Owned by lawyer Manuel Meyer Cantero, a descendant of Justo Cantero ▲ *186*, this house still has its 19th-century furniture, lamps and paintings. (Visits available on request.)
CASA DE LA CALLE IZQUIERDO, NO 105. This house belongs to the Echemendia Font y Herr family, of Catalan and German origin. In the early 20th century, the lawyer José Antonio Font y Herr was the town's official photographer. The 19th-century furniture, lamps and other decorative objects are worth a look. (Visits available on request.)
CASA DE LA CALLE MÁRQUEZ, NO 48. This was where María Encarnación Ruiz de Porra y Suárez del Villar was born. This famous pianist was better known in Trinidad by her

nickname Néné. Her 18th-century house has many beautiful features, including an attractive inner garden. (Visits available on request.)

CASILDA AND THE PENÍNSULA DE ANCÓN
The port of Casilda, four miles south of Trinidad, was the economic hub of the region at a time when the sugarcane industry was flourishing. Now it provides a modest living for several fishermen. Sun-worshippers and scuba-divers should head south, where there are two lovely beaches: Playa María Aguilar and Playa Ancón.

CASA DE LA CALLE ECHERRI, NO 31. This is the home of Isabel Bécquer, better known as *La Profunda*. This descendant of one of the region's potentates is a musician, like many members of her family before her. Near the Casa de la Trova ▲ *187*, her house is imbued with the same unconventional spirit, which finds expression in a style of decoration combining bohemian touches with traditional Trinidadian architecture. (Visits available on request.)
CASA DE LA CALLE BOLÍVAR, NO 411. This 18th-century house is next to the Palacio Cantero and opposite the Palacio Iznaga ▲ *186*. Its renowned owner, Teresa Paulette Cajigas, nicknamed 'Tété', is one of Trinidad's most emblematic figures. The pious images decorating every room in her house attest to her unusual passion: representations of Christ. Almost one hundred years old, she proudly takes tourists on a voyage of discovery of Trinidad's religious heritage. (Visits available on request.)

Although Trinidad's renown is based on its palaces, its appeal has a great deal to do with its many low-roofed houses clustered together (*above*), their appearance typical of the 17th and 18th centuries. These houses are quite plain, with tiled roofs – their only form of

ornamentation are the grilles covering their windows. One characteristic feature is that, being raised by 16 to 20 inches above street level, they enabled their inhabitants to sit at their windows and watch the world go by. In the 18th century, doors and windows were protected by *barrotes* or turned wooden bars; these were replaced in the early 19th century by elegant wrought-iron grilles.

189

THE TORRE DE MANACA IZNAGA
Symbol of the Iznaga family's influence throughout the entire region, this eight-story tower (148 feet) raises as many questions as it has spawned legends. The most plausible relates to the rivalry between the two Iznaga brothers: it is said that Alejo built the tower in the first half of the 19th century as a response to an enormous well dug by his brother, Pedro. It is more likely that it was used to watch the slaves laboring in the sugar fields. The bell at the top was rung at intervals to regulate work on the plantation.

VALLE DE LOS INGENIOS ★

The 'Valley of the Sugar Mills', which comprises the three small valleys of Santa Rosa, San Luis and Meyer, extends over nineteen miles between Trinidad and Sancti Spíritus. It owes its name to the large number of *ingenios* (sugar mills) ● *50* built here in the 19th century during the sugar industry boom in Trinidad. Productivity was increased by the proximity of forests which supplied wood for the fuel used in processing the sugar. Named, like Trinidad, a World Heritage Site by UNESCO, this historical valley remains a potent symbol of slavery in Cuba: over 11,000 Africans from many different ethnic groups once worked here.

VISITING THE VALLEY. A TOY STEAM TRAIN ★ runs morning and evening from Trinidad to the main ruins in the valley, providing an opportunity to admire the glorious scenery. Some fifteen haciendas attest to the immense wealth of the farming families: that of MANACA IZNAGA (converted into a bar-restaurant) and JESÚS DE NAZARENO DE BUENAVISTA (an estate owned by the Cantero family ▲ *186*), with its Italianate architecture, as well as the *casonas* (tropical mansions) of DELICIAS, GENIA DE SOTO, SABANILLA and GUACHINANGO. The CASA DEL INGENIO GUÁIMARO (currently being restored) contains a 19th-century mural decoration by the Italian painter Daniel D. Laglio. Beside these stately mansions stand the *barracónes* ● *88* which housed slaves.

SANCTI SPÍRITUS

The fourth largest of the seven original colonies ● *32*, Sancti Spíritus was founded by Diego Velázquez in 1514 on the banks of the Río Tuinucú, then moved in 1522 to its current site on the Río Yayabo. Like Trinidad, forty-three miles away, it rapidly prospered on sugar and the slave trade and was twice sacked by pirates. Although its architecture is less imposing and less well preserved than that of its famous neighbor, the provincial capital still radiates a certain colonial charm (one of the city's streets, *below*).

PARQUE SERAFÍN SÁNCHEZ. This immense square was named after the local hero of the independence movement, who died in battle in 1896. It is lined with attractive neoclassical buildings including the magnificent Hotel Perla (closed). In the evenings, the inhabitants congregate here and, sitting on the benches, chat into the small hours of the morning. The other hotel on the square, the Plaza, is an excellent observation post for anyone

wanting to watch the world go by in the lively heart of the city. (Walk down Calle Máximo Gómez toward the Río Yayabo.)

IGLESIA PARROQUIAL MAYOR DEL ESPÍRITU SANTO ★. Towering over the Parque Honorato, this church (*right*) with its 400-year-old foundations (1522) was originally made of wood. Destroyed by pirates, it was rebuilt in 1680. Its 98-foot-high spire was added in the 18th century and its dome in the 19th century. Inside, the wooden ceiling of the nave and choir is well worth a look.

PALACIO DE VALLE IZNAGA. At the corner of Calles Gómez and Plácido stands the most prestigious house in the city. The Valle Iznagas, a wealthy family who made its fortune in sugar, built this three-story house in the 18th century. It provides a particularly felicitous setting for the MUSEO DE ARTE COLONIAL ★, which shows the sophisticated lifestyle of the aristocracy of the time: sumptuous colonial furniture, porcelain, paintings and stained-glass windows dating from the 18th and 19th centuries.

SANTA CLARA

The city was founded inland on July 15, 1689 by the inhabitants of San Juan de los Remedios who wanted to avoid attack by pirates. It has less of a colonial heritage than Trinidad or Camagüey, but the proximity of one of the largest universities in the country, the Universidad Central de la Villa (five miles to the east), makes it a warm and lively city. Santa Clara holds an important place in the collective memory of the Cuban people because it was here that the last great battle of the revolutionary guerrilla war, led by Ernesto 'Che' Guevara, was fought ▲ *192*.

PARQUE LEONCIO VIDAL. Until 1894, strict racial segregation was imposed on this pleasant tree-lined square: a fence separated the sidewalks assigned to blacks from those reserved for whites. Only the latter could enter the central area and listen to concerts performed on its bandstand.

TEATRO DE LA CARIDAD ★. This theater (1885–6), which stands on the northwest corner of the park, is aptly named (Theater of Charity) as it was built 'for the poor of Santa Clara' at the instigation of Martha Abreu de Estévez. This noblewoman improved the life of women working in the laundries and founded Santa's Clara first free clinic and first state school. The beautiful fresco adorning the theater's dome is the work of Spanish artist Camilio Zalaya.

MUSEO DE ARTES DECORATIVAS. The museum beside the Teatro de la Caridad is housed in the finest colonial building in Santa Clara: a palace erected in the 18th century by an illustrious local family. The collections – furniture, paintings, porcelain and other decorative objects – are displayed by period, from the 18th century to the 20th century, in rooms that give onto the patio.

THE HISTORIC CENTER OF SANCTI SPÍRITUS ★ Now restored, the cobbled streets between Calle Panchito Jiménez and the Río Yayabo invite visitors to take a stroll: in the former colonial quarter the small, low-roofed houses painted in pastel colors and adorned by fine wrought-iron balconies have been given a new lease of life. Nearby, the Puente Yayabo (*above*), built by the Spanish in the early 19th century, is the only vaulted bridge made of brick in the country.

SANCTI SPÍRITUS, GATEWAY TO CENTRAL CUBA Before the highway was built, Sancti Spíritus truly deserved the key that figures on its arms and symbolizes its position at the center of the island: people traveling across Cuba from east to west had to go via the Carretera Central and were obliged to pass through the city.

191

Ernesto Guevara (1928–67) is buried in Santa Clara. The legend of 'Che', a nickname given by his *compañeros* because of his frequent use of this typically Argentine interjection, actually originated in this city. On August 31, 1958, Guevara left the Sierra Maestra for Havana at the head of the 144 men in Column 8. They had to march for forty-seven days, brave two hurricanes, hunger and Batista's troops to rally Las Villas province. On October 15, Guevara linked up with the second front at Escambray, effectively cutting the island in two. In mid-December, he launched a lightning attack and liberated towns and villages in Central Cuba. Defended by 3000 soldiers, Santa Clara was the last obstacle blocking the route to the capital. The battle that raged here from December 28 to 31, 1958, assured the *Barbudos'* victory.

ERNESTO 'CHE' GUEVARA (1928–67) Ernesto Guevara was born in Rosario in Argentina, to a middle-class family with enlightened ideas. A student of medicine, he explored Latin America by motorbike and this voyage of discovery through the subcontinent sharpened his political vision. In 1955, in Mexico, he met Fidel Castro, leader of the 26th of July Movement. In November 1956, they both boarded the yacht *Granma* ● 44 with the aim of

CHE WITH A BROKEN ARM
An enormous statue by José Delarra stands in the Plaza de la Revolución. It was erected in 1987 for the 20th anniversary of Che's death. The bronze work was financed by the people of Villa Clara Province. The *comandante* is represented with his arm in a sling, because it had been broken during the Battle of Santa Clara. His motto is inscribed on the gigantic concrete pedestal: *Hasta la victoria, siempre* ('Ever onward to victory'). An illustration of his battles and the text of his last letter to Castro are carved on a bas-relief (*below*). A guerrilla mausoleum has been built beneath his statue.

MONUMENT IN HOMAGE TO THE ATTACK ON THE ARMORED TRAIN
On December 29, Guevara and eighteen guerrillas attacked the armored train dispatched by Batista to stop the advance of the revolutionary columns. The train was derailed and nearly four hundred soldiers surrendered; the clash lasted around one-and-a-half hours. Only four carriages of the convoy remain, exhibited near the railroad west of Parque Vidal. One has been converted into a museum.

THE RETURN OF CHE
In 1997, thirty years after his death ● 45, Guevara's mortal remains were collected from Bolivia. Brought back to Cuba in a climate of popular excitement, they were exhibited on July 12 in Havana. They were laid to rest in the marble mausoleum, where a perpetual flame burns near the mortal remains of his companions in arms.

starting a revolution in Cuba. After their victory, Che held govermental positions including Head of the National Bank (1959) and Minister of Industry (1961).

IN THE FOOTSTEPS OF CHE ✪
Spend an afternoon visiting the memorials dedicated to Che: they are all situated in the Plaza de la Revolución, just one mile west of Parque Vidal, the central square. The monument in homage to the attack on the armored train, which is not quite as moving, is on the other side of the city.

THE LETTER TO FIDEL

On April 1, 1965, just before he departed for Bolivia, Che Guevara wrote to Fidel Castro: 'Other nations are calling for the aid of my modest efforts [...] The time has come for our separation. I want it to be known that I do this with a mixture of joy and sorrow [...] I formally renounce my duties in the national leadership of the party, my post as minister, my rank of major, and my Cuban citizenship [...] In new fields of battle, I will bear the faith you instilled in me.'

ALEJANDRO GARCÍA CATURLA (1906–40) This composer is famous for being the first to introduce African rhythms to classical music ● 52. The museum devoted to him in Remedios was set up in his grandparents' house, where he lived. He shocked the local bourgeoisie by marrying a black woman and frequenting the homes of the poor of the city. He was murdered at the age of thirty-four for refusing bribes from a local politician.

REMEDIOS

Founded in 1514, San Juan de los Remedios remained the main colony in the region until the foundation of Santa Clara ▲ *191, 192* in 1689, whose location was designed to avoid raids by pirates. Overshadowed by Santa Clara, Remedios has not changed much in the 20th century. Its peace is only broken each year by the Parrandas Remedianas, which are to this city what the carnival is to Santiago. The most interesting sights are concentrated around Parque José Martí.

IGLESIA DE SAN JUAN BAUTISTA ★. This imposing building was rebuilt in 1692. Its interior is breathtaking. The mahogany coffered ceiling, decorated with stylized flowers, was discovered during the restoration program (c. 1940) carried out by architect Aquiles Maza and sculptor Rogelio Atá. The carved cedar altar is lavishly adorned with 24-carat gold leaf.

MUSEO DE LAS PARRANDAS REMEDIANAS. Near Parque Martí, the museum retraces the history of the musical event which takes place on the Saturday before Christmas. Its origins date back to 1835: the Franciscans sent children out into the streets to summon the parishioners to midnight mass by banging on cans. This practice has been transformed into a musical battle between musicians from the Carmen and San Salvador neighborhoods: the winner is the one who has the finest float and makes the most noise with an array of firecrackers and fireworks.

FROM MORÓN TO CAYO GUILLERMO

GREATER FLAMINGOS ■ 27 Punta del Perro on the north coast of Cayo Coco is home to the largest colony of greater flamingos (*right*) in Cuba (more than 2000). The birds only migrate in the month of April, the start of the wet season, to breed. During the dry season (November to March), they live on the south coast of the island, mainly in the salt marshes of the Zapata Peninsula ▲ *174*.

MORÓN. An unremarkable stopping place along the 'road of the Cayos', Morón lies twenty-five miles from Ciego de Ávila. In 1896, during the war for independence ● 39, the *mambises* crossed the Morón-Júcaro line of defense erected by the Spanish to divide the island and block the advance of the rebels.

LAGUNA DE LA LECHE ★. A road and a canal link Morón to the largest expanse of salt water (*left*) on the island (twenty-six square miles), two miles to the north. This lake, teeming with fish and water birds, owes its milky color to the storms which stir up the chalky deposits on its bed.

CAYO COCO ★. Separated from the mainland of Cuba by the Bahía de Perros, Cayo Coco (143 square miles) is a paradise for divers and bird-watchers and central to Cuba's ecotourism program. Over three-quarters of this Cay ■ 28 has been designated a nature reserve. Stretching for fourteen miles, nine beautiful beaches protected by a coral reef edge the north coast, which is a major tourist center.

CAYO GUILLERMO. This small island to the west of Cayo Coco can also be reached by road. Its beach (*top*) and its fish-filled waters have secured its fame. Hemingway ▲ *148* came here to fish: 'See that big coral head to starboard that's just awash? [...] On the inside gentlemen is Guillermo. See how green she is and full of promise?' (*Islands in the Stream*).

CAYO COCO ✪
One of the most beautiful islets in Cuba, Cayo Coco has 14 miles of beaches and great fishing. The Pedraplein, a 16-mile road that links Cayo Coco, Cayo Guillermo and the Cuban coast, offers some spectacular views.

CITY OF CHURCHES
Seen from the roof of the hospital of San Juan de Dios ▲ *196*, Camagüey looks like a 'city of churches', a result of the great wealth accrued by

CAMAGÜEY

The province of Camagüey, the largest in the country, extends across the central plains of the island. Its economy has revolved around cattle breeding since the 18th century. Steeped in history, Camagüey is Cuba's third largest city with 300,000 inhabitants. It was also the birthplace, in 1902, in Calle Príncipe, of Nicolás Guillén ▲ *103*.

A LABYRINTHINE TOWN. Founded in 1514 by Diego Velázquez ● *32*, Santa María del Puerto Príncipe was moved further up the Río Caonao in 1516, then again to its current site in 1528, when the colony was renamed Camagüey. The irregularity of its street layout, with its many cul-de-sacs and winding lanes, sets it apart from other colonial towns on the island. The aim of this plan was to prevent raids by pirates, but the city was sacked in 1668 by Henry Morgan ● *33* and in 1679 by the French pirate François Granmont. At the end of the 18th century a thriving trade in smuggled goods made it the second largest city in Cuba.

UNDEFEATED BY TRADITION. In the 19th century, many *Camagüeyanos* took part in the wars for independence, the most famous being Ignacio Agramonte (1841–73), general-in-chief of the rebel troops.

notable families in the livestock sector: these include the cathedral of Nuestra Señora de la Candelaria, dating from the second half of the 19th century, overlooking Parque Agramonte; and the churches of Nuestra Señora de la Merced and de la Soledad, both built in the mid-18th century, although the former was rebuilt in the 19th century. (Iglesia de la Caridad, *above*.)

The restaurant
*La Campana
de Toledo*, Plaza
San Juan de Dios,
top.

**THE CITY OF
'TINAJÓNES'** ✪
Potters during the
colonial period
developed giant clay
jars, called *tinajónes*,
to solve the region's
problem of chronic
drinking water
shortages. Modeled
on the large oil and
wine jars imported
from Spain, these
receptacles
measuring almost
five feet tall and ten
feet in diameter were
partly buried in the
ground to ensure the
water remained cool.
You can still find
tinajónes in the patio
of the *La Campana
de Toledo* restaurant,
in the Casa Natal de
Ignacio Agramonte,
and in the cloister at
the Hospital de San
Juan de Dios.

PARQUE IGNACIO AGRAMONTE. During the wars for
independence, the former Plaza de Armas in Camagüey was
the scene of many executions. A huge EQUESTRIAN STATUE OF
IGNACIO AGRAMONTE stands at the center of the square, and
the nearby palms were planted in honor of the men who fell
in battle under his command.

CASA NATAL DE IGNACIO AGRAMONTE ★. At the corner of
Calles Cisneros and Agramonte, the house where the local
patriot was born has become one of the most impressive
museums in Cuba. Confiscated when the revolutionary fighter
took up arms and neglected for many long years, it was
restored in the second half of the 20th century. The museum's
varied collection of objects charts Agramonte's short but
eventful life: this aristocrat, leader of the local rebel forces
against the Spanish, attacked Camagüey in 1869 and died in
battle in 1873. The museum's main attraction, however, is its
setting, a beautiful 18th-century house with period furniture
and decoration.

PLAZA SAN JUAN DE DIOS. This square south of Parque
Agramonte is undoubtedly the finest colonial monument in
the city and the only one that has been fully restored. Most of
the buildings on the square are typical 18th-century structures
with their brightly painted façades (*above*), single-story
construction and restrained style of ornamentation.
Two of the houses have now been combined and converted
into a popular restaurant.

**HOSPITAL DE SAN JUAN DE
DIOS**. This architectural
complex occupies an entire
corner of Plaza San Juan de
Dios, but only the former
hospital and its CLOISTER,
dating from 1728 ★ (*right*) can
be visited. Until 1972, it
functioned as a children's
hospice, then a nursing
college, before providing a
home, in 1991, for the CENTRO
PROVINCIAL DE PATRIMONIO,
in charge of restoring the city's
monuments. A hotel is being
built in the second cloister,
dating from the 19th century.

Oriente

François Missen

▲ ORIENTE

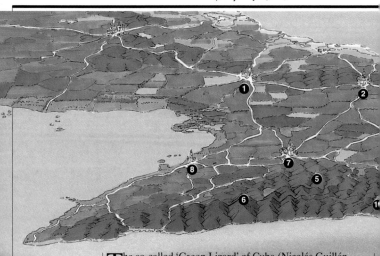

1. LAS TUNAS
2. HOLGUÍN
3. GUARDALAVACA
4. BANES
5. SIERRA MAESTRA

The so-called 'Green Lizard' of Cuba (Nicolás Guillén ● *103*) has a very wide head: Cabo Cruz in the south is 186 miles away from Guardalavaca in the north. The eastern part of the island also marks the greatest distance between the two seas in which this tropical lizard seems to sprawl. The border separating Oriente (the eastern part of the island) from the rest of Cuba is further west. This quarter of the island is divided into five provinces: Las Tunas, Holguín, Granma, Guantánamo and Santiago. Las Tunas is memorable only for its abundant sugar harvests (*zafra*) ● *49*, and Holguín for its flourishing tourist industry. The Cubans prefer the

WALTER BETANCOURT
In 1959, this young architect from New York (1932–78) declined an offer from Frank Lloyd Wright to join his architectural practice, and instead moved to Cuba in support of the Revolution. 'Because it evolved in the eastern provinces, far from the center of power [...], [he] found margins of space for his designs' (G. Seguí). Betancourt designed fifteen buildings in Oriente ▲ *201*.

latter three eastern provinces. Their mountainous topography has played a key role in Cuban history, helping in the battle for independence: the Sierra Maestra ● *44*, ▲ *202*, in southeastern Oriente, has harbored five centuries of rebellion, epic achievement, cruelty and passion. From Pico Turquino, the highest mountain in the range, to the coastal road linking Marea del Portillo to Santiago de Cuba, the dense vegetation has lent itself to all types of covert activity.

AT THE HISTORICAL HEART OF CUBA

The Sierra Maestra, at the gates of Santiago, and the north coast of Oriente have earned their place in the history books. Two vital dates and places hold the key to understanding this land: in 1492, Christopher Columbus landed in Cuba for the first time in the Bay of Bariay ● *32*, ▲ *201*; in 1953, Fidel Castro attacked the Moncada Barracks ● *44*, ▲ *215* in the town of Santiago de Cuba. Between these two dates, many

6. PICO TURQUINO
7. BAYAMO
8. MANZANILLO
9. SANTIAGO DE CUBA
10. EL COBRE
11. PARQUE BACONAO
12. GUANTÁNAMO
13. LA FAROLA
14. BARACOA
15. BOCA DE YUMURÍ
16. PLAYA MAGUANA
17. MOA

⊇ c. 300 miles

One of Oriente's great historical heroes: Carlos Manuel de Céspedes ● *39, below*. In 1868, he triggered the first war for independence.

LA DEMAJ
UN LUGAR
para encon
con la HIS

THE HUNT FOR 'CIMARRONES' ● 37
In February 1815, in response to frequent desertions by slaves fleeing the coffee plantations, 'orders were given to destroy the enclosures on the estates of Toa and Mayarí, because the *cimarrones* had begun to invade other areas. They treat the owners roughly […] then loot the haciendas. Arrest them, hang them.'

formative events took place: the genocide of the Indians, the forced immigration of African slaves to work on the plantations, the immigration of French settlers following the rebellion in Haiti ● *38* and the two wars for independence ● *39*. The first, the so-called Ten Years' War, ended in a peace treaty with Spain because the resistance fighters were unable to come to an agreement about the country's future. However, these ten years did at least serve to bring two great leaders of Oriente, generals Antonio Maceo and Máximo Gómez ● *39,* a Dominican, to the fore, not to mention the *mambises* ● *39*, an entire army of people ready to join the resistance. Victory came with the second war, which secured the fame of poet and orator José Martí ● *40*, who emigrated to the United States. In contact with the leaders and instigators of the first war, Martí began the second war for independence; a large-scale, instantaneous rebellion took place in 1895. After two years of harassment, the *mambises* decimated the Spanish army. On the pretext of mediating between Spain and the rebels, the United States intervened in Cuba and declared war on the Spanish Crown. The Spanish fleet was imprisoned in the Bay of Santiago de Cuba. Spain was crushed and, four months later, on December 10, 1898 the Treaty of Paris ● *39* agreed to the US occupation of the island. Cuba's independence was officially proclaimed in 1902.

199

HOLGUÍN

CALIXTO GARCÍA
(1832–98)
The general reigns supreme in Holguín, sitting on horseback in the middle of the square that bears his name. This statue is a well-earned tribute to a man who snatched his native town from the hands of the Spanish in 1872 and returned here in 1898 at the end of the war for independence after playing a vital role in the battle of Santiago de Cuba ▲ 207. The house where he was born, to the east of the Parque Calixto García, can be visited.

The *zafra* (sugar harvest) ● *49* assumes particular importance in the province of Holguín. This region, which plays a decisive role in the national economy, is the most important area for the Cuban sugar industry. And it is no coincidence that Holguín is the only city in the country to support a heavy industry: it is the only place on the island where sugarcane cutting machines are made, impressive, practical models worthy of the former Soviet Union. In the eastern part of Holguín, the province's industrial calling is still apparent: the nickel mines of Moa and Nicaro account for fifteen percent of the state's income. Nicknamed the 'City of Squares', Holguín has paid homage to its local hero by naming its central square Parque Calixto García.

PARQUE CALIXTO GARCÍA. Before the Revolution, it was good form for men to walk on one side of the park and women on the other. As an elderly shoe-shiner waiting for customers by his seat remarked roguishly: 'The rebellion was hard ... but it certainly changed things.'

MUSEO DE HISTORIA PROVINCIAL. Before becoming a chronicle of the city's past, this building, built in 1860, was a casino. The wealthy gentry came here to play for high stakes and to dance the night away. Converted into military barracks, it was besieged in 1868 by the first patriots who answered the call of Carlos Manuel de Céspedes ● *39*. Before the arrival of reinforcements sent to liberate the city from the rebels, the Spanish soldiers were imprisoned for several days under the mocking eye of the *Holguineros*. Their multicolored uniforms gave rise to the building's nickname: the Periquera (the 'Parrot Cage'). The museum's main attraction, a stone axe from the Pre-Columbian period, has become the city's symbol.

THE 'MACHETEROS'
The tireless cane cutters derive their name from their principal tool, the *machete* ● *48*. Since the sugar harvest has been mechanized, they stand braced against the base of the stalks and finish off the work done by the machines which, like steel giraffes, collect the bundles stacked at the edge of the fields.

CASA DE LA TROVA ★. Performances of *música campesina* (country music) by all the great artists of this genre can be heard in the attractive patio of this building in Calle Maceo overlooking Parque Calixto García. El Guayabero (born in 1911), sometimes performs here when he returns to his native town after one of his many trips.

PARQUE DE LAS FLORES. This city square, two blocks to the south of Parque Calixto García, is dominated by the impressive CATEDRAL DE SAN ISIDORO (1720), dedicated to the town's patron saint.

His festival is held on April 4, when believers lay palm leaves at the foot of the altar.

PLAZA DE LA REVOLUCIÓN. This square, the arena for large popular rallies, two miles to the east of the historic center, was built in honor of Holguín's generals of the independence movement. Calixto García was laid to rest here in a mausoleum built in 1980.

AROUND HOLGUÍN. Architecture buffs should take a trip to Velasco, around fifteen miles northeast of Holguín, to see its magnificent and unusual CULTURAL CENTER ★. This building, begun in 1964 by Walter Betancourt, an American architect of Cuban origin, was completed by Gilberto Seguí in 1991.

A family from Holguín in 1888.

FROM GUARDALAVACA TO BANES

GUARDALAVACA. Some thirty-four miles from Holguín, this seaside resort was created in the mid 1980s and is now one of Cuba's two major tourist sites, along with Varadero ▲ *168*. In its early days, it was very popular with Soviet officials. Now exclusively used by foreigners, it stretches for thirty-one miles along a turquoise coast that boasts the lovely beaches of Don Lino and Estero Ciego in the west.

CHORRO DE MAITA. Some four miles east of the resort, on top of a small hill, is the largest aboriginal necropolis discovered in Cuba, Chorro de Maita, 525 feet above the Atlantic Ocean. Among the hundred skeletons exhumed in 1930, archeologists have found the presumed remains of a European who was buried naked, unlike the early Cubans who were interred with clothes and jewelry.

BANES ★. This small well-preserved town, twenty miles from Guardalavaca, owes its fame to its MUSEO INDOCUBANO BANI, which holds the largest collection of objects (tools, ceramics, jewelry) belonging to the island's first civilization ● *34*. Famous in Cuba, the 'TAÍNO IDOL' is a solid gold 13th-century statuette discovered in the area. The presence – the oldest in the island – of a North American population in Banes accounts for the large number of American classic cars which have more or less escaped the ravages of time, including Chryslers, Cadillacs, Chevrolets and Studebakers.

'HE HAD NEVER SEEN SUCH A BEAUTIFUL LAND'
Christopher Columbus is supposed to have landed in the Bay of Bariay, some fifteen miles west of Guardalavaca, on October 28, 1492. 'The Admiral said that he had never seen such a beautiful land. Close by a stream were a great many fine green trees, different from ours, and each had the flowers and fruits of their species. Many birds, large and small, sang very sweetly. There were many different types of palms to ours.' A strange collection of sculptures and porticos have been erected to commemorate the arrival of Columbus.

The Sierra Maestra, 155 miles long and 19 miles wide, straddles the provinces of Granma and Santiago de Cuba and is the largest mountain range on the island. Often shrouded in mist, Pico Turquino (6470 feet), the highest point in the country, was witness to the revolutionary war led by Fidel Castro and his men, who took refuge here between December 1956 and August 1958. Access is now strictly controlled from the Hotel *Villa Santo Domingo*, the point of departure for many walks. Remarkably well-appointed paths (ladders, ramps, rock-hewn stairs) make it easier to explore this mountainous range, which boasts some spectacular scenery.

'All the rifles, all the bullets, all the resources for the sierra!'

Fidel Castro

HIKING FROM THE BELVEDERE D'ALTO DEL NARANJO

VISITING THE COMANDANCIA DE LA PLATA IN THE WEST
It takes an hour to get to the base of the former *Barbudos'* command post (*below*) ● *44*, two miles from Alto del Naranjo. Fidel Castro's headquarters, now converted into a museum, has a hospital and the Radio Rebelde transmitter.

CLIMBING PICO TURQUINO IN THE EAST
Pico Turquino is eight miles from Alto del Naranjo. This arduous trek along two ridgetops running east-west and north-south takes two days with a night in a mountain shelter at an altitude of 5000 feet. The main stages are as follows:
1. La Platica: first village.
2. Palma Mocha.
3. Loma del León: fine panoramic view of Pico Turquino and Pico Cuba (6142 feet) further west, as well as the Caribbean sea.
4. Aguada del Joaquín mountain shelter.
5. Pico Joaquín.
6. Paso de los Monos.
7. Pico Turquino.
The descent via Las Cuevas, on the coast, is difficult.

IN THE PARQUE NACIONAL DE LA SIERRA MAESTRA
The Sierra Maestra is covered with dense tropical rainforest ■ *20*, remarkable for the indigenous orchids growing there. There is also a wide variety of bird life: *tocororo* (Cuban trogon ■ *20*), *zunzuncito* (bee hummingbird ▲ *175*), various *carpinteros* (woodpeckers) and *palomas* (pigeons).

BAYAMO

'LA BAYAMESA'
The music and words of the Cuban national anthem are the work of Pedro Figueredo (1819–70). Manuel Muñoz Cedeño conducted the orchestra on June 11, 1868 for the Corpus Christi celebrations:

To the battle, run, Bayameses,/
Let your country proudly observe you./

A small city sandwiched between sugar fields on the south coast and the Sierra Maestra ▲ *202* in the east, Bayamo is an important destination for anyone wanting to relive the great events in Cuban history. Writing about Bayamo, the second town founded by Diego Velázquez in 1513, historian Rafael Rodríguez Ramos commented: 'The settlers would never have guessed that this city being built by the Spanish was to become the nerve center of a province legendary for its role in the birth of Cuban identity and even less that the immense house built by the first head of the Céspedes family, who came to the island in the first half of the 17th century, was to become the house of the Father of the Nation.' Bayamo was in fact the birthplace of Carlos Manuel de Céspedes ● *39*: ten days after proclaiming independence on his estate, *La Demajagua*, he seized the town on October 20, 1868. The first Assembly of the Republic in arms was constituted, and the Cuban national anthem, *La Bayamesa*, was sung. On January 12, 1869, however, Bayamo's independence fighters preferred to burn their city down rather than see it fall to the Spanish.
PLAZA DE LA REVOLUCIÓN. In this square, at the heart of the city, two figures dear to the residents of Bayamo stand face to face: Carlos Manuel de Céspedes, looking solemn in his

bronze uniform, and Pedro Figueredo, author of the national anthem. The words of *La Bayamesa* are engraved beneath his bust. Out of respect for the former settlers, the authorities do not sing the last two verses of the anthem at official ceremonies. On

Fear not a glorious death,/
To die for your country is to live./

Fear not the ferocious Iberians,/
They are cowards, like all tyrants,/
They cannot withstand the brave Cubans./
Their empire is dead and gone forever./

Cuba is free, Spain is dead,/
Where now are their power and pride?/
Listen to the bugle calling you./
To arms, brave ones, run!'

the façade of the AYUNTAMIENTO (city hall), a plaque commemorates the first declaration of the abolition of slavery in 1868, although this was not made official until 1886. In the city center, the former chapel houses the TEATRO JOSÉ JOAQUIN PALMA, the work of Betancourt.
CASA NATAL DE CARLOS MANUEL DE CÉSPEDES. On the north side of the Plaza de la Revolución stands the house where the 'Father of the Nation' was born. This fine building, which survived the fire of 1869, has been converted into a museum and holds a collection of documents retracing the fight of the man who was not only a planter, an ideologist and an orator but also a journalist on at least one occasion: he published the *Cubano Libre*, the first newspaper of the independence movement. The printing press he used is on display here.
PLAZA DEL HIMNO NACIONAL. This square, the first to be built in Bayamo and the most important, was originally named Plaza de la Iglesia Mayor after the church of IGLESIA MAYOR DE SAN SALVADOR (1613). Rebuilt in 1740, it was almost entirely destroyed by the fire of 1869, except for the CAPILLA DE LA DOLOROSA (*above*) ★, to the left of the altar. Its rich

ornamentation serves as a setting for one of the finest baroque retables in the country. On November 8, 1868, a group of Bayamese sang the national anthem for the first time on the square of the church after a priest blessed the flag raised by Carlos Manuel de Céspedes.

MANZANILLO

The scenery opens out towards Manzanillo (*below*) and a pleasant breeze blows in from the Caribbean sea. However, the road passes through YARA, twenty-three miles from Bayamo, which recalls the island's first great tragedy: this was where the Indian chief Hatuey was burned at the stake by the Spanish conquistadors ● 32, ▲ 221.

ONE OF THE BIRTHPLACES OF 'SON' ● 55. This phrase still applies; various famous groups have made the city's name, including the Original de Manzanillo, one of the first to be signed abroad. Manzanillo is also the birthplace of troubadour Carlos Puebla, the author-performer of the popular *Hasta Siempre*, an homage to Ernesto 'Che' Guevara ● 44, ▲ 192. Before leaving Manzanillo, visit the local Pinilla rum factory and enjoy a taste of one of the best rums on the island.

MUSEO HISTÓRICO LA DEMAJAGUA. Along the seven-mile road linking Manzanillo with the sacred site of *La Demajagua*, a poster entitled 'Encounter with History' depicts a noble-looking Carlos Manuel de Céspedes, posing for eternity. It was here, on this estate which is now a museum, on October 10, 1868, that he rang the bell of his *finca* – which can still be seen – not to summon his slaves to work but to free them. Another of the plantation's interesting relics is a notched mill wheel from the former sugar mill.

THE ORGANS OF MANZANILLO

Lino Borbolla is an organ maker, a long tradition that runs in the Borbolla family. Lino's uncle, Francisco, and Santiago Fornaris acquired organs first brought into the Cienfuegos region by the French fleeing Haiti ● 38. Francisco sent his son to France to learn how to make them, then built the first organ factory in Manzanillo. For many years Manzanillo was, with Holguín, the only town able to meet demand in Latin America. Three instruments, including a prestigious Pollereau, made in Nancy, France, are still in working order and provide music for the region's popular dances.

The flag of the 26th of July Movement ● *44, below*. José Martí, Máximo Gómez and Antonio Maceo; Fidel Castro in liberated Santiago; the achievements of the Revolution, *right, from left to right*.

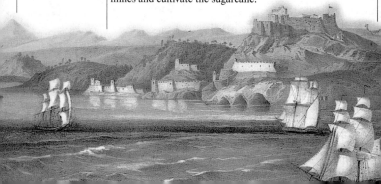

26 - JULIO

SHELTERED FROM PIRATES AND CORSAIRS
During the 16th century, the port of Santiago de Cuba played an important role in the trade between Spain and its colonies. As a result, it was continually under attack from corsairs and pirates and in 1554, Jacques de Sores ● *33* looted the city. The Spanish crown, fearing an equally unsettled future, fortified Santiago in 1639: the bay was now watched by the Castillo de San Pedro de la Roca, known as El Morro ▲ *217*. However, this did not stop the English corsair Henry Morgan ● *33*, from destroying and setting fire to the city in 1662. El Morro in the 18th century (*below*).

The high temperatures and sweltering heat of the town nestling between the Sierra Maestra ▲ *202* and an immense bay come as something of a surprise. Santiago, the second largest city in Cuba with 420,000 inhabitants, spins out its inextricable tangle of lanes, neighborhoods and housing estates from Parque Céspedes, the heart of the city.

Santiago belongs to a more distant continent than the one in the Caribbean: Africa is its foster mother. In his *Negro Chant in Cuba*, Federico García Lorca said: 'Oh Cuba! Oh rhythm of dry seeds!/I'll go to Santiago./Oh warm waist, and a drop of wood!/I'll go to Santiago./Harp of living trees. Crocodile. Tobacco blossom!/I'll go to Santiago./I always said I would go to Santiago/in a carriage of black water./I'll go to Santiago./Wind and alcohol in the wheels,/I'll go to Santiago./My coral in the darkness,/I'll go to Santiago./The ocean drowned in the sand,/I'll go to Santiago./White heat and dead fruit,/I'll go to Santiago.'

HISTORY

FOUNDATION AND COLONIZATION. Santiago de Cuba was founded in 1514 by Diego Velázquez ● *32* on the other side of the bay and was not moved to its present site until 1522. Many old buildings have disappeared, destroyed by successive earthquakes. Figures who played a key role in the Spanish colonization came to prominence in this city: Pánfilo de Narváez, Vasco Porcallo de Figueroa, Bernal Díaz del Castillo and Hernán Cortés ● *33*, ▲ *180*, who was the city's first mayor. In 1515, Santiago was declared capital of Isla Ferdinanda, Cuba's first name, before the title was given to Havana in 1553 ● *33*. Following in the footsteps of Cortés, other expeditions left Santiago to discover new lands in the Americas. Because the indigenous Cubans had been eliminated, forced immigration from Haiti and Africa was the only way of obtaining manpower to work the gold and copper mines and cultivate the sugarcane.

FRENCH IMMIGRATION. In 1791, a vast number of French settlers, fleeing the slave revolt in Haiti, arrived in Cuba and made their homes around Santiago. Many of them were accompanied by the slaves who had remained loyal to them. This settlement, the last in Cuba, was to change the future of Oriente, until then exclusively Spanish. Having made their fortune – coffee farming imported from Haiti was a great success – the immigrants moved to an area of Santiago which acquired the nickname of 'Little France': it is now called Tívoli.

'REBELLIOUS THEN, HOSPITABLE NOW, HEROIC ALWAYS.'
The first part of Santiago's motto relates to events that took place in the second half of the 19th century. At this time, French revolutionary ideas spread through the coffee and sugar plantations, inciting the slaves to rebellion. The *cimarrones* ● *37*, ▲ *199* undermined the equilibrium of a region that was rousing itself and preparing to throw off the Spanish yoke. In Santiago, the many Catalan immigrants, who had imbibed ideas of autonomy and independence in Spain, founded Masonic lodges. Among others, they were to be the pioneers of the rebellion against the Spanish crown. The city responded enthusiastically to Carlos Manuel de Céspedes' call for independence in 1868. The inhabitants of Santiago enlisted en masse in the rebel battalions for the *Guerra Chiquita* ('Little War'). This war, which broke out in Santiago on August 25, 1879 and ended in 1880, was the last attempt at insurrection after the surrender at Zanjón ● *39*. On April 25, 1898, at the end of the war for independence, the United States declared war on Spain and, on July 3, the fleet of Admiral Pascual Cervera, which had taken refuge in Santiago Bay, was put to rout by the American squadron. The Spanish finally surrendered on July 17. The victory of the *mambises* ● *39* was snatched from them at the last moment by the American conquerors, who refused to allow them into the city. The American occupation continued until May 20, 1902, which marked the start of some hard times for the rebel capital of Oriente. Later, the fight against Gerardo Machado ● *42*, removed from power in 1933, began in Santiago. It was here also, on July 26, 1953, that Fidel Castro and a group of conspirators tried to capture the Moncada Barracks. During the island's final 'liberation' by the *Barbudos* ● *44*, Castro insisted on entering liberated Santiago first, before rallying Havana. All these momentous events have earned Santiago the title of 'heroic city'.

A TALE OF SANTIAGO
In the western area of Santiago, between the railway station and the port, a 656-foot-long fresco retraces Cuba's history in thirty scenes. It charts the long battle for independence fought by key figures from rebellious Oriente – twenty-six generals were born in the city of Santiago.

SANTIAGO, A LIVELY, COSMOPOLITAN CITY
'Interracial mixing goes much deeper than skin-color, it has had a profound impact on ideas, emotions, arts and costumes' (Fernando Ortiz). In Santiago, ethnic diversity has shaped an extremely rich and varied culture: notable examples include the famous carnival, embodied by Chan, the director of the Comparsa de les Hoyos ● *63*, and the Ballet Folklórico Cutumba, founded in 1961, which keeps traditional Afro-Cuban dance alive.

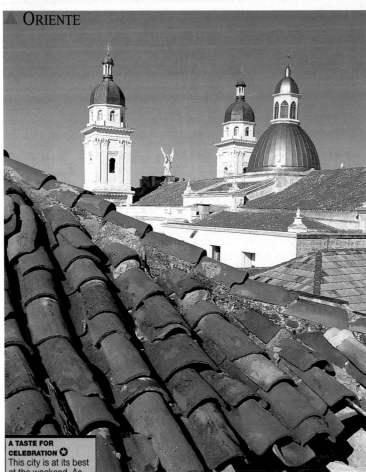

PARQUE CÉSPEDES

'Peace to men of good will!' For many years, these words, on a huge banner strung between two balconies, greeted people taking a stroll in Parque Céspedes, Santiago's central square. It encapsulated the city's guiding spirit: rebellion and authority, faith and history. The former Plaza de Armas was renamed Parque Céspedes in honor of the 'Father of the Nation': his statue keeps a watchful eye over the buildings that line the square and attest to the city's past glory.

HOTEL CASA GRANDA. The rooftop bar of this luxury hotel, a luminous spot when the calm of night descends, affords a fine view of the entire square. It is an ideal observation post for those who want to watch the *Santiagueros* go about their everyday business, including their visits to the ice cream parlor beneath the cathedral's arches. The *Casa Granda* of the 1950s, a '...hotel of real spies, real police-informers and real rebel agents', is thus described in Graham Greene's novel, *Our Man in Havana* ● *103*.

Santiago city hall

CASA DE DIEGO VELÁZQUEZ ▲ *210* ★. This fine mansion, opposite the Casa Granda, is named after the man who is said to have lived here: Diego Velázquez, first governor of Cuba. It is one of the oldest houses in Latin America (1516).

> 'As soon as a mulatto woman starts swaying her behind close to a male dancer, everyone present will provide a beat for their moves by clapping their hands, or tapping on a box, a door, the wall.'
>
> Alejo Carpentier

Catedral de Nuestra Señora de la Asunción. The first cathedral, built in 1522, faced the bay. Damaged by several earthquakes and rebuilt, it acquired its present appearance in 1922 (*left*): its raised, neoclassical façade is flanked by two steeples between which stands the *Angel of the Annunciation*. It is worth a visit for the magnificent coffered ceiling and carved wooden choir stalls. In February 1998, on his visit to Cuba, Pope John Paul II ● *46* celebrated his 'reconciliation mass' here.

CALLE HEREDIA ★

This street, on the right as you come out of the cathedral, is one of the liveliest in the city. A more secular type of mass is celebrated here, but with no less fervor. Every porch and street corner along Calle Heredia is alive with music. On Saturday evenings, before going home to watch their beloved *telenovela* (soap opera), the Cubans flock to this informal stage for the *son*, the *trova* ● *55* and poetry.

Casa de los Estudiantes (N⁰ 204). Every Saturday, this discotheque becomes a showcase for Afro-Cuban dances and music. Watch the kings of the *bata* drum leading hip-swaying *Santiagueras* in a merry dance with their frantic beat.

Casa de la Trova (N⁰ 208). This Santiago institution has always been connected with music. The composer Rafael Pascual Salcedo (1844–1917) entertained his troubadour friends here for many years. In 1950, Virgilio Palais transformed it into a meeting place for fans of the *trova*.

It was only in 1968 that *El Cafetín de Virgilio* officially became the *Casa de la Trova*. Some of the original charm of this 19th-century house has been lost since its atmospheric decor of wood panels and yellowing photos (*right*) was modernized and repainted in 1995. The portraits of the old troubadours who made it famous are still in their place, but the kings of *son*, cousins of El Guayabero ▲ *200* (*right*) and Compay Segundo, do not perform here anymore. The latter, a musician and state official since the Revolution, retired in 1970, although he continues to play in Europe.

UNEAC (N⁰ 206). The best *son* on the island can be heard in the patio of the National Union of Writers and Artists of Cuba.

COMPAY SEGUNDO
The patriarch of *son* was born Francisco Repilado Muñoz in 1907, near Santiago. At the age of fourteen he studied musical theory and the clarinet and joined Santiago's wind and brass band. It was at this time that he made his *armónico*, a cross between the *tres* ● *54* and the classical guitar. In 1934, Muñoz moved to Havana and began playing with the Nico Saquito quintet. He then became guitarist with the Cuarteto Hatuey, was clarinetist with the Conjunto Matamoros and founded the duo Los Compadres with L. Hierrezuelo. Around 1955 he formed his own band, Compay Segundo y sus Muchachos. The record *Buena Vista Social Club*, on which he sang *Chan Chan*, received a Grammy Award.

The Casa de Diego Velázquez is considered to be the oldest house in Cuba (1516–30). Built by the conquistador Velázquez, the Spanish crown's first representative in Cuba, it originally housed the command post of the Spanish colony and a gold foundry downstairs, as well as the governor's private apartments upstairs. The current museum, which illustrates the development of Cuban furniture from the 16th to the 19th centuries, occupies both Casa de Diego Velázquez and the adjoining 19th-century residence. Listed as a historic monument, this complex was restored in 1965.

THE PATIO
Behind the sober dressed-stone façade, an imposing courtyard in mudéjar-style immediately transports visitors to the heart of Seville or Cordova. Notice the central well, in keeping with Moorish tradition, and a clay jar, or *tinajón*, similar to those in Camagüey ▲ *196*.

THE UPPER STORY
The rooms upstairs showcase typical 16th- and 17th-century furniture. In the early days of the colony few pieces of furniture were imported into Cuba; the country possessed a rich stock of all types of wood and the basic essentials were made on the island. Family life revolved around the *estrado*: a wooden platform used as a bed at night and a work surface during the day. A priest's chair and an intricately-carved chest present excellent examples of Moorish style. The only trace of the Velázquez family is a tapestry with the family arms.

THE 19TH-CENTURY HOUSE
The style of furniture in this house betrays a marked French influence ▲ *213* and expresses an obvious taste for comfort. Notice the small rocking chairs as well as a Charles X console table and mirror.

Detail of the cedar roof structure, *above*, in Mudéjar style, dating from the 16th century.

Vast 17th-century hall, furnished with Creole-style furniture, *right*. The inner space is divided by two eye-level partitions. This characteristic layout of the period made it possible to ventilate the rooms naturally.

19th-century dining room, *above*.

18th-century dining room, *below*.

THE FIRST STORY

A collection of 18th-century furniture which boasts, for the first time, a distinctive Cuban flavor called 'Luis Las Casas' style is on display downstairs. The island's wealth encouraged the emergence of this style which combined English and French rococo influences: this heavy furniture was decorated with ornate motifs and massive protruding bases shaped like claws.

BALCÓN DE VELÁZQUEZ
This corner of Calles Mariano Corona and Bartolomé Masó, affords a magnificent panoramic view over the picturesque quarter of Tívoli. The stairs in Calle Padre Pico (*below*, beginning of the 20th century) were commissioned by Emilio Bacardí.

EMILIO BACARDÍ THE JUST
Founder of the famous Bacardí distillery ● *51*, Emilio (1844–1922) fought for independence and paid for it with two stays in prison. At the end of the Spanish-American war ● *39*, after a yellow fever epidemic, a decree was published threatening thirty days' imprisonment for anyone who did not notify the authorities of any deaths. Emilio wrote to the mayor: 'Thirty days of hard labor for the martyrs, mothers, sisters and friends who gave us our homeland. As a man and as a Cuban, I venture to inform you that the duty of any authority is to be near those who are suffering.' He was to be the first mayor of Santiago, after independence.

CASA NATAL DE JOSÉ MARÍA DE HEREDIA. The poet José María de Heredia (1803–39) was born in this 18th-century house. He is not to be confused with his cousin of the same name, the Parnassian and author of *Les Trophées* who was born near Santiago (1842–1905), but left his native island at an early age. This museum, a place of pilgrimage for artists and poets, retraces the life of the man who was as famous for his odes to nature as he was for his fight for independence.

MUSEO DEL CARNAVAL (N⁰ 303). This large museum, housed in a fine 18th-century colonial mansion, charts the history of the famous Santiago carnival ● *62* from its religious origins to its more revolutionary character from 1959 onward. When the republic was in its infancy, floats were used as promotional tools for Pilón, Bacardí, etc. On display in the various rooms are costumes, *cabezones* (large heads), banners, floats and a great many musical instruments. There are often performances by folk groups on the patio.

MUSEO EMILIO BACARDÍ-MOREAU. At the corner of Calle Aguilera and Calle Pío Rosado, this temple to Cuban identity has a surprisingly wide neoclassical columned façade. Founded in 1899 by Emilio Bacardí ● *50*, this is the oldest museum in Cuba. The first story contains a large collection of personal effects belonging to three heroes of the wars for independence ● *39*, José Martí, Carlos Manuel de Céspedes and Antonio Maceo. The basement houses the Bacardí collection, including an Egyptian mummy and several pieces of Pre-Columbian art. The second story is devoted to Cuban and European art (including several paintings by Wifredo Lam ● *99* and René Portocarrero ● *99*).

PARQUE DOLORES AND VICINITY. Leaving the historic center and journeying toward the east of the city, you will find a more open area of Santiago. Calle José A. Saco climbs toward Parque Dolores, passing a row of stores such as El París and El Gallo whose unlit neon signs still attest to the city's past splendor. This busy shopping street owed a debt of gratitude to the French *émigrés* from Haiti. Quickly prospering, they imported fine clothes, glassware, rare ceramics and furniture

from Europe. Parque Dolores, surrounded by buildings with wrought-iron balconies, is an attractive place to stop. Try one of the many restaurants and cafés, such as the Isabelica, renowned for its coffee.

TÍVOLI, A FRENCH ENCLAVE ★

Tívoli, southwest of Parque Dolores, is probably the most working-class quarter in Santiago, a symbol of Cuban multiculturalism: it accommodated Spaniards with modest incomes, Jamaicans, Dominicans, Puerto Ricans, Arabs, Chinese as well as a sizable French population. Local people proudly claim that the first ever *santiaguero* carnival was held here. The quarter was named after a theater in which labyrinthine corridors led from the bar to the auditorium, thereby justifying this allusion to Tivoli in Italy. The French immigrants made this hill above the port an extremely desirable address, much sought after by *Santiagueros*. The quarter was extremely well-appointed with businesses, music schools, fashionable boutiques, studios, theaters and hotels. The pace of life has now slowed considerably. The only hot spot offering a good night out is the CASA DE TRADICIÓN, Calle Rabí, a popular haunt of local musicians.

MUSEO DE LA LUCHA CLANDESTINA ★. This lovely house on Calle Rabí was burned down in 1956 and completely 'reinvented' by architect Walter Betancourt in 1976. The

museum is devoted to the rebel fight against Batista and depicts the events that took place in this former police station on November 30, 1956: the attack led by Frank País in order to enable Castro and his men to land in Oriente. Castro himself once lived in Calle Rabí.

Sale of Bacardí rum, in 1955.

THE 'TUMBA FRANCESA' GROUPS
The 'French Blacks' first organized their festivals in the coffee plantations, then in the cities. Two groups still exist, in Santiago and Guantánamo. Their choreography is based on the formal dances of French settlers in the 18th century (minuet, rigaudon, quadrille); the songs are sung in Creole and the music played on specific instruments. Three of the drums used are also found in Haiti: the *tambora*, struck on both sides, the *catá*, of Bantu origin (hollow tree trunk hit with sticks) and the *chachás* (metal bells decorated with ribbons) shaken by the chorus. Two dances still exist: the *masón* and the *yubá*.

In the once lively port of Santiago, a heavy lethargy has descended over the quays that were a hive of activity during the Soviet era.

NAPOLEON'S DOCTOR
A Corsican-born Frenchman lies in the Santa Ifigenia cemetery: Francesco Antommarchi (1780–1838), Napoleon's last doctor on Saint Helena. On the death of Napoleon in 1821, he exhibited a death mask that he claimed had been made from a mold taken of the emperor's face. Accused of producing a fake, he traveled to Cuba and decided to settle in Santiago, the cornerstone of the French colony: many of the officers and soldiers who had served under the emperor had turned to coffee farming. 'El Doctor's' dedication earned him the friendship of the *Santiagueros*. A month before his death, he petitioned the mayor of Santiago to give beds to the poor with trained staff to look after them.

SANTA IFIGENIA CEMETERY ★

Taking one of the horse-drawn carriages waiting in Parque Alameda, south of the station, makes a visit to this cemetery even more rewarding. Opposite are the warehouses of the former Bacardí rum distillery (staff gathered in front of the cellars, around 1920–30, *top right*) which now produces Caney Rum.

HEROES' NECROPOLIS. Santiago's cemetery is almost as prestigious as the Cristóbal Colón cemetery in Havana ▲ *145*. Two important historical figures from the wars for independence are buried here: JOSÉ MARTÍ ● *40* and CARLOS MANUEL DE CÉSPEDES ● *39*, ▲ *204*. The former was initially laid to rest in Dos Ríos, the place of his death. His remains were then moved to the capital of Oriente and interred in a white marble mausoleum (1951). The tomb of the 'Father of the Nation', easily recognizable by its column topped by an eternal flame, stands next to that of MARIANA GRAJALES, Antonio Maceo's mother and 'Mother of the Nation'. It is also near the monumental group dedicated to the twenty-six generals from Santiago who died in the battle. The tombs of the 'Martyrs of the Revolution', such as FRANK PAÍS and his brother Josué, are draped with a red and black flag, the colors of the 26th of July Movement ● *44*, ▲ *206*. Also worthy of note is the pyramid-shaped tomb of EMILIO BACARDÍ.

FROM PLAZA DE MARTE

TO PLAZA DE LA REVOLUCIÓN

PLAZA DE MARTE. The third largest square in the heart of Santiago, east of Parque Dolores, links the city center with the city's other historical area. Built in the 19th century, it played a part in the Cuban revolutionary movement, since it was the site of executions during the colonial era. Many people were shot here during the dictatorship of Gerardo Machado ● *42*. **MONCADA BARRACKS** ● *44*. This building, on the corner of Calle General

Portuondo and Avenida Moncada, dates from the 19th century but was enlarged in the 1930s. The attack on what was at that time the second most important garrison in Cuba, organized by Fidel Castro on July 26, 1953, at the height of carnival, sparked off a general rebellion on the island. To provide cover for the operation, it had been decided that two groups, led respectively by Abel Santamaría and Raúl Castro, would attack the Saturnino Lora hospital and the Law Courts, near the barracks. Outnumbered by Batista's soldiers, the hundred men led by Castro began a desperate shoot-out which ended in failure: eight men killed and fifty-five taken prisoner, tortured and executed. Castro, who managed to escape, was captured a week later and judged at closed hearing, on October 16, 1953 ● *44*, in a small room in the Saturnino Lora hospital. Converted into a school after 1959, the building has been home to the MUSEO HISTÓRICO DEL 26 DE JULIO ★ since 1967. (Its outer façade, scarred by bullet holes, was repaired by Batista. After his overthrow, Castro put the holes back, painstakingly placed according to photographs taken shortly after the original failed attack.) This museum, devoted mainly to the attack on the Moncada Barracks, contains a model illustrating the sequence of events. A torture room has been recreated with photographs providing supporting evidence. Newspaper articles, uniforms (stained with blood) and weapons are all on display.

PLAZA DE LA REVOLUCIÓN. History has already honored Antonio Maceo ● *39*, the general of the Cuban liberation army who was such a source of inspiration for Castro. This son of a black merchant is Santiago's true godfather. Astride his rearing horse, the 'BRONZE TITAN' (*opposite*) dominates the Plaza de la Revolución, a vast esplanade at the junction of three main avenues leading into the city. His machete in his belt, he motions his companions to follow him. The machete was the rallying sign of the *mambises* ● *39* and Maceo, who declared: 'Liberty is not begged for but won with the blade of a machete.' The bunch of twenty-three steel stalks, whose central piece measures 26 feet, alludes to March 23, 1878, the date of the *Protesta de Baraguá* ● *39*.

Picturesque scenes await visitors exploring Santiago's streets. A barber cutting hair in the open, *below*.

CASA NATAL DE ANTONIO MACÉO
The house where the general was born (Calle Los Maceos, Nº 207), now converted into a museum, is a humble abode. Maceo was born on June 14, 1845 and died in combat at the battle of Punta Brava (southeast of Havana) on December 7, 1898. For Cubans, he symbolizes the refusal to compromise in the armed fight for independence ● *39*. The museum shows photographs of the Macéo family: José, Antonio's brother, also a general nicknamed the 'Lion of Oriente', and Mariana Grajales, his mother. The two mango trees on the patio were brought back from Baraguá ● *39* and from Magos de la Roque, two key places in Maceo's military career.

VISTA ALEGRE

This residential quarter of Santiago is on the east side of the city and can be reached by taking Avenida Victoriano Garzón from Plaza de Marte. Avenida Manduley, which runs through the center of this grid street layout, is lined with some fine houses built in the 1920s and 1930s (*right*) but abandoned by the wealthy families of Santiago after 1959. Many of these residences have been converted into cultural centers – the Alliance Française, for example, at Calle 6, Nº 253 – schools, museums, or clinics; some house foreign consulates.

PALACIO DE LOS PIONEROS. A Mig in a garden with children for fighter pilots? Although the Mig is real, it has no jet engines and no rocket launchers. The *pioneros* ('pioneers') of this school are merely playing on this former fighter plane. This building, which resembles a castle, is located on the corner of Avenida Manduley and Calle 11. It is not open to the public.

CASA DEL CARIBE. This house is on Calle 13, near Avenida Manduley. Founded around fifteen years ago, this fascinating showcase of regional culture studies customs, delves deep into memories, and questions the descendants of these long-neglected mixed cultures. The researcher José Millet has won a great deal of renown for his work here; an expert in cults of African origin (*santeria* ● 58 and voodoo), he has the well-earned respect of the Haitians in Oriente. Another ethnological enclave near the Casa del Caribe, is the CENTRO CULTURAL AFRICANO FERNANDO ORTÍZ (Nº 106, Avenida Manduley) which exhibits a range of African objects (masks, musical instruments, etc).

SAN JUAN HILL. It is a wrench to leave Vista Alegre, an oasis of peace perched on a hill above the road heading east. The exhaust fumes from cars climbing the gentle slope of Avenida Raúl Pujol produce an almost constant fog and conceal San Juan hill to the south. It was on this site – a ridge like a donkey's back, with its perfectly kept lawns that, on July 1, 1898, the

AN ARCHITECTURAL GEM
The Castillo del Morro (1637) is a striking example of the Spanish-American school of military architecture. This classical bastioned fortification, designed by Italian engineer Juan Bautista Antonelli, applies principles put forward by Renaissance theoreticians: geometrical forms, symmetry and a respect for balanced proportions.

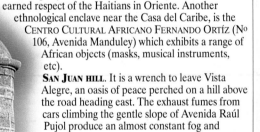

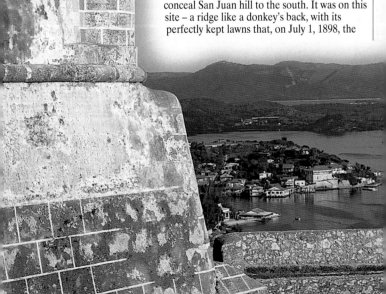

Many Cubans drive American classic cars.

battle of San Juan took place, following the blockade of the Spanish fleet in Santiago Bay. One of the 6000 American foot soldiers who attacked the hill was to become famous in later life: his name was Theodore Roosevelt, the future president of the United States. The memorial, which consists of cannons and engraved marble plaques, has now become a substitute garden for the Hotel *San Juan*.

CASTILLO DEL MORRO

The magnificent guardian of the harbor, the citadel of El Morro, six miles from the center of Santiago, is at the end of the airport road. The Carretera Turística also leads to the castle and affords a series of wonderful views over the bay. Around the mid-16th century, pirates and corsairs posed a serious threat to the city ▲ *206*.

In 1637, after a visit the year before by renowned military engineer Juan Bautista Antonelli ▲ *146*, the governor of Santiago, Pedro de la Roca y Borja, followed his lead and began building a stone fortress, the Castillo San Pedro de la Roca. Antonelli linked it to the ravelin built between 1590 and 1610 on the *morro* (promontory). Destroyed by the English in 1662 ▲ *206*, it was rebuilt and enlarged between 1663 and 1669. The current fort, restored in the 1960s by Francisco Prat Puig, is the result of many reconstructions, repairs and additions carried out from the early 18th century until the end of the 19th century. It served as a prison from 1775 and many *mambises* were imprisoned here during the wars for independence. In 1898, after the Spanish defeat, the American troops took up residence here until Cuba's independence. The fortress now houses the fascinating MUSEO DE LA PIRATERÍA, which charts the eventful history of the numerous privateers during the 16th and 17th centuries.

Residences in neo-classical or eclectic style in the Vista Alegre quarter in Santiago. Many of these elegant houses were built to plans designed by American architects.

CAYO GRANMA
A ferry service links this tiny island in Santiago Bay (*left*) with Marina Punta Gorda, five miles south of the center of Santiago, at the end of the Carretera Turística. Cayo Granma, which looks like a water lily floating in the middle of the bay, boasts a delightful little fishing village with cabins and brightly colored houses on stilts. This is an ideal destination for a day trip, providing a breath of fresh air after walking through the city center or visiting the nearby Castillo del Morro. There is a restaurant for temporary islanders.

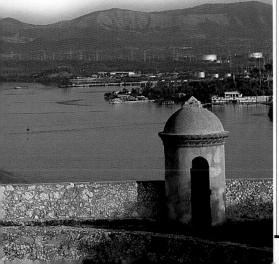

'The drought that year was so bad that the river and spring had run hopelessly dry. The villagers decided to beseech the Virgin and, to do so, carried her statue across the fields. They had not

gone any further than two leagues when a high wind came up: it started to rain so heavily that they found it extremely difficult to transport the statue back to the church.' (Sanchez Moya, *Accounts of the Miracles of the Virgin of Charity*.)

NUESTRA SEÑORA DEL COBRE ★

The basilica of Nuestra Señora de la Caridad del Cobre (*above*), twelve miles northwest of Santiago, is the most important pilgrimage center on the island. Cubans call it 'El Cobre' (the copper) and it is sacred to them: since May 10, 1916, the Vírgen de la Caridad del Cobre has been the patron saint of the country.

THE MINING VILLAGE OF EL COBRE. In 1534, stonemason Luis Espinosa obtained permission to work a small copper mine at the foot of Cardenillo Hill. He soon abandoned the mine, leaving it in the hands of his slaves. The latter, with a group of Spaniards from Santiago, founded the village of El Cobre. Toward the end of the 17th century, the slaves revolted, following the example of the *cimarrones* ● 37. After several attempts to reach an agreement with their masters, the *Cobreros* were given the right to stay on the land they were mining. They were freed in 1807, some seventy-five years before the abolition of slavery.

THE VÍRGEN DE LA CARIDAD DEL COBRE. In 1605, three young fishermen ● 33 discovered a Virgin and child in the Bahía de Nipe. One of them, Juan Moreno, reported that the wooden statue had the following inscription: 'I am the Virgin of Charity'. The relic was taken to the village of El Cobre, where it immediately became an object of worship for the villagers

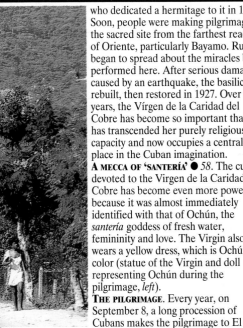

who dedicated a hermitage to it in 1608. Soon, people were making pilgrimages to the sacred site from the farthest reaches of Oriente, particularly Bayamo. Rumors began to spread about the miracles being performed here. After serious damage caused by an earthquake, the basilica was rebuilt, then restored in 1927. Over the years, the Vírgen de la Caridad del Cobre has become so important that she has transcended her purely religious capacity and now occupies a central place in the Cuban imagination.

A MECCA OF 'SANTERÍA' ● *58*. The cult devoted to the Virgen de la Caridad del Cobre has become even more powerful because it was almost immediately identified with that of Ochún, the *santería* goddess of fresh water, femininity and love. The Virgin also wears a yellow dress, which is Ochún's color (statue of the Virgin and doll representing Ochún during the pilgrimage, *left*).

THE PILGRIMAGE. Every year, on September 8, a long procession of Cubans makes the pilgrimage to El Cobre, bringing medals, crutches, locks of hair, clothes, photos and all kinds of ex-voto offerings which are placed in her shrine alongside those left by the *barbudos* ● *44*. Look out particularly for the medallion that Hemingway ▲ *149* received for his Nobel Prize and which he himself laid in the showcase for gifts to the Vírgen de la Caridad del Cobre from her worshippers.

MOUNTING AN ASSAULT ON GRAN PIEDRA
If you want the chance to experience one of the finest views in Cuba and see the islands of Jamaica and Haiti in the distance (on a clear day), you must climb to an altitude of more than 3300 feet. Once out of Santiago, take the narrow unmarked fork before reaching Siboney. Although this humble road seems to peter out in a field, it eventually leads to the foot of a pass worthy of an alpine stage of the Tour de France: seven miles of tortuous road will take you to Gran Piedra. This huge rock, at an altitude of 4,048 feet, is the highest point in the Gran Piedra mountain range. This was where the French settlers from Haiti planted their first coffee trees on the island. Nearby, *La Isabelica* ★, an old coffee plantation built in the early 19th century, now houses a meager museum devoted to the coffee industry. The coffee beans were dried on three platforms above the defensive ditch surrounding the plantation.

PARQUE BACONAO

Parque Baconao, an area of 200 acres designated a Biosphere Reserve by UNESCO, lies to the east of Santiago and extends to the Río Baconao. The park contains many interesting historical and artistic sights.

PRADO DE LAS ESCULTURAS. This sculpture garden containing twenty monumental works by Cuban and foreign artists was erected in the 1980s and lies about ten miles from Santiago on the road to Gran Piedra. It is possible to drive around them for a closer look.

GRANJITA DE SIBONEY. The road that leads from Santiago to the 'small farm' of Siboney is lined with twenty-six white stone stele, in memory of the heroes who lost their lives in the attack on the Moncada Barracks ▲ *215* on July 26, 1953. The farm, which was where they planned the attack, has been converted into a museum. The weapons – some of which are exhibited – were hidden in the well.

PLAYA SIBONEY AND PLAYA DAIQUIRÍ ★. Many *Santiagueros* head for Playa Siboney, which is their favorite beach. Playa Daiquirí, a tiny, secluded cove with the evocative name of a famous cocktail ● *66*, ▲ *150*, is the loveliest beach in Oriente. This was where the American troops ● *39* landed in 1898, before heading for Santiago.

**THE 'BALSEROS'
CRISIS ● 46**
In August 1994, some 35,000 Cubans tried to reach Florida on board makeshift rafts (*balsas*). They remained on the Guantánamo naval base for almost a year, until May 1995, when 22,000 were allowed to leave for the United States.

GUANTÁNAMO

'*Yo soy un hombre sincero* […] *Guantanamera.*' There is no mistaking that the fame of Guantánamo, the chief town of an agricultural province, owes a great deal to this rhythmic ballad by Joseíto Fernández (*left*), but it is much less well known than the chorus borrowed from *Versos Simples* by José Martí ● *40*. The hero of the independence movement wrote: 'I am a sincere man, from the land of the palm tree' – and the cactus, you could add. In Guantánamo, this plant is used in two different ways: planted on the roofs of houses, it is supposed to ward off bad luck; if it survives, the year will be good, but if not, it is said anything could happen. It has also been planted around the American naval base and forms an impenetrable hedge, nicknamed the 'cactus curtain', to prevent unofficial immigration.

THE AMERICAN NAVAL BASE. Plaza de la Revolución and Parque Martí are nothing out of the ordinary, so Guantánamo's main claim to fame is the 100-year-old bone of contention between Cuba and the United States: 'the Base' ● *46*. The forty-five square miles of land were ceded to the Americans in 1903 as part of the Platt Amendment ● *39*. Cubans are not allowed inside the base, with the exception of around thirty men, who inherited their parents' jobs before 1959. Since that date, Castro's government has not cashed the annual rent of $4,085, thereby contesting the legitimacy of the American enclave. Although Guantánamo has 200,000 inhabitants, the naval base, equipped with two airdromes, houses around 7,000 people, who benefit from sports and leisure facilities, schools, a supermarket and places of worship. A road lined with salt marshes leads to the pretty neighboring village of Caimanera.

TOWARD BARACOA ALONG THE COAST

The stunning coast road linking Guantánamo to the village of Cajobabo crosses one of the most arid regions on the island, densely covered with cacti for the last nineteen miles.

LA FAROLA ★. From Cajobabo, this thirty-mile-long winding road climbs through increasingly lush vegetation to the town of Baracoa, on the north coast of Guantánamo Province. This highway, a genuine technical feat when it was built in the 1960s, has been cut into the slopes of the Sierra del Plurial, providing road access to Baracoa, which formerly could only be reached by sea.

THE 'CHANGÜÍ'
This musical genre, peculiar to Guantánamo Province, is a variant of the *son* ● *54*, which was born on the Yateritas coffee plantations in the mountains. Many contemporary bands endeavor to preserve this traditional genre. Instead of the guitar or the *claves*, the main instrument used in this distinctive variant is the *tres*. (*left to right: bongó, tres, marímbula* and *maracas*.)

'CUCURUCHO'
This typical delicacy is made with coconut, guava, orange and papaya and wrapped in palm leaves. It is made by hand in every household of Baracoa.

THE EXECUTION OF HATUEY
Bartolomé de Las Casas ● 32 related: 'He was tied to a stake. A monk from the order of St Francis who was present spoke to him about God and our faith […] After some thought, the cacique asked the priest whether Christians went to heaven […] The priest replied that good Christians did. The cacique immediately said that he would rather go to hell than be in heaven with people who were so cruel.'

MUSEO MUNICIPAL DE BARACOA ❂
This is one of the most interesting museums on the island. Among other things, it boasts a collection of objects owned by 18th-century settlers, some of whom made their fortunes in sugar . Allow at least one and a half hours.

BARACOA ★

THE FIRST OF THE COLONY'S SEVEN TOWNS. Baracoa, known variously by nicknames such as the 'Forgotten Town' or the 'Real Cuba', was the first city founded by Diego Velázquez in 1511. Visitors are likely to experience the strange sensation of having stepped back in time to the early days of the settlement: for over four centuries, Baracoa was completely cut off from the rest of the island. Unable to defend itself from raids by pirates, it built three fortresses in the 18th century, which are a familiar sight in Baracoa today.

AN EXTRAORDINARY SITE. The dilapidated façades and rusty metal roofs of this small city with its many coconut palms (*above*) attest to the harsh weather that batters the easternmost tip of the island. Curving around a wide bay, it appears to have been sheltered from time immemorial by the huge hill covered in a dense tropical forest that looms over it in the west. Its flat summit, a natural citadel known as El Yunque (the Anvil), was used as a landmark for the fleet captained by Christopher Columbus, who described a mountain of similar shape in his captain's log. El Yunque may have been the sanctuary for the Taíno Indians ● 32.

THE MOST INDIAN TOWN IN CUBA. Baracoa, an Indian name meaning 'where the sea begins', was profoundly influenced by the Taíno civilization: some of their descendants still live in the region's traditional *bohíos*. The town has dedicated a cult to the cacique Hatuey ● 32, who attempted to stand against the conquistadors. His bronze bust, erected on a

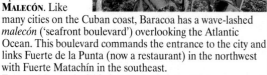

In Cuba are varieties of snails (*below*) that change color according to their position on the tree

column, faces the the cathedral square.

MALECÓN. Like many cities on the Cuban coast, Baracoa has a wave-lashed *malecón* ('seafront boulevard') overlooking the Atlantic Ocean. This boulevard commands the entrance to the city and links Fuerte de la Punta (now a restaurant) in the northwest with Fuerte Matachín in the southeast.

FUERTE MATACHÍN. This fortress houses the MUSEO MUNICIPAL ★, headed by Alejandro Hartman, the official city historian, who is an inexhaustible font of anecdotes about the Spanish occupation. Much of the museum is devoted to the flora and fauna in the area, which is of a richness and diversity unequaled in Cuba (around 100 species of wood).

CATEDRAL DE NUESTRA SEÑORA DE LA ASUNCIÓN. Consecrated in 1512, this is the oldest religious building in Cuba. Sacked by pirates in 1652, it was restored at the end of the 19th century. It contains one of the most valuable relics in the country: the CRUZ DE LA PARRA (15th century), said to have been placed here by Christopher Columbus.

FUERTE DE SEBORUCO. Perched above the town, this fortress houses the Hotel *El Castillo*, which is the best observation point for admiring El Yunque. At its foot, the cocoa plantations (*right*), along the banks of the Río Duaba, supply the chocolate factory and the CASA DEL CHOCOLATE in Calle Maceo.

AROUND BARACOA

Two rivers flow through Baracoa, the Toa and the Yumurí, but the latter is by far the dearest to the Baracoans' heart.

BOCA DE YUMURÍ ★. This delightful cluster of *bohíos* (*above*), fifteen miles east of Baracoa, is a fishing village on the edge of a lake into which the Río Yumurí flows. After crossing the river by boat, you disembark on a beach where children, most of them Taíno descendants, offer visitors brightly colored snails called *polimitas* (*above*).

PLAYA MAGUANA. In this village of *bohíos*, twelve miles west of Baracoa, washerwomen smack their laundry against bowls identical to those of their Indian ancestors. The men fish, bringing in enough to feed the village and supply the Villa Maguana inn, hidden beneath the palms. The nearby BEACH ★ is one of Baracoa's tourist gems.

Archipiélago de los Canarreos

Monique Peainchau

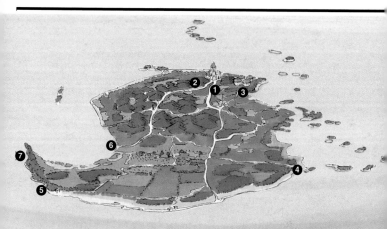

THE AMERICAN PRESENCE
In 1955, dictator Batista declared the Isle of Youth, at that time the Isle of Pines with a population of 11,000 inhabitants, a free zone. Americans hastened to build hotels, vacation villages and a private airport, which was inaugurated just before the · 'Revolution'. There are still traces of American settlement: wooden houses with verandas and the American cemetery.

The Archipiélago de los Canarreos, the largest group of islands in Cuba, lies south of Havana Province. This vast scattering of tiny islands floating in the Caribbean sea was inhabited well before the arrival of the conquistadors ● *32*, but the latter neglected it: 'The solitude of these regions differs widely now from their appearance in the time of Columbus, when they were inhabited and frequented by large numbers of fishermen.' wrote Alexander von Humboldt. Most of its 350 *cayos* ■ *28* are today uninhabited, except for the Isle of Youth (*Isla de la Juventud*) and the Cayman Islands, which belong to Great Britain. The archipelago has become one of Cuba's major tourist centers because of its excellent diving.

HISTORY OF THE ISLE OF YOUTH

The Isle of Youth, the largest island in the archipelago at 850 square miles, is in the Gulf of Batabanó, sixty-five miles from the coast. It has around 80,000 inhabitants and is a 'special municipality' administered by the government, like all the neighboring *cayos*. The Sierra de Caballo and the Sierra de Casa, whose highest point is the Loma de Cañada (1020 feet), dominate the flat open countryside of the north. The karstic southern plain, south of the Ciénaga de Lanier swamp, is composed of virgin territory and dense tropical rainforest.
THE ISLAND OF A THOUSAND NAMES. The island has an interesting toponymic history. The aborigines called it successively Camargo, Guanaja, Siguanea, Ahao and Reylla. Christopher Columbus named it La Evangelista (1494), then Diego Velázquez renamed it Santiago. Its characteristic flora and fauna earned it the names of Parrot Island and the Isle of Pines. It owes its current name to Fidel Castro: the *Comandante* wanted to pay homage to the young people of Cuba who contributed to its economic development.
THE REFUGE OF PIRATES AND CORSAIRS. In the 16th and 17th centuries, pirates, corsairs, freebooters and

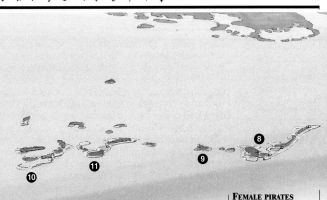

buccaneers used the island as a base because, with its coves, woods, abundant fresh water and food, it was strategically placed on the route taken by the galleons. Among the many corsairs, pirates and seamen who frequented this island were British subjects Francis Drake, Thomas Baskervill and Henry Morgan ▲ 206, Dutchmen Pieter Peterzon and Oliver Esquemeling – this pirate and surgeon left behind a large body of writings about the buccaneers – and the Frenchmen Jacques de Sores ● 33, L'Olonnais and Latrobe. The latter reputedly buried a fabulous treasure trove, looted from two Spanish galleons, in the southwestern part of the island near the Bay of Siguanea. It was never found.

A PLACE OF DETENTION THEN HOPE. On December 17, 1830, the island, under Spanish control, became the Colonia Reina Amalia. It was used as a detention center for Cuban patriots, the most famous of whom being José Martí ● 40. In 1898, Cuba wrested its independence from Spain with the Treaty of Paris. But the United States, within the framework of the Platt Amendment ● 39, temporarily excluded the Isle of Pines from national territory and it was not until March 13, 1925, after a long battle by the Cubans, that it was restored to the nation with the Treaty of Hay-Quesada. In 1926, during Machado's dictatorship ● 42, the island was again used for detention and a massive penitentiary, the Model Prison, was built. Fidel Castro and his companions were imprisoned here from 1953 to 1955. After the Revolution, under the aegis of Fidel Castro, the island endeavored to make up for its slow economic development with the help, in the 1960s and 1970s, of thousands of youngsters from Cuba and abroad who came here to study and work the fields. Although this initiative has now been abandoned, the Isle of Youth is still known for the warm welcome it offers many students from the Third World, particularly Africa.

FEMALE PIRATES
Some dangerous female pirates who disguised themselves as men used the Isle of Youth as a hideout. Among the many tales of these pirates is that of Mary Read and Anne Bonny. The latter was the mistress of a pirate called Rackham, whose nickname was 'Calico Jack'. The pregnant Anne disembarked in Cienfuegos Bay ▲ 177, gave birth and abandoned her child to its fate before returning to the ship to be with her lover. She then succumbed to the charms of a sailor who, during a duel, proved to be Mary Read, a woman in disguise.

225

A LAND WREATHED IN LEGEND
The island abounds in stories about pirates and their hidden treasure. In the Bay of Siguanea in the west, the inhabitants shiver with fear when they see a light moving at night over the beaches of Punta Rincón del Guanal, said to be haunted by the tormented soul of the pirate L'Olonnais.

Nueva Gerona

Nueva Gerona, the main town of the 'special municipality', was founded in 1830 on the banks of the Río Las Casas in the northern part of the island. This quiet provincial village is dominated by hills containing marble mines. The polychromatic marble is one of the town's key local resources.

Iglesia de Nuestra Señora de los Dolores. This church dedicated to Our Lady of Sorrows stands on the northwest side of Parque Central, the hub of the town and a popular meeting place for foreign students. Originally neo-classical (1853), this building was almost entirely destroyed by the hurricane of 1926. The current church (*below*), in colonial style, dates from 1929.

Museo Municipal. This museum is housed inside the former town hall, on the south side of Parque Central. A collection of stuffed birds is displayed beside historical objects and documents relating to the age of piracy and the Revolution. The fight against Fulgencio Batista's dictatorship ● *44* is charted in the Museo de la Lucha Clandestina, on the corner of Calles 24 and 25.

Museo de Historia Natural. Built at the southwest end of town, on Calle 41, this museum takes visitors on a voyage of discovery of local natural history, geology and archeology. Anyone who does not have the time to visit the southern part of the island will enjoy the reproductions of the prehistoric cave paintings from Punta del Este. The astronomy room of the planetarium reveals that this is one of the few places in the world where the North Star in the Northern Hemisphere and the Southern Cross in the Southern Hemisphere can be seen at the same time.

Around Nueva Gerona

Finca del Abra. This farm is southwest of Nueva Gerona. In 1870, at the age of seventeen, José Martí was kept under house arrest here for nine weeks, before being deported to Spain. The property of a wealthy Catalan, the house has been converted into a museum.

Presidio Modelo ★. The Model Prison, a copy of the famous American penitentiary of Joliet (Illinois), was one of the first maximum security prisons in Latin America. Built between 1926 and 1931, under Machado's regime, two miles from Nueva Gerona, it has gone down in history because of the revolutionaries who were incarcerated here during the 1950s. Four circular towers several stories high provided accommodation for around 5000 prisoners. Each had a central tower which served as a watchtower for the guards and was reached by an underground tunnel to avoid any contact with the prisoners. The most famous 'guests' at the Presidio Modelo were Fidel Castro and his companions, who were imprisoned in the medical wing from October 1953 to May 1955, after the attack on the Moncada Barracks ● *44*, ▲ *215*. In 1967, the building was converted into a museum. You can visit Castro's cell (prisoner number 3859) at the entrance to wing Nº 1 (*above*).

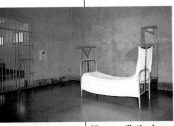

From Punta del Este to Hotel *Colony*

Cueva de Punta del Este ★. This site, the most picturesque on the south coast, is thirty-seven miles southeast of Nueva Gerona. Its seven caves open onto a magnificent secluded white-sand BEACH ★. Discovered in 1910 by a Frenchman of English origin who had taken shelter here after being shipwrecked, the pictograms and paintings were painted on the walls by Siboney Indians ● *34* well before 1492. The main cave, which has 235 paintings on the walls and ceiling, was nicknamed the 'Caribbean Sistine Chapel' by ethnologist Fernando Ortíz ● *42*. Ortíz studied these paintings in 1925: one of the largest, composed of twenty-eight red and black concentric circles, appears to represent a solar calendar. Their purpose, however, remains shrouded in mystery. Cited a historical monument, the cave has been damaged by unscrupulous visitors and by a charcoal-burner who lived here for some thirty years.

Hotel *Colony* ★. The HOTEL *COLONY* INTERNATIONAL DIVE CENTER has some of the best facilities in the country. It can be found at PLAYA ROJA, a large beach lined with coconut palms in the southwestern part of the island, at the back of the Bay of Siguanea. Two hours' sailing between Cabo Francés and Punta de Pedernales will take divers to fifty-six dive sites along the COSTA DE LOS PIRATAS, an area of stunning beauty and tranquillity with a teeming diversity of sealife. The coral reef contains over forty species of coral. Its main attraction, the Black Coral Wall, is at a depth of ninety-eight feet. Spanish boats sunk by pirate ships can still be seen northwest of Cabo Francés.

CASTRO IN PRISON
Fidel Castro and his friends lost no time when they arrived at the Presidio Modelo. They set up a library, analysed their failure and began planning for the future. It was here that Castro wrote the text of

History will Absolve Me. A campaign calling for an amnesty to be granted gathered momentum. In April 1955, demonstrations were held in the capital and, in May, Batista amnestied the men involved in the attack on the Moncada Barracks.

'PIRATE COAST' ✪
Where there are pirates, there is treasure… the treasures of the sea off the coast near the Hotel *Colony*. The evocative names of the dive sites speak for themselves: Parrot Valley, Stingray Paradise, Caribbean Cathedral, etc. Underwater photography poses no problems here because the fish are used to being fed by the divers.

COCODRILO
Once called Jacksonville, this fishing village was settled in the 19th century by inhabitants from the British Cayman Islands. It can be reached by boat from the Hotel *Colony*.

CAYO
LARGO ★

The Caribbean Sea is sprinkled with *cayos* (from the English 'key' or islet) along the northeast coastline of the Isle of Youth and south of the Zapata Peninsula ▲ *174*. The easternmost island in this long string of uninhabited windswept islands, basking in sunshine and silence, is Cayo Largo.

A LONG RIBBON OF CORAL. Cayo Largo, fifteen miles long and thirteen square miles in area, is seventy miles from the Isle of

Youth. It is the best known of the *cayos* in the archipelago. Very popular for its watersports, it is exclusively a tourist resort and is the only island operating regular flights to Havana and Varadero. It has seven idyllic beaches washed by clear, warm water (78°F) which is such a deep blue that it seems almost unreal. The most beautiful beach, PLAYA SIRENA, on the west side of the island (*left*), boasts over a mile of fine white sand and is well sheltered from waves and wind. Further east, on the south coast, PLAYA LINDAMAR and PLAYA BLANCA, the two longest beaches on Cayo Largo, are the site of most of the hotel complexes built since the 1980s. PLAYA LOS COCOS, which owes its name to its many coconut palms, has sandy shallows and is full of coral rocks making it a paradise for divers. The

trees. The scanty fauna includes palm trees, coconut palms and mangroves.

remains of a shipwreck that happened over half a century ago can still be seen here. PLAYA TORTUGAS, the easternmost beach on Cayo Largo, is a refuge for turtles which come to lay their eggs in the warm sand.

SMALL 'CAYOS'. The small uninhabited *cayos* scattered around are ideal for hikers and can be reached by boat from Cayo Largo. CAYO AVALOS, with its white sandy beach lined with coconut palms, is probably the most beautiful island in the Canarreos. The explorer Cyrus Wicker, when looking for treasure here, discovered a cannon dating from the era when pirates had the run of the archipelago. Between Cayo Largo and the Isle of Youth, CAYO RICO, a superb islet whose bright green water owes its color to beds of molluscs and colonies of crayfish, is inhabited by iguanas, turtles and pelicans. In CAYO IGUANA, the iguanas can grow to more than three feet. CAYO

CANTILES is home to monkeys and all kinds of birds, while some very beautiful species of seabirds nest and breed in the rocks of CAYO PÁJARO. Last but not least, divers can marvel at an endless cavalcade of different types of fish off CAYO ROSARIO.

GRANJA DE TORTUGA
This turtle farm in Combinado, on the northwesternmost tip of Cayo Largo, is open to visitors.

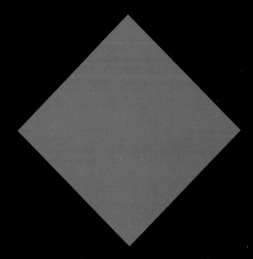

Practical information

Ⅲ	Air conditioning	P	Parking
🏃	Reductions for children	♿	Access for disabled people
☎	Telephone in the rooms	🌱	Garden
📺	TV in the rooms	🎵	Music
🐾	Pets not allowed	❀	View
🔇	Quiet	C	City center
🌂	Terrace	🌊	Swimming pool

◆ PREPARATIONS

USEFUL INFORMATION

→ IN LONDON
■ **Cuban consulate**
15 Grape Street
London WC2 8DR
Tel. 020 7240 2488
■ **Cuban embassy and Tourist Office**
167 High Holborn,
London WC1V
Tel. 020 7379 1706

→ IN THE USA
■ **Amcham cuba**
910 17th Street
NW Suite 422
Washington
DC 20006-2601
Tel. 202 833 3548

ENTRY REQUIREMENTS

→ 'TOURIST CARD'
All visitors, including children, must have a 'tourist card', which replaces the visa. It can be obtained from travel agencies and is valid for one month.

→ HOTEL VOUCHER
Customs officials will ask you the name of your hotel for your first two nights, so it i better to book accommodation before departure. If you do not have a reservation, the Cuban tourist office will allocate a hotel of its choice.

→ PASSPORT
You need a passport with at least six months validity.

→ AIRPORT TAX
$20 in cash payable on leaving Cuba.

AIRLINE COMPANIES

> BRITISH AIRWAYS
> Information
> Tel. 0345 222787
> Reservations
> Tel. 0345 222111

→ IN LONDON
■ **British Airways**
156 Regent Street
London W1R 5TA
Tel. 020 7434 4700
■ **Cubana**
49 Conduit Street
London W1R 9FB
Tel. 020 7734 1165

■ **Iberia**
Change at Madrid.
27–9 Glasshouse St,
London W1R
Tel. 020 7830 0011

→ IN THE USA
There are no direct flights to Cuba from the US. However there are special charter flights for which American citizens must obtain government permission.
■ **From Canada**
CUBANA AIRLINES
Tel. 1-514-871-1222
CANADA 3000
Tel. 1-905-612-2100
■ **From Mexico**
CUBANA AIRLINES
Tel. 1-514-871-1222
MEXICANA AIRLINES
Tel. 52-5-325-0990

→ PRICES
Approx. £450 from London; $500 from Canada, depending on season.

→ CONFIRMATION
You must confirm your return flight with the airline two or three days before your return.

WHEN TO GO?
Tourist seasons: July, August, Christmas and Easter.

→ JULY-AUGUST
High season, very hot. Higher prices. Carnivals in Havana and Santiago de Cuba.

→ DECEMBER-FEB
Cuban winter: not so hot, fresher, fewer tourists, can be overcast and rainy.

AVERAGE TEMPERATURES (°F)		
Month	Sea	Air
Jan.	75	72
Feb.	75	72
Mar.	77	75
Apr.	79	77
May	82	79
June	86	81
July	86	81
Aug.	86	81
Sep.	81	81
Oct.	77	79
Nov.	75	77
Dec.	75	73

→ **MARCH-JUNE AND SEPTEMBER**
Very pleasant, fewer tourists. Heavy, brief showers are likely.
→ **OCTOBER-NOVEMBER**
Hurricanes possible but they do not occur every year.

CLIMATE
→ **SUBTROPICAL**
■ **Sunshine**: around 330 days per year.
■ **Nightfall**: winter 6pm, summer 8pm.
■ **Humidity levels**: up to 78 percent. Nov.-May: dry season. June-Oct.: wet season.

TIME DIFFERENCE
GMT minus five hours: when it is 5pm in London or 11am in Los Angeles it is midday in Havana. Havana and New York City share the same time.

ITINERARIES
→ **ONE WEEK**
Much too short. A quick tour of Havana, the Viñales Valley, Varadero and Trinidad.

→ **TWO WEEKS**
You can also take in Cienfuegos, Santa Clara, the Zapata Peninsula.

→ **THREE WEEKS +**
Ideal if you also want to explore Oriente; Camagüey, Holguín, Santiago de Cuba and Baracoa can be added to your two-week program.

TOUR OPERATORS & TRAVEL AGENCIES
→ **IN THE UK**
■ **Caribtours**
161 Fulham Road
London SW3
Tel. 020 7581 3517
■ **Exodus Travels**
9 Weir Road
London SW12
Tel. 020 8675 5550
■ **Journey Latin America**
14-16 Devonshire Rd
London W4 2HD

Tel. 020 8747 8315
Fax 020 8747 1312
■ **South American Experience**
47 Causton Street
London SW1P 4AT
Tel. 020 7976 5511
Fax 020 7967 6908

→ **IN THE USA**
■ **Marazul Tours**
4100 Park Avenue
Weehawken,
NJ 07087
Tel. 201 840 6711
Fax 201 840 6719
www.marazultours.com
■ **Cubatravel**
Tijuana, Baja California, Mexico
Tel. 526 686 5298
■ **Atevo Travel**
1633 Bay Shore Highway, Suite 225, Burlingame, CA 94010, USA.
Tel. 650 652 1000
All are specialists for US citizens wanting to travel to Cuba.

→ **MUSIC AND DANCE SPECIALISTS**
Planet Cuba
1254 Olive Street Road, Suite 241, St Louis,
MO 63141, USA
Tel. 877 665 4321

→ **HUNTING SPECIALISTS**
International adventure
308 Mikel, Maryland Heights, MO 63043, USA
Tel. 314 209 9800

MONEY
→ **CURRENCY: 3 TYPES OF CURRENCY**
■ **Cuban pesos**
The national currency is divided into centavos.
1 Cuban peso = 100 centavos
£1 = 35 Cuban pesos
$1 = 20 Cuban pesos
(March 2000)
■ **Dollars**
All tourist services must be paid for in dollars.
Organized tours: no point in changing into Cuban pesos.
■ **Convertible pesos**
Currency on a par with dollars.

BUDGET TYPE
■ **Inexpensive**
Room in a family home: $10-$30
Hotel: $20-$40
Paladar: $6-$8
■ **Mid-price**
Hotel: $40-$60
Restaurant: $8-$10
■ **Upscale**
Hotel: $80 or more
Restaurant: $20 or more

HOW MUCH THINGS COST
■ **Beer**
In a café or hotel costs between $0.50 and $2.
■ **Coca-Cola**
In a café or hotel costs between $0.50 and $2.
■ **Coffee** Around $1.
■ **Bottle of water** Between $0.50 and $2.
■ **Sandwich** Between $1 and $3.
■ **Meal**
In a *paladar*, expect to pay $3 to $10, in a reasonable restaurant or hotel, between $15 and $30.
■ **Bus ticket** 10 cents.
■ **Postcard** 25 cents.
■ **Stamp** 40 cents.
■ **Discotheque** Admission costs between $5 and $10, depending on the venue.
■ **Cabaret** Between $25 and $50.

GIFTS
The Cubans are legendary for their hospitality and give presents easily: they will appreciate similar treatment in return.

→ **GIFT SUGGESTIONS**
Bathroom essentials: beauty products, razors, shaving foam, toothpaste, bar of soap, perfume. Sweets, toys, school equipment, clothes, puncture repair kits...

USEFUL ITEMS
Sunglasses and sun hat, torch, flat plug

adapter, camera film, padlocks and keys for your suitcase...

HEALTH
→ **REMEMBER TO PACK**
■ **Health care items**
Tampons and sanitary towels, sun cream, mosquito repellent, sticking plasters, antiseptic cream.
■ **Medications**
Pharmacies in Cuba often run low on stock. Antibiotics, pain-killers, medication for gastroenteritis, ENT medication, antihistamines and treatment for insect bites and stings.
Travel tip
Before you return, give any unused medication to a Cuban family or family practitioner.

→ **AIDS**
Cuba is not a high risk country but AIDS is on the increase, particularly due to the growth of tourism.
→ **CONTRACEPTION**
Do not forget to pack condoms: they are extremely hard to buy in Cuba and are of very poor quality.
→ **VACCINATIONS**
It is recommended to be immunized against Hepatitis A and typhoid.

■ **Where to find out in London**
British Airways Travel Clinics
156 Regent Street
London W1R 5TA
Tel. 020 7439 9584;
■ **Where to find out in New York**
Travel Medicine Center of New York
311 East 79th Street, Suite A, NY 10021.
Tel. 212 879 6086
For other cities in US Division of Quarantine
Fax 888 535 3599
www.cdc.gov/travel

Santa Cruz del Norte · Varadero · **HAVANA** · San Antonio de los Baños · Artemisa · **Matanzas** · Cárdenas · Corralillo · Güines · Sagua la Grande · Minas de Matahambre · **Pinar del Río** · Colón · **Santa Clara** · Mantua · Jagüey Grande · Aguada de Pasajeros · Cienfuegos · Placetas · La Fé · Isabel Rubio · **Nueva Gerona** · Trinidad · Isle of Youth · Cayo Largo

GETTING AROUND CUBA

→ FINDING AN ADDRESS

The city is organized in *cuadras* (blocks).

■ **Example 1**
Calle Humboldt #263, apto. 3 e/ O y P (Vedado) La Habana
This means:
263, Humboldt Street, between streets O and P (perpendicular to Humboldt Street) apartment 3, in the Vedado quarter of Havana.

■ **Example 2**
Calle San Ignacio #22 esq. Empedrado
This means:
22, San Ignacio Street, at the corner of Empedrado Street.

→ STREET NAMES

In some cities, the streets have been renamed, often at the time of the Revolution. In Havana, Santiago de Cuba and Trinidad, however, the old names are still in use.

■ **Example**
In Havana, 'Paseo del Prado' is still used despite its official name of 'Paseo de Martí'.
Travel tip
In the provinces, there are often no street names. You will therefore have to depend on the kindness of locals for directions.

BY AIR

→ AIRPORTS

■ **José Martí airport in Havana**
Av. Van Troi y Boyeros
Tel. (7) 45 31 33
Three terminals:
1st: domestic flights
2nd: flights to Miami
3rd: international flights.
■ **Varadero**
Tel. (5) 6 21 33
■ **Santiago de Cuba**
Tel. (226) 9 10 14

→ RESERVATIONS FOR DOMESTIC FLIGHTS

■ **Cubana de Aviación**
Calle 23 #64, esq. Infanta (La Rampa) Vedado, Havana
Tel. (7) 33 49 49
Fax (7) 66 23 17
Some representative prices (single ticket from Havana):
Santiago: $90
Varadero: $29
Cayo Largo: $50
■ **Aerotaxi**
Calle 27 #102 e/ M y N, Vedado, Havana
Tel. (7) 33 40 64
Customized travel. Airplane (11 seats) and crew. Example: Havana: $490 (1 h)

'BOTELLA' (HITCH-HIKING)

Most people hitch as public transport is so poor.

BY BUS

■ **Bus terminal**
Ave. Independencia y 19 de Mayo (Vedado), Havana
Tel. (7) 70 33 92
Tickets
Buy these at least an hour before departure.

■ **Viazul**
Ave. 26 y Zoológico (Nuevo Vedado), Havana
Tel. (7) 81 14 13
Ideal for exploring the island from Havana. Air-conditioned buses to all the main tourist cities. Affordable, punctual, comfortable.

BY TWO-WHEELED VEHICLE

You can hire scooters and small mopeds (not motorbikes) in all the tourist resorts.

→ BY BICYCLE

Excellent way of seeing the island. Inquire at hotels in the provinces and ask locals in Havana. Average price: $2–3/day.
Precautions
Remember to take a sturdy anti-theft device.

BY TAXI

→ WHERE TO FIND THEM

Used widely for short journeys in the city, found near hotels and tourist centers.

→ BASIC PRICE

In Havana, depending on the distance, $2–5.

→ DIFFERENT CATEGORIES

■ **State taxis**
With meter.
■ **Several companies**
PANATAXI
(air-conditioned vehicles)
Tel. (7) 55 55 55 to 59
HABANA TAXI
Tel. (7) 41 96 00
CUBATAXI
Tel. (7) 79 16 42
TURISTAXI
Tel. (7) 33 55 39 to 42
■ **Private official taxis**
No meter.
Fix the price of your journey before you leave. These are often 1950s classic American cars.
■ **Unofficial taxis**
No meter.
Fix the price of your journey before you leave.

BY TRAIN

Not advised.
Not punctual and uncomfortable.

→ RAILWAY STATION

Egido y Arsenal (Old Havana)

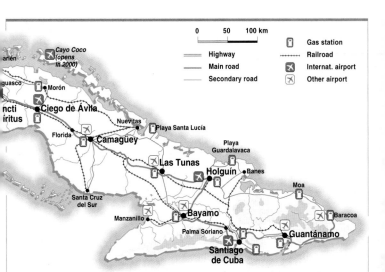

Reservations:
8am–5pm
Tel. (7) 61 42 59
■ **Hershey train**
Tel. (7) 62 48 88
Original carriages
(1918). Catch
the train from
Casablanca or
Muelle de la Coubre
(Old Havana).
Runs to Matanzas
and vicinity.
■ **Estación 19 de
Noviembre**
Calle Factor
e/ Canill y Tulipán
Havana
Tel. (7) 81 44 31
Tickets: 1 hour
before departure.
Trains to villages in
Havana Province.

BY CAR
→ **ROAD INFORMATION**
One highway:
Ocho Vías;
and a Carretera
Central.
Well-developed
road network
(but not always
well maintained).

→ **MAPS OF THE
COUNTRY**
■ **El Navegante**
Calle Mercaderes,
#115 e/ Obispo y
Obrapía
(Old Havana).
But also from
hotels and tourist
centers.

→ **CAR RENTAL**
Price
Depends on the
season, number
of days and
class of car.
Example for a
week: between
$45 and $80 per
day, insurance
an extra $5 to
$20 per day.
■ **Companies
Havanautos**
Ave. 1a e/. O,
Miramar
Tel. (7) 24 06 47
The most reliable.
■ **Cubanacán OK**
Tel. (7) 24 16 46
■ **Rex Reservation**
Tel. (7) 33 91 60 to
63
■ **Gaviota**
Tel. (7) 20 46 50
■ **Transtur (24 hrs)**
Tel. (7) 24 76 44

→ **GAS STATIONS**
■ **Nationwide**
There are only
eighty Cupet/Cimex
gas stations in
the whole of Cuba
(*see map above*), so
make sure you fill
up in the cities
before you set off
on a long journey.
■ **In Havana**
RIVIERA (Malecón y
Paseo); L Y 17;
TANGANA
(Línea y Malecón);
5 Y 112 (Miramar);

SANTA CATALINA
(Cerro);
BOYERO Y AYESTARÁN
(Nuevo Vedado);
EL CHIQUITICO
BOYERO
(near the airport).

GETTING TO THE
ISLE OF YOUTH
→ **BY AIR**
■ **Airport Nueva
Gerona**
Tel. (61) 22 690
One-way
ticket $22
■ **Aerotaxi**
Charter an
eleven-seater
airplane $550
(return journey).

→ **HYDROPLANE
OR BOAT**
To Batabanó port.
Hydroplane
2 h/$11
Boat: 6 h/$8

GETTING
AROUND HAVANA
→ **VAIVÉN BUS**
9am–9.15pm
Every 50 mins.
Leaves from
Plaza de Albear,
opposite the
Floridita.
Visits all the
city's tourist
sights (23 stops).
Use as often as
you want on the
same day for
$4 per day.

→ **CYCLOBUS**
Park El Curita:
Águila y Dragones.
Bus taking cyclists
through the Havana
tunnel with their
bicycles.

→ **TAXIS COCO**
(Two people)
These yellow and
coconut-shaped
conveyances are
opposite the
Hotel Inglaterra.
$5 to cross Old
Havana as far as
Miramar.

→ **BICITAXI**
Bicycle-taxi,
around $5 per
hour. Fix a price
before you leave.

→ **FERRY**
To get to the
other side of
Havana Bay,
Regla and
Casablanca.
■ **Embarkation**
Muelle de Luz
(Old Havana).
■ **Frequency**
Every 30 mins or
every hour.

→ **HORSE-DRAWN
CARRIAGE**
Mainly in
Old Havana.
$5 per hour.
Fix a price before
you leave.

233

USEFUL ADDRESSES
- **British embassy**
Calle 34 #708, Miramar, Havana. Tel. (7) 24 17 71 (open daily)
- **United States Special interest section**
Calzada e/ L y M, Vedado, Havana Tel. (7) 33 35 31

MONEY
→ **CURRENCY EXCHANGE**
- **Banks**
Usually open daily from 8am to 3pm. The most efficient networks are: BFI (Banco Financiero Internacional) and BANDEC
- **Bank cards**
Only International Visa, Mastercard and Eurocard credit cards are accepted in the major hotels and restaurants. American cards are not accepted.
- **Buying dollars**
With international credit cards in banks and large hotels (more flexible opening hours).
- **Other currencies**
Other international currencies, such as sterling, can be exchanged in foreign banks, but US dollars are the recommended currency to bring into Cuba.
- **Travelers checks**
There is an average commission charge of 3 percent.

Travel tip
You are not allowed to exchange money in the street. If you want to change dollars into pesos, try one of the Cadeca banks, which are located all over major cities in Cuba.

→ **PAYMENT METHODS**
Paying by credit card: luxury restaurants, hotels, car hire. Travelers checks can also be used.

→ **LOSS OR THEFT OF BANK CARDS**
Centro de tarjetas de crédito (fincimex)
Calle 23 e/ L y M, Vedado, Havana Tel. (7) 33 44 44 Fax (7) 33 40 01 Open Mon.–Fri. 8.30am–5.30pm

COMMUNICATION
→ **MAIL**
Standard letters and postcards take three weeks or sometimes more to get from Cuba to the United Kingdom or the United States, and vice versa.

→ **EXPRESS MAIL**
- **Cubanacán**
Unit 49, Skylines, Limeharbour, London E14 9TS Tel. 020 7537 7909 Fax. 020 7537 7747 Sending packages and letters usually takes 48 hours to Havana, 92 hours at the most to the provinces.
- **Cubanacán Express**
Ave. 31 #7230, esq. 41 (Playa) Havana Tel. (7) 24 78 48 Fax (7) 24 24 99 Branches of Cubanacán are found in all the main cities in Cuba. Also swift dispatch of standard mail.

→ **FAX**
In all the large hotels: around $8/min.

→ **TELEPHONE**
- **Phone cards**
$10 and $20 On sale at all Etecsa offices, banks, airports, international post offices, tourist sites.
- **Mobile phones Cubacel**
You can hire mobiles in the main cities on the island. Inquiries in Havana, to Calle 28 #510 e/ 5 y 7 (Miramar) and at the José Martí international airport. Tel. (7) 80 22 22. Open Mon.–Fri. 8am–5pm, Sat. 8am–noon.
- **Directory enquiries**
Tel. 113
- **Telegrams**
Tel. 81 88 44

ELECTRICITY
Single-phase current: 110 volts (recent hotels: 220 volts). Remember to bring American standard flat pin plugs. *Apagones* (power cuts) only affect private homes.

TOURIST INFORMATION
- **Infotour**
Calle Obispo #358 e/ Habana y Compostela Old Havana Tel. (7) 33 33 33 Open 9am–noon and 1–8.30pm
- **Infotour**
Calle 112 y 5a Ave. (Miramar) Open 8.30am–8pm

Dialing codes	
Isle of Youth	61
Sancti Spiritus	41
Pinar del Río	82
Havana Province	64
Havana City	7
Guantánamo	21
Matanzas	52
Santiago de Cuba	226
Cienfuegos	432
Granma	23
Santa Clara	422
Holguín	24
Trinidad	419
Las Tunas	31
Ciego de Ávila	33
Camagüey	322

BOOK STORES
- **La Internacional**
Calle Obispo #526 (Old Havana)
- **Librería Internacional Fernando Ortiz**
Calle L #202 esq. 27 (Vedado)
- **La Bella Habana**
Calle O'Reilly #4 (Old Havana)
- **Librería Cervantes**
Calle Bernaza #9 esq. Obispo (Old Havana) Secondhand books at attractive prices (closed Sun.).

MARKETS
Open-air craft markets (*ferias*)
- **Calle Tacón**
(Old Havana, close to the cathedral) Open daily except Sun.
- **Malecón y D**
(Vedado) Open daily except Mon.

PHOTOS
Buy camera film in the stores in large hotels. You must not photograph military areas and some museums (most of them charge for taking photos).

FOREIGN NEWSPAPERS
International Press Center
Calle 23 e/ O y Havana Tel. (7) 32 05 26

HEALTH
→ **WATER**
Do not drink tap water.

→ **CLINICS**
A network of international clinics reserved for tourists. Excellent health care. Consultation: $20–30.

→ **CITY CLINICS**
- **Havana**
Calle 20 #4101 esq. 43 (Miramar) Tel. (7) 24 28 11 to 14 Fax (7) 24 28 56

■ **Santiago de Cuba**
Calle 13 y 14 Rpto
Vista Alegre
Tel. (226) 33 50 15
■ **Cienfuegos**
Calle 37 #202 e/ 2 y
4 Punta Gorda
Tel. (432) 33 50 71
■ **Trinidad**
Calle Lino Pérez
#130, esq. Reforma
Tel. (419) 33 91
■ **Varadero**
Calle 60 y 1a
Tel. (5) 66 77 10

→ EMERGENCIES
All hotels have a
medical team on
hand and there is
an accident and
emergency
department in all
Cuba's hospitals.

**→ INTERNATIONAL
PHARMACY**
In every
international clinic:
Havana
Calle 41 e/ 18 y 20
(Miramar)
Tel. (7) 24 43 50
Open 9am–9pm.

→ FOR DIVERS
Decompression
chambers in
Santiago de Cuba,
the Isle of Youth,
Varadero, Havana.

USEFUL TIPS
A cheerful smile will
help to iron out
most difficulties.
Dress smartly when
you go out in the
evening; the Cubans
will appreciate the
effort.
Do not disturb
Cubans from 9pm to
10.30pm as this is
when they watch
the *novela* (soap
opera). Cubans like
to take their time
and it is regarded as
quite acceptable to
keep someone
waiting an hour!
If you are invited to
someone's home,
your hosts will
appreciate a small
gift: Coca-Cola,
cakes, ice-cream,
chocolate, rum…
Piropos, gallant
compliments

paid by men
to women,
particularly in
the street, may be
amusing, poetic,
original, but are
rarely vulgar…

SAFETY
Watch out for
pickpockets
(cameras, cash,
jewelry…). Leave
valuable objects
and passports
in the hotel
safe or in a
padlocked
suitcase.

SOUVENIRS
→ CRAFTS
Traditional objects
made of leather,
basketwork, marble.
Dolls representing
figures from the
santería religion.
■ **Palacio de la
Artesanía**
Calle Cuba #64
e/ Peña Pobre y
Cuarteles (Old
Havana). All types
of souvenirs.
■ **Bazar 43**
Calle 22 #4109 e/ 41
y 43 (Miramar)
Typical Afro-Cuban
objects.
■ **El Quitrín**
Obispo y San Ignacio
(Old Havana)
Arts and crafts
center. Woven
products,
embroidery,
dresses, tablecloths,
guayabera…

→ ART
You need an export
permit to take
paintings and objets
d'art out of the
country (a means of
protecting national
works of art).

**Fondo de Bienes
Culturales**
Calle Muralla, #107
(Old Havana)
Paintings, ceramics,
jewelry, sculptures
and objets d'art by
Cuban artists.

→ JEWELRY
Superb pieces of
jewelry made of
black coral at prices
to suit all pockets.

→ COFFEE
Cubita is the most
common brand of
Cuban coffee.

→ CIGARS
These are much less
expensive in Cuba
than in the United
Kingdom or the
United States.
Wide choice.
Examples:
Cohiba Lanceros
(box of 25 cigars):
$320;
Montecristo #4
(box of 25 cigars):
$65.
Do not buy cigars
in the street.
Although they may
look authentic and
may be much less
expensive, they are
often made at home
(unsmokable) or
stolen, and lack the
necessary guarantee
and rigorous quality
control. Customs
officials may ask you
to produce invoices
for all purchases.
Without these
documents, the
cigars will be
confiscated.
In the large hotels,
there is often a *Casa
del Tabaco* selling a
wide range of
products.

■ **Casa del Habano**
Calle Mercaderes,
esq. Obrapía
(Old Havana)
■ **Casa del Habano**
Fábrica Partagás
Calle Industria #520
(Old Havana)
■ **El Patio Colonial**
Obispo, esq.
Baratillo (Old
Havana)
■ **La casa del Tabaco
y Ron**
Obispo, esq.
Monserratte
(Old Havana)
■ **El Palacio del
Tabaco**
Fábrica La Corona
Zulueta, esq. Morro
(Centro Habana)

→ MUSIC
Cassettes, CDs with
a Cuban beat: salsa,
merengue, cha-cha-
cha, *Nueva Trova*,
rumba, conga;
musical instruments
(bongo,
tumbadora…).
Artex Stores
L y 23 (Vedado)
CDs, cassettes,
musical instruments,
tee-shirts…

→ RUM
Its price varies
according to the
brand and age.
Examples:
Havana Club
Silver Dry: $4.
Seven-year-old
Havana Club: $10.
**La Casa del Tabaco y
Ron**
Obispo, esq.
Monseratte
(Old Havana)

→ CLOTHES
■ **Guayabera**
Traditional Cuban
men's shirt. Sisal hats.
■ **La Maison**
Calle 16 e/ 7a y 9a
ave., Vedado
Exclusive store.
Bags, accessories,
silver, jewelry
(antique and new),
Cuban designer
clothes…

→ AS WELL AS
Stamps, posters,
coins, machetes,
hammocks…

◆ ENTERTAINMENT

CULTURAL ACTIVITIES
■ **Mercadu SA**
Specialist seminars, language classes, conferences, lectures, workshops, courses in Cuban culture.
Calle 13 #951 esq. 8 (Vedado) Havana
Tel. (7) 33 3893
Fax (7) 33 2028
■ **Casa del Caribe**
Courses on Cuban culture, Afro-Cuban religions, history, music, dance and ecotourism.
Calle 13 #154 Vista Alegre, Santiago de Cuba
Tel. (226) 42 285
Fax (226) 42 387
■ **ISA/Instituto Superior de Arte**
Classes in percussion, dance, visual arts, music, theater, esthetics.
Calle 120 #110 Cubanacán Havana
Tel. (7) 21 60 75
Fax (7) 33 66 33
■ **Folkcuba**
International forum of Havana folklore. Classes in dance, music and Cuban folk culture given by the Conjunto Folklórico Nacional de Cuba.
Calle 4 e/ Calzada y 5a Havana
Tel. (7) 31 34 67
■ **Prodanza**
The Cuban modern dance company in Havana.
Classes for foreign visitors.
Tel. (7) 20 91 42

HORSE RIDING
At hotels, clubs, seaside resorts or with locals.
■ **Club Hípico Iberoamericano**
On the northwest corner of Parque Lenin (southern Havana)
Tel. (7) 44 10 58
■ **Ranches**
Ranches reserved for tourists.

■ **El Oasis**
Baconao
■ **La Casa del Campesino**
Trinidad
■ **Hacienda Los Molinos**
One of the best cattle farms, between Trinidad and Sancti Spíritus.

FISHING
Guide and equipment on site.
Charge for fishing permit.

Hoteles Horizontes
Calle 23 #156 e/ y O (Vedado) Havana
Tel. (7) 33 40 042

→ **SEA FISHING**
With heavy tackle (spring/summer) and light tackle (November/April): Playa del Este, Varadero, Cayo Largo.

→ **FRESHWATER FISHING**
Lake Zaza (Sancti Spíritus) Lake Hanabanilla (Villa Clara) and Lake Redonda (Ciego de Ávila)

DIVING
Fresh water diving possible in the underwater caves.

Travel tip
Aim to head for the south and west coast from November to April (when it is much quieter) and the north coast from May to September.

■ **International Dive Centers**
HOTEL COLONY (Isle of Youth)
MARÍA LA GORDA (Pinar del Río). For the latter, inquiries to Marsub, Calle B #310, esq. 15
Tel. (7) 33 30 55
CLUB BARRACUDA Cubanacán
Tel. (7) 61 34 81
MARINA GAVIOTA Gaviota Group
Tel. (7) 66 77 55
ACUA DIVING CLUB Puerto Sol
Tel. (7) 66 80 63

HIKING
Although registered hiking trails are currently being laid in the nature reserves, there are not many signposted paths and large-scale maps are rare. Pony trekking is also available.

Remember
You must be accompanied by a guide at all times.

→ **SEA HIKING SUGGESTIONS**
■ **From three days...**
SIERRA MAESTRA Authorization essential.
Admission: from $8 to $15 depending on the hike. The walk is both beautiful and taxing. Guides at the Villa Domingo or La Platica. There are several footpaths, camping sites and mountain shelters along the way.
■ **... to several hours**
SIERRA DEL ESCAMBRAY Picturesque circular walks leaving from Trinidad. Inquire at: Gaviota Tours of Topes de Collantes
Tel. (419) 40 117 or the Trinidad and Ancón Hotels.

SIERRA DEL ROSARIO AND SIERRA DE LOS ÓRGANOS
A large number of caves and limestone *mogotes* afford the chance to indulge in the more specialized pursuits of speleology and rock-climbing.
LAS TERRAZAS Several short, gentle walks (from one to five miles) to the island's huge coffee plantations.

SPELEOLOGY
Inquiries to the travel agencies or hotels.
Cubatour
Calle L, esq. 23 (downstairs at the Hotel Habana Libre)
Tel. (7) 33 41 35
Offers trips lasting several days in the cave system of Majagua-Canteres.

Remember
You are not allowed to visit the caves alone. You must go with a Cuban guide.

SAILING
Winter is the best season for sailing. Many organizations hire out boats including Cubanacán, Puerto Sol, KP Winter. Mooring and offices in most of the island's marinas:
■ **Marina Tarará**
Playas del Este, 14 miles east of Havana
■ **Marina Acua**
Ave. Kawama e/ 3 y 4, Varadero

Precautions
The American government will not allow ships to put in at US ports if they have already made a stopover in Cuba. It is therefore preferable to charter a yacht on the island.

THREE CULTURAL INSTITUTIONS

There are three cultural, traditional and creative institutions in virtually all Cuba's cities.

→ LA CASA DE LA CULTURA

Community arts center. Varied range of artistic activities in the main cities and all the quarters of the capital: *bolero*, rock, salsa, lectures, exhibitions, ballets...

→ LA PEÑA

Typical cultural gathering which may be organized in a Cuban institution or, more spontaneously, at someone's home. Artistic evening during which people read poems, play music and sing.

→ LA CASA DE LA TROVA

This is where you will find the *trovadores*, writers, composers and performers who sing and play the guitar. This is the place for the best performances of the Cuban musical genre called the *trova*.

PINAR DEL RÍO

→ CABARET/ RESTAURANT

Rumayor
Carretera Viñales, 1 mile, Pinar del Río Restaurant open noon–10pm; shows at 11pm and 1.30am, followed by a discotheque. Admission: $5. Excellent open-air show.

HAVANA

→ CABARETS

■ **Tropicana**
Calle 72, esq. ave. 43 #4504 Marianao Tel. (7) 27 01 10 Daily 9pm–2am Admission $50 and $60 (show and a cocktail).Bookings

taken in all hotels. A spectacular open-air cabaret in a Cuban garden. Cuban and Caribbean show lasting 1½ hours. The entertainment is a slick blend of classical dance, Cuban rhythms and acrobatics.

■ **Cabaret Parisien**
Hotel Nacional, Calle O, esq. 21 Tel. (7) 33 35 64. Open 9.30pm–2.30am. Two shows nightly, followed by a discotheque. Admission $30. Plush, intimate cabaret. The show, based on the history and music of Cuba, is called *L'Ajiaco* (a Cuban meal in which everything is thrown in together), a symbol of the Cuban cultural melting pot. It finishes with a boisterous carnival on stage and in the auditorium.

→ DISCOTHEQUES

■ **Salón Internacional**
Hotel Riviera (former Palacio de la Salsa) Ave. Paseo y Malecón Tel. (7) 33 40 51 Show and disco 10pm–3am. Admission $5.

■ **Café Cantante**
Teatro Nacional de Cuba, Paseo y 39, Plaza de la Revolución Tel. (7) 33 57 13 Open daily 10.30pm–2am Admission: $15–20. A discotheque frequented more by

Cubans than tourists.

→ JAZZ

La Zorra y el Cuervo
Calle 23 #155 e/ N y O, Vedado Open daily 9pm–4am. Admission $5. The home of Latino jazz in the heart of la Rampa.

→ BOLERO

Pico Blanco, Rincón del Feeling
('the corner of feeling') Hotel St John's, 15th story, Calle O e/ 23 y Humboldt, Vedado Tel. (7) 33 37 40 Open 9.30pm–3am Admission $5. An evening of *boleros*, intimate atmosphere, ideal for a romantic night out. Perfect for the slightly older age group.

→ SHOWS

El Gran Palenque
Calle 4 #103 e/. Calzada y 5, Vedado Tel. (7) 30 39 39 Fax (7) 33 38 10 Open every second Sat. from 3pm to 5pm. Admission $5. Home of the famous Conjunto Folklórico Nacional de Cuba, which keeps Cuba's cultural and folk traditions alive, whether of Spanish, French (*tumba francesa*) or African origin. An open-air show in a large tree-lined patio. Not to be missed!

→ ARTS CENTERS

Casa de la Amistad
Calle 17 y Paseo, Vedado Superb setting: neoclassical house surrounded by a garden. A lively showcase for bands and vocalists. Excellent atmosphere.

→ AND IN THE STREET...

El Callejón de Hammel
Aramburu y Hospital (Centro Habana) Open Sun from noon. Admission free. A cul-de-sac transformed into an arts center and decorated with frescos by Salvador González. Afro-Cuban shows in which the *rumba* reigns supreme!

TRINIDAD

→ DISCOTHEQUE

Cueva Ayatala
Carretera Hotel Las Cuevas Open daily 10pm–4am. Admission $3. A narrow stony path leads to this ultra-fashionable venue in a cave. You can dance among stalagmites and stalactites to Cuban and techno music. Range of cocktails.

SANTIAGO DE CUBA

■ **Casa de la Trova**
Calle Heredia e/ San Félix y San Pedro Open Tues.–Sun. from 11am. Admission $1. Traditional musicians and salsa bands.

■ **Casa de las Tradiciones**
Calle Rabi #154 e/ Princesa y San Fernando (Tívoli quarter) Open Mon.–Fri. except Tues. from 7pm. Admission $1. Unusual cultural hotspot in an apartment. Traditional music and dancing. A must!

◆ ENGLISH-SPANISH GLOSSARY

Addresses (abbreviations)
e/: between; **avenida (ave., avda.)**: avenue; **via**: road;
reparto (rpto.), barrio: quarter; **esq.**: at the corner of
two streets; **apartamento (apto.)**: apartment

A

address: dirección
airplane: avión
airport: aeropuerto
all inclusive: todo
incluido
arrival: llegada

B

**bank note (travel
ticket):** tickete (boleto)
bank: banco
bath towel: toalla
bathroom: sala de baño
beans: frijoles
bed: cama
beef: res
beer: cerveza
bill: factura
**black coffee (white
coffee):** café solo
(café con leche)
boat: barco
bread: pan
breakfast: desayuno
bureau de change:
cambio
butter: mantequilla

C

cake: pastel
car: máquina, carro
check: cuenta
cheese: queso
chicken (fried): pollo
(frito)
chocolate: chocolate
city: ciudad
closed: cerrado(a)
credit card: tarjeta
crédito
customs: aduana

D

date: fecha
departure: salida
dessert: postre
(to) drink: beber
driving license: licencia
de conducir

E - F - G

(to) eat: comer
egg: huevo
envelope: sobre
expensive: caro, cara
fall: otoño
far from: lejos de
fish: pescado
fruit juice: jugo
fruit: fruta
gas: gasolina
glass: vaso
good day: buenos días
good evening: buenas
tardes

H - I - J

ham: jamón
hotel: hotel

house: casa
ice cream: helado

L - M

letter: carta
luggage: equipaje
lunch: almuerzo
madam: señora
mailbox: buzón
map, plan: mapa
meat: carne
menu: menú,
carta
minced meat:
picadillo
miss: señorita
money: dinero
month: mes

January:	enero
February:	febrero
March:	marzo
April:	abril
May:	mayo
June:	junio
July:	julio
August:	agosto
September:	septiembre
October:	octubre
November:	noviembre
December:	diciembre

Mr.: señor
museum: museo

N

near: cerca de
now: ahora
number: número

one:	uno
two:	dos
three:	tres
four:	cuatro
five:	cinco
six:	seis
seven:	siete
eight:	ocho
nine:	nueve
ten:	diez
eleven:	once
twelve:	doce
thirteen:	trece
fourteen:	catorce
fifteen:	quince
sixteen:	dieciseis
seventeen:	diecisiete
eighteen:	dieciocho
nineteen:	diecinueve
twenty:	veinte
hundred:	cien
thousand:	mil

O - P - Q

oil: aceite
omelet: tortilla
open: abierto(a)
place setting/meal:
cubiertos
plate: plato
pork: cerdo
post office: oficina
de correos
postcard: postal
potato: papa
price: precio

R - S

**railroad station (bus
terminal):** estación de
ferrocarriles (terminal
de ómnibus)
red wine (white): vino
tinto (blanco)
restaurant: restaurante
round trip: ida y
vuelta
rice: arroz
road: carretera
salad: ensalada
salt: sal
sauce: salsa
seafood: mariscos
serviette: servilleta
sheet: sábana
shower: ducha
shrimps: camarones
single room (double):
habitación sencilla
(doble)
spring: primavera
stamp: sello
store: tienda
straight ahead: todo
derecho
street: calle
sugar: azúcar
summer: verano
supper: cena

T - V - W - Y

table: mesa
tea: té
(to) telephone: llamar
por teléfono
theater: teatro
tip: propina
today: hoy
toilets: servicios, baños
tomorrow: mañana
(to) travel: viajar
travel agency: agencia
de viajes
travelers' checks:
cheques de viaje
vegetables: verduras
village: pueblo
water: agua
week: semana

Monday:	lunes
Tuesday:	martes
Wednesday:	miércoles
Thursday:	jueves
Friday:	viernes
Saturday:	sábado
Sunday:	domingo

winter: invierno
year: año
yesterday: ayer
yucca: yuca

COMMON
EXPRESSIONS

Book a room: reservar
una habitación
**Can you give me a
wake-up call?:** ¿Puede
despertarme?
Cheap: barato(a)
How are you?: ¿Cómo
está?

How long?: ¿Cuánto
tiempo?
How much is this?:
¿Cuánto cuesta?
I don't speak Spanish:
no hablo español
I don't understand:
no entiendo
I'm sorry: disculpe
I would like: quisiera
Please: Por favor
Pleased to meet you:
encantado(a)
See you soon: hasta
luego
Thank you (very much):
(muchas) gracias
To the right, to the left:
a la derecha,
a la izquierda
What is the time?:
¿Qué hora es?
When?: ¿Cuándo?
Where is (are)...?:
¿Dónde está(n)...?
Yes, no: sí, no

CUBAN DICTIONARY

agromercado: farmers'
market
apagón: power cut
babalao: priest
(santería)
balseros: Cuban boat
people
barbudos: (lit. the
bearded ones)
revolutionaries
bodega: store
bohío: peasant's house
buró de turismo:
tourist office
camello: large coach in
Havana
cayo: tiny island
comprobante: invoice
guagua: bus
guajiro (a): peasant
hacer la cola: to queue
jinetero (a): man or
woman who pursues
tourists, often a
prostitute
libreta: book of food
vouchers
mambí: independence
fighter during the
wars in the 19th
century
machete, machetero:
machete, cane cutter
mogotes: karstic
hillocks
orisha: deity in santería
paladar: restaurant at
an inhabitant's house
pedir botella: to
hitchhike
pelota: baseball
santería: Afro-Cuban
religion
sillón: rocking chair
tabaco: cigar
trusa: bathing trunks
vega: tobacco
plantation

FESTIVALS AND CULTURAL EVENTS ◆

FESTIVALS

FEB.	Festival del habano (cigars)	HAVANA
APR.	Festival Huella de España (Spanish culture)	HAVANA
MAY	Guitar Festival and International Competition	HAVANA
JUNE	Boleros de Oro International Festival (every two years)	HAVANA AND SANTIAGO
JULY	Fiesta del Fuego – Festival of Caribbean Culture	SANTIAGO DE CUBA
AUG.	Beny Moré International Festival (every two years)	CIENFUEGOS
SEP.	International Drama Festival	HAVANA
SEP.	Matamoros International Festival (every two years)	SANTIAGO DE CUBA
OCT.	Fiesta de la Cubanía (Cuban identity)	BAYAMO
OCT.	Fiesta de la Cultura Iberoamericana	HOLGUÍN
OCT.	Contemporary Music Festival	HAVANA
OCT./NOV.	International Ballet Festival (every two years)	HAVANA
NOV.	Festival de raíces africanas Wemilere	CIUDAD DE LA HABANA
NOV.	Festejos de San Cristóbal de La Habana	HAVANA
NOV.	International Barmen's Competition (every two years)	HAVANA
NOV./DEC.	National Barmen's Competition (Havana Club Grand Prix)	HAVANA
DEC.	Parrandas Remedianas	VILLA CLARA
DEC.	Jazz Festival (every two years)	HAVANA
DEC.	International Choir Festival (every two years)	SANTIAGO DE CUBA
DEC.	International Festival of New Latin-American Cinema	HAVANA

CARNIVALS

JUNE	Festivals of San Juan y San Pedro	CAMAGÜEY
JULY	Havana Carnival	HAVANA
JULY	Santiago de Cuba Carnival	SANTIAGO DE CUBA
DEC.	Parrandas Remedianas	REMEDIOS ▲ 194

RELIGIOUS FESTIVALS

3 MAY	Las Romerías de Mayo (May processions)	HOLGUÍN
8 SEP.	Festival of the Virgin of El Cobre (Afro-Cuban religion)	EL COBRE I 58, ▲ 218
24 SEP.	Festival of La Merced (Afro-Cuban religion)	HAVANA
3-4 DEC.	Festival of Santa Bárbara (Afro-Cuban religion)	ALL OF CUBA ● 58
8 DEC.	Festival of la Virgen de Regla (Afro-Cuban religion)	REGLA I 58, ▲ 147
17 DEC.	Festival of San Lázaro (Afro-Cuban religion)	EL RINCÓN ● 58

SPORTS EVENTS

OCT./MAR.	International Baseball Championships	HAVANA
APR.	Giraldo Córdova Cardín Boxing Tournament	VILLA CLARA
MAY	Hemingway International Marlin Fishing Tournament	MARINA HEMINGWAY ▲ 162
JULY	International Offshore Boats Championship	CUBA'S PORTS
NOV.	Marabana: International Marathon	HAVANA

FAIRS

FEB.	FIART (International fair of popular art)	HAVANA
FEB.	International Book Fair	HAVANA
NOV.	FIHAV (Havana International Fair)	HAVANA

NATIONAL HOLIDAYS

1 JAN.	Liberation Day and Anniversary of the 'Triumph of the Revolution'
1 MAY	Labor Day
26 JULY	National Rebellion Day and Anniversary of the attack on the Moncada Barracks
10 OCT.	Anniversary of the outbreak of the first war for Independence
25 DEC.	Christmas

To take part in festivals, fairs, dance or music classes, inquiries to
Paradiso: Promoter of Cultural Tourism (Artex),
Calle 19 #560, esq. C (Vedado)
Tel. (7) 32 69 28 and Fax (7) 33 39 21.
We have listed the festivals, fairs and cultural events that
are the most popular and that best represent Cuban cultural life.
To take part in sports events, inquiries to
Cuba Deportes, Calle 20 #706, e/ 7 y 9 (Miramar),
Tel. (7) 24 09 45

◆ PLACES TO VISIT

The letters and figures after each entry for a city or
quarter (example: Museo de la Ciudad **E** E3) give grid
references for the maps at the end of the guide.

HAVANA

HABANA VIEJA · MAP E

MUSEO DE LA CERÁMICA Castillo de la Real Fuerza Calle O'Reilly y Ave. del Puerto Plaza de Armas	*Open Mon.–Sat. 8.30am–4.45pm* *Ceramic works by contemporary artists and* *a collection of Cuban paintings.*	▲ *122* **E** E2-3
EL TEMPLETE Plaza de Armas Calle Baratillo e/ O'Reilly y Enna	*Open daily 9.30am–4pm*	▲ *123* **E** F3
MUSEO DE LA CIUDAD Palacio de los Capitanes Generales Plaza de Armas Calle Tacón e/ O'Reilly y Ave. del Puerto Tel. (7) 61 28 76/61 50 62	*Open daily 9am–7pm* *Roundup of historical and cultural events from the* *foundation of Havana to the present day.*	▲ *124* **E** E3
CATEDRAL DE SAN CRISTÓBAL Empedrado #158, e/ Mercaderes y San Ignacio Plaza de la Catedral	*Open daily 10.30am–3pm; Sun. 8am–noon*	▲ *126* **E** E3
MUSEO DE ARTE COLONIAL Palacio de los Condes de Casa Bayona San Ignacio, #61 Plaza de la Catedral, e/ Empedrado y O' Reilly Tel. (7) 62 64 40	*Open Tue.–Sat. 10am–6pm; Sun. 9am–1pm* *Exhibition focusing on the colonial period and a* *collection of mediopuntos (semicircular stained-* *glass windows).*	▲ *127* **E** E3
CENTRO WIFREDO LAM Calle San Ignacio #22 esq. Empedrado Tel. (7) 61 34 19	*Open Mon.–Fri. 10am–5pm* *Showcase of art from Asia, Africa, the Middle East,* *Latin America and the Caribbean.*	▲ *127* **E** E3
FUNDACIÓN ALEJO CARPENTIER Casa de la Condesa de la Reunión Calle Empedrado #215 e/ San Ignacio y Cuba	*Open Mon.–Fri. 8.30am–4pm* *Museum devoted to the great Cuban writer: many* *mementos of the author on display.*	▲ *128* **E** E3
CASA DE LA OBRA PÍA Calle Obrapía #158 esq. Mercaderes Tel. (7) 61 30 97	*Open Tue.–Sat. 10.30am–5.30pm* *Sun. 9.30am–12.30pm*	▲ *129* **E** E3
CASA DE ÁFRICA Calle Obrapía #157 e/ Mercaderes y San Ignacio Tel. (7) 61 57 98	*Open daily 9am–7pm*	▲ *129* **E** E3
CASA SIMÓN BOLÍVAR Calle Mercaderes #156 e/ Obrapía y Lamparilla Tel. (7) 61 39 88	*Open Tue.–Sun. 9am–6pm*	▲ *129* **E** E3
MUSEO NUMISMÁTICO Casa del Obispo Calle Oficios °8 e/ Obispo y Obrapía Tel. (7) 61 58 57/62 21 05	*Open Tue.–Sat. 10am–5pm; Sun. 10am–1pm* *Collection of Cuban coins and banknotes dating* *from the 16th century to the present day.*	▲ *129* **E** E3
CASA DE LOS ÁRABES Calle Oficios e/ Obispo y Obrapía Tel. (7) 61 58 68	*Open daily 9am–5pm* *Objects donated by twelve Arab countries.*	▲ *129* **E** E3
CASA DE LOS CONDES DE JARUCO Fondo Cubano de Bienes Culturales Plaza Vieja Muralla, #107–111, esq. San Ignacio	*Open 9am–6pm*	▲ *130* **E** E4
MUSEO/CASA NATAL DE JOSÉ MARTÍ Calle Paula #314 e/ Egido y Picota Tel. (7) 61 37 78	*Open Tue.–Sat. 9am–5pm; Sun. 9am–1pm*	▲ *131* **E** D6

CENTRO HABANA · MAP E

CAPITOLIO NACIONAL Prado e/ San José y Dragones Tel. (7) 60 34 11/61 02 01	*Open daily 9am–6pm*	▲ *132* **E** B4-5

To decipher an address, refer to page 232.

GRAN TEATRO FEDERICO GARCÍA LORCA Paseo del Prado, esq. San Rafael Tel. (7) 61 30 78	Performances and shows at 8.30pm during the week and at 5pm on Sun.	▲ 133 E B-C4
FÁBRICA DE TABACOS PARTÁGÁS Calle Industria #520 e/ Dragones y Barcelona Tel. (7) 62 46 04	Guided tours at 9am. Admission: $5. Subject to unpredictable closures.	▲ 134 E B5
MUSEO DE LA REVOLUCIÓN Y MEMORIAL GRANMA Former Presidential Palace Calle Refugio #1 e/ Monserrate y Zulueta Tel. (7) 62 40 91 to 96	Open Tue.–Sun. 10am–5pm Comprehensive overview of the history of the Cubans's fight for independence from the time of the Indians to the Revolution of 1959.	▲ 137 E C2
MUSEO NACIONAL DE LA MÚSICA Casa de Pérez de la Riva Calle Cárcel #1 e/ Aguiar y Habana Tel. (7) 61 98 46	Open Mon.–Sat. 9.30am–4.45pm History of Cuban music and instruments from the 16th to the 20th centuries.	▲ 137 E D2
VEDADO	**MAP E**	
MUSEO ANTROPOLÓGICO MONTANÉ Edificio Felipe Poey, Planta baja Universidad de La Habana	Variable opening hours.	▲ 142 D B2
MUSEO NAPOLEÓNICO Calle San Miguel #1159 esq. Ronda, Vedado, 100 yards from the university Tel. (7) 79 14 12/79 14 60	Open Mon.–Sat. Winter 10am–5.30pm, summer 11am–6.30pm Admission: $5. English–speaking guide. Open Tue.–Sat. 9am–5pm; Sun. 9am–noon	▲ 142 D B2
MUSEO MÁXIMO GÓMEZ Quinta de los Molinos Ave. Salvador Allende (Ave. Carlos III) e/ Infanta		▲ 142 D B3
CEMENTERIO CRISTÓBAL COLÓN Calle 12 y Zapata Tel. (7) 34 196	Open Mon.–Sat. 9am–5pm English–speaking guide.	▲ 144 D A4
MÉMORIAL JOSÉ MARTÍ Plaza de la Révolución Tel. (7) 84 05 51	Open Mon.–Sat. 9am–5pm	▲ 145 D A4
MIRAMAR	**A D2**	
MUSEO DEL MINISTERIO DEL INTERIOR Ave. 5a y Calle 14, Miramar	Open Tue.–Fri. 9am–5pm; Sat. 9am–4pm	▲ 146
MODEL OF HAVANA Calle 28 #113 e/ 1a y 3a Miramar	Open Tue.–Sat. 9am–5pm Wonderful miniature model of the city covering a surface area of 200 square meters.	▲ 146
HABANA DEL ESTE	**D EF1**	
CASTILLO DE LOS TRES REYES DEL MORRO Carretera de la Cabaña (east bank) at the entrance to Havana Bay	Open daily 8.30am–8pm The lighthouse can be visited.	▲ 146 D E1
MUSEO DE LAS ARMAS MUSEO DE LA COMANDANCIA DE CHE GUEVARA EL CAÑONAZO Fortaleza de San Carlos de la Cabaña Carretera de la Cabaña (east bank) at the entrance to Havana Bay	Open daily 10am–10pm Cannon fired daily at 9pm.	▲ 147 D F1
SAN FRANCISCO DE PAULA	**A E2**	
FINCA VIGÍA/MUSEO HEMINGWAY San Francisco de Paula Eastern Havana Tel. (7) 91 08 09	Open daily 9am–4pm, Sun. 9am–noon	▲ 148

WESTERN CUBA: PINAR DEL RÍO PROVINCE

SOROA	A C3	
ORQUIDEARIO (ORCHID GARDEN) Carretera Soroa 5 miles	Visits 9am–4.30pm	▲ 155

SAN DIEGO DE LOS BAÑOS	A C3	
CUEVA DE LOS PORTALES A couple of miles from San Diego de los Baños	Che's former headquarters during the Cuban Missile Crisis.	▲ 155

VIÑALES	A C3	
MURAL DE LA PREHISTORIA Mogote Dos Hermanas 2 miles west of the village of Viñales	Open air Anthropological and geological evolution painted on the side of a rock. Guided tours.	▲ 157
CUEVA DEL INDIO 4 miles north of Viñales	One of the longest caves in Cuba.	▲ 156

PINAR DEL RÍO	A B-C3	
MUSEO PROVINCIAL DE HISTORIA Calle Mart, #58 e/ Isabel Rubio y Colón Tel. (82) 43 00	Open Tue.–Sat. 9am–4pm; Sun. 9am–1pm	▲ 158
MUSEO DE CIENCIAS NATURALES SANDALIO DE NODA Palacio Guasch Calle Martí #202 esq. Comandante Pinares	Open Mon.–Sat. 9am–5pm; Sun. 8am–noon Exhibition of stuffed models of the fauna of Pinar del Río and the rest of the country.	▲ 158
CASA GARAY Guayabita del Pinar factory Calle Recreo #189	Open daily Mon.–Fri. 8am–4pm; Sat. 8am–noon Factory manufacturing the region's liquor.	▲ 158
FÁBRICA DE TABACOS FRANCISCO DONATIÉN Calle Antonio Maceo, #157	Open Mon.–Fri. 7.30am–noon and 1–4.30pm; Sat. 7.30am–noon	▲ 158

THE NORTH COAST

MATANZAS	A F2	
MUSEO HISTÓRICO PROVINCIAL Palacio del Junco Plaza de la Vigía	Open Tue.–Sat. 10am–noon and 1–5pm; Sun. 8am–noon	▲ 167
TEATRO SAUTO Plaza de la Vigía	Performances from 8.30pm.	▲ 167
MUSEO FARMACÉUTICO Calle Milanés #4951 e/ Santa Teresa y Ayuntamiento Tel. (52) 31 79	Open Tue.–Sun. 9am–5pm Former pharmacy. Furniture and de Sèvres porcelain.	▲ 167
CUEVAS DE BELLAMAR 2 miles from Matanzas and 31 miles from Varadero	Open daily 9am–5pm Tours every 90 minutes	▲ 167

VARADERO	A F2	
MUSEO MUNICIPAL Calle 57 y Playa	Open daily 9am–5pm Paintings by local artists and well-known painters.	▲168
DELPHINARIUM Carretera Las Morlas	Dolphin show; it is possible to swim with them.	▲ 169

CÁRDENAS	A F2	
MUSEO MUNICIPAL ÓSCAR MARÍA DE ROJAS Calzada °4 Tel. 52 2417	Open daily Tue.–Sat. 9am–5pm, Sun. 9am–1pm One of the oldest museums in Cuba. History of Cárdenas. Furniture and objets d'art.	▲ 170

CENTRAL CUBA

GIRÓN	B A3	
MUSEO GIRÓN Playa Girón	Open Tue.–Sun. 9am–5pm	▲ 176

CIENFUEGOS — B B3

TEATRO TOMÁS TERRY Calle 25 y ave. 56	*Open daily 9am–4pm*	▲ 178
PALACIO FERRER Casa de la Cultura, on the east side of Parque José Martí	*Opening hours depend on the cultural activities on the program.*	▲ 178
MUSEO PROVINCIAL Parque Martí	*Open daily 9.30am–5.30pm*	▲ 179
PALACIO DEL VALLE At the tip of Punta Gorda Calle 37 e/ O y 2 Opposite Hotel Jagua	*Open daily 10am–11pm* *Although converted into a restaurant, it can still be visited.*	▲ 179
CASTILLO DE JAGUA Cienfuegos Bay Tel. (432) 45 10 03/45 12 10	*Motorboat opposite the Hotel Pasacaballos or a launch from Cienfuegos (boarding on the quay at the bottom of Calle 25).*	▲ 179
JARDÍN BOTÁNICO LA SOLEDAD 9 miles east of Cienfuegos e/ San Antón and Guaos	*Open daily 8am–4pm*	▲ 179

TRINIDAD — B C4

IGLESIA PARROQUIAL **DE LA SANTÍSIMA TRINIDAD** Plaza Mayor	*Mass on Sunday morning at 10am*	▲ 182
MUSEO DE ARQUITECTURA COLONIAL Casa de los Sánchez-Iznaga Calle Desengaño #83 Plaza Mayor	*Open daily 8.30am–5pm* *Mon. and Thurs. 8.30am–10pm* *Closed Fri.*	▲ 183
GALERÍA DE ARTE Casa de Aldemán Ortiz Plaza Mayor	*Open daily 8am–5pm* *Free admission.*	▲ 183
MUSEO DE ARQUEOLOGÍA GUAMUHAYA Casa Padrón Calle Simón Bolívar #457 Plaza Mayor	*Open daily 9am–5pm,* *Mon. and Wed. 8.30am–10pm* *Closed Fri.*	▲ 183
MUSEO ROMÁNTICO Palacio Brunet Calle Fernando Hernández #52 e/ Piro Guinart and Simón Bolívar Tel. (419) 43 63	*Open Tue.–Sun. 8.30am–5pm*	▲ 184
MUSEO MUNICIPAL DE HISTORIA Palacio Cantero Calle Simón Bolívar #423 esq. Callejón de Peña Tel. (419) 44 60	*Open Sun.–Fri. 8.30am–5pm*	▲ 186
MUSEO DE LA LUCHA CONTRA **BANDIDOS** Convento San Francisco de Asís Calle del Cristo esq. Boca Tel. (419) 41 21	*Open daily 8.30am–5pm,* *Wed. and Fri. 8.30am–10pm* *Closed Mon.*	▲ 187

VALLE DE LOS INGENIOS — B C4

HACIENDA DE LA MANACA IZNAGA Carretera de Sancti Spíritus 7 miles. Take the train: 9-mile route between Trinidad and the Valle de los Ingenios	*Tour of the tower 8.30am–5pm* *Leave from La Pastora, stop at Las Ruinas del Ingenio Magua, then a stop for lunch in Manaca Iznaca, arrive in Guachinango.*	▲ 190

SANCTI SPÍRITUS — B D4

MUSEO DE ARTE COLONIAL Palacio de Valle Iznaga Calle Plácido y Menéndez Tel. (41) 25 455	*Open daily 10am–5pm* *Closed Tue.*	▲ 191

SANTA CLARA — B C3

TEATRO DE LA CARIDAD Parque Leoncio Vidal Northwest corner of the park	*Performances from 8.30pm.*	▲ 191
MUSEO DE ARTES DECORATIVAS Calle Martha Abreu esq. Luis Estévez Tel. (422) 53 68	*Open daily 9am–5pm* *Closed Tue.*	▲ 191

MONUMENTO DEL TREN BLINDADO Carretera Camajuaní y Línea del Ferrocarril	*This monument commemorates one of the high points in the battle of Santa Clara.*	▲ 192
MUSEO DEL CHE **MAUSOLEO DEL CHE** Ave. de los Desfiles e/ Danelito y Circunvalación Plaza de la Revolución	*Open daily Mon.–Sat. 9am–noon and 2–5pm, Sun. 9am–noon* *Mausoleum containing Che's mortal remains.*	▲ 192

REMEDIOS	**B** D3	
MUSEO DE LAS PARRANDAS REMEDIANAS Calle Máximo Gómez #71	*Open daily 10am–4.30pm* *Photos, models, musical instruments, traditional costumes associated with the region's local festivals.*	▲ 194
MUSEO DE MÚSICA A. GARCÍA CATURLA Parque José Martí	*Open 10am–4.30pm*	▲ 194

CAMAGÜEY	**B** F5	
MUSEO CASA NATAL DE I. AGRAMONTE Calle Ignacio Agramonte #59 esq. Independencia Tel. (322) 97 116	*Open Tue.–Fri. 10am–5.45pm; Sat. 10am–10pm; Sun. 8am–11.45am*	▲ 196
CENTRO PROVINCIAL DE PATRIMONIO Plaza de San Juan de Dios	*Open Mon.–Sat. 9am–5pm*	▲ 196

ORIENTE

HOLGUÍN	**C** C4	
CASA NATAL DE CALIXTO GARCÍA Calle Miró #456 e/ Frexes y Martí	*Open Mon.–Fri. 9am–5pm; Sat. 9am–1pm*	▲ 200
MUSEO DE HISTORIA PROVINCIAL 'LA PERIQUERA' Calle Frexes #198 e/ Libertad y Maceo (opposite the park)	*Open Mon.–Fri. 9am–5pm; Sat. 9am–1pm* *Mementos and accounts relating to the city's hero.*	

GUARDALAVACA	**C** D3	
CHORRO DE MAITA 4 miles east of Guardalavaca	*Open Mon.–Sat. 9am–5pm; Sun. 9am–1pm*	▲ 201

BANES	**C** D4	
MUSEO INDOCUBANO BANI Calle General Barrero #305 e/ Martí y Céspedes	*Open Tue.–Sat. 9am–5pm; Mon. 2–5pm; Sun. 9am–2pm* *Collections of objets d'art by the early Indians.*	▲ 201

BAYAMO	**C** B5	
CASA NATAL DE CARLOS MANUEL DE CÉSPEDES Calle Maceo #57 Tel. (23) 42 38 64	*Open daily 9am–5pm*	▲ 204

MANZANILLO	**C** B5	
MUSEO HISTÓRICO LA DEMAJAGUA 7 miles south of Manzanillo	*Ruins of the estate of Carlos Manuel de Céspedes. Now a museum of History and Archeology.*	▲ 205

SANTIAGO DE CUBA	**C** D5	
MUSEO DE AMBIENTE HISTÓRICO CUBANO Former Casa Diego Velázquez Calle Felix Peña #610 e/ Heredia y Aguilera, near Parque Céspedes	*Open Mon.–Sat. 9am–5pm; Sun. 9am–1pm* *Furniture, decorative objects, porcelain and ornamental objects.*	▲ 210
MUSEO CASA NATAL DE JOSÉ MARÍA DE HEREDIA Calle Heredia #260 Next to Parque Céspedes	*Open Tue.–Sat. 9am–9pm; Sun. 9am–1pm and 4pm–8pm*	▲ 212
MUSEO DEL CARNIVAL Calle Heredia #303 e/ Pío Rosado y Porfirio Valiente	*Open Tue.–Sun. 9am–5pm* *Photos, costumes and musical instruments charting the history of the Santiago carnival.*	▲ 212
MUSEO EMILIO BACARDÍ-MOREAU Calle Pío Rosado esq. Aguilera Tel. (226) 28 40 02	*Open Mon.–Fri. 9am–6pm; Sun. 9am–noon*	▲ 212

MUSEO DE LA LUCHA CLANDESTINA Calle Rabí, #1, Tívoli Quarter Tel. 24 689/28 244	*Open Tue.–Sun. 9am–5pm* *Former police station under Batista.*	▲ 213
TUMBA FRANCESA Calle Los Maceo #501 esq. San Bartolomé	*Public rehearsals on Thu. 8am–noon and 5–11pm*	▲ 213
SANTA IFIGENIA CEMETERY Ave. Crombet (northwest of Santiago)	*Open daily 7am–6pm*	▲ 214
MUSEO HISTÓRICO DEL 26 DE JULIO BARRACKS MONCADA Calle Gal Portuondo e/ Moncada y Ave. de los Libertadores	*Open Mon.–Sat. 9am–5pm, Sun. 9am–1pm* *Former historic barracks converted into a school and museum.*	▲ 215
CASA NATAL DE ANTONIO MACEO Calle los Maceo, #207 e/ Coronay Rastro Tel. (226) 23 750	*Open Mon.–Sat. 9am–5pm* *Museum devoted to the life and work of one of the key figures in Cuba's war for independence.*	▲ 215
CASA DEL CARIBE Calle 13 #154 esq. Calle 8 Vista Alegre Tel. (226) 42 285/42 387	*Organizes the Festival of Caribbean Culture.*	▲ 216
CENTRO CULTURAL AFRICANO FERNANDO ORTÍZ Ave. Manduley #10 esq. Calle 5, Vista Alegre Tel. (226) 42 487	*Open daily 9am–6pm*	▲ 216

AROUND SANTIAGO   C D5

MUSEO DE LA PIRATERÍA CASTILLO DEL MORRO 6 miles south of Santiago	*Relatively meager collection.*	▲ 217
BASILÍCA DE NUESTRA SEÑORA DE LA CARIDAD DEL COBRE 12 miles west of Santiago	*Sculpture garden measuring nearly 100 acres: twenty works by Cuban and foreign artists.*	▲ 218
PRADO DE LAS ESCULTURAS Parque Baconao, 10 miles from Santiago, in the direction of Gran Piedra, between Las Guásimas and El Sapo	*Open daily 9am–5pm*	▲ 219
GRANJITA DE SIBONEY Small Siboney farm, 8 miles along the road to Siboney	*Open Tue.–Fri. 10am–4.30pm; Sun. 9am–1pm. Museum devoted to coffee farming.*	▲ 219
CAFETAL LA ISABELICA Carretera de la Gran Piedra, 9 miles	*Open daily 10am–5pm*	▲ 219

BARACOA   C F5

MUSEO MUNICIPAL Fuerte Matachín-Bahía de Miel	*Open Tue.–Sat. 9am–5pm; Sun. 9am–1pm Former Casa del Gobierno. Collection of aboriginal objects.*	▲ 222

ISLE OF YOUTH

NUEVA GERONA AND VICINITY   A D4-5

MUSEO MUNICIPAL South side of Parque Central Calle 30 e/ 37 and 39	*Open Tue.–Sat. 8am–5pm; Sun. 8am–noon History of the clandestine war waged against Batista.*	▲ 226
MUSEO DE LA LUCHA CLANDESTINA Calle 24 y 45 Tel. (61) 24 582	*Open Tue.–Thu. 8am–7pm; Fri. 2–10pm; Sat. 1pm–5pm; Sun. 9am–1pm*	▲ 226
MUSEO DE HISTORIA NATURAL Calle 41 y 52 Tel. (61) 23 143	*The island's geology and archeology, with prehistoric paintings.*	▲ 226
MUSEO FINCA DEL ABRA In the Sierra Las Casas Carretera Siguanea, 1 mile	*Open Tue.–Sun. 9am–5pm*	▲ 227
PRESIDIO MODELO 2 miles east of Nueva Gerona, Reparto Chacón	*Open Tue.–Sun. 9am–5pm Penitentiary where Castro was imprisoned.*	▲ 227
CUEVA DE PUNTA DEL ESTE 37 miles southeast of Nueva Gerona	*Works by Ciboney Indians, cave paintings.*	▲ 227

◆ HOTELS AND RESTAURANTS
HAVANA

◒ : the editors' choice

The grid references (for example: Hotel Inglaterra **E** B4)
refer to the maps at the end of the guide ◆ 265.

Hotels and restaurants in Cuba are state-run establishments and, as such, are given an official rating. However, the charm of a place, a good meal or a lively atmosphere cannot be reduced to a simple 'official' standard. The prices of hotels are given as a guide and do not take into account special discounts and seasonal rates. Please remember that the price given for a double room should be multiplied by the number of occupants. The food in official restaurants is improving but remains generally basic. *Casas particulares*, (rooms in family homes) and *paladares* (private restaurants) are found mainly in the city centers. We have provided some addresses of these family establishments, which number around 3500 in Havana alone. However, *paladares* often have a very short life span, being subject to state supervision and supply difficulties. Nevertheless, whenever possible, visitors are advised to sample the Creole cuisine offered in *paladares*, taking care to fix the price of the meal, including drinks, in advance. Opt for pork or chicken rather than lobster (often mediocre), which these establishments are not authorized to sell.

HAVANA
A D–E2
→ **ACCOMMODATION**
Convento de Santa Clara
E E5
Calle Cuba #610 e/ Luz y Sol
Habana Vieja
Tel. (7) 61 33 35
Fax (7) 33 96 56
This is the former 'Sailors' cloister' within the Residencia Académica. A studious atmosphere in the heart of the old city and well priced accommodation.
1 suite and 8 rooms ($25 with breakfast)
☎

Hotel Ambos Mundos★★★★
E E3
Calle Obispo #153 esq. Mercaderes, Habana Vieja
Tel. (7) 66 95 30
Fax (7) 66 95 32
Luxury hotel
Ernest Hemingway lived here from 1932 until 1939. He wrote For Whom the Bell Tolls in room 511 of this legendary hotel. Two restaurants.
49 rooms ($57/$87)
Ⅲ ▣

Hotel Colina
D B2
Calle L e/ 27 y Jovellar Vedado
Tel. (7) 334071
Fax (7) 334104
Tourist hotel
Close to the University and La Rampa, this is ideal for those who prefer an intimate, family atmosphere to the splendor of the grand palaces.
79 rooms ($35)

Hotel Habana Libre
D B2
Calle L y 23, Vedado
Tel. (7) 33 40 11
Fax (7) 33 31 41
Luxury hotel
One of the finest establishments in the Hilton chain, this is also one of the

leading hotels in Havana. Completed in 1959, renovated in 1997, it is now run by a Spanish group. A meeting place for businessmen and visiting celebrities.
540 rooms ($85)
▣ ⊠

◒ **Hotel Inglaterra**
E B4
Paseo del Prado #416 e/ San Rafael y San Miguel, Habana Vieja
Tel (7) 33 85 93 to 97
Fax (7) 33 82 54
Hotel with character
Built in 1875, this was the first modern hotel in Havana. Its design shows the influence of colonial art, combined with Arab and Andalusian references in the azulejos that decorate the restaurant and bar, the Sevillana. The spacious terrace becomes just as lively at mealtimes as it did when García Lorca, Caruso and Sarah Bernhardt, guest performers at the nearby National Theater, used to stay here. You might be inclined to wallow in nostalgia for this hotel's past glory but the generous mojitos served on the terrace help to see things in a rosier light. The best rooms are those overlooking the square. The restaurant serves several Creole specialties and international cuisine.
69 double rooms ($58/$78) 4 single, 10 triple.
▣ ☎ ⌂

Hotel Meliá Cohiba★★★★★
A E2
Ave. Paseo e/ 1ra y 3ra Vedado
Tel (7) 33 36 36
Fax (7) 33 45 55
Luxury hotel
In a tower, near

the Malecón. The hotel's facilities, boutiques and swimming pool are situated on the mezzanine level and the paved area outside. Despite its plush decor, it lacks character. Those who like the old city will not warm to its anonymity, while visitors pressed for time will appreciate its functionality. Several restaurants.*
342 rooms ($74/$120) and 64 suites.
Ⅲ ▣ ⌖ ♫ ⊠

Hotel Meliá Habana★★★★★
A D2
Ave. 3ra e/ 76 y 80, Miramar
Tel. (7) 24 85 00
Luxury hotel
The most recent of the great Cuban palaces (twelve stories), opened in fall 1998. Luxurious rooms with a view of the city or the ocean.
409 rooms with balcony or terrace ($85/$123)
⌂ Ⅲ ▣ ⊠

Hotel Nacional★★★★★
D B–C1
Calle O esq. 21, Vedado
Tel. (7) 33 35 64 to 67
Fax (7) 33 50 54
Luxury hotel
Good location in the Vedado quarter, with a view of Havana Bay and the seafront, this prestigious hotel still radiates 1930s charm. Several restaurants, each with their own culinary specialties: the Aguiar serves international cuisine; the Veranda is more relaxed; La Pérgola is outdoors and the Arboleda café is more intimate.
488 rooms, $89/$106 p/p, 15 suites
⊠

Hotel Neptuno-Tritón
A D2
Ave. 3ra y 74,
Miramar Playa
Tel. (7) 24 16 06
Fax (7) 24 00 42
Tourist hotel
*One hotel complex,
but two slightly
old-fashioned
establishments by
the sea, with shared
facilities: the chance
to relax and enjoy a
little leisure, near
the center. Cabaret.
Neptuno: 187
double rooms
($41/$61),
34 triples, 6 suites
Triton: 260 double
rooms ($61), 6 suites.*

Hotel Plaza★★★★
E C3
Calle Agramonte
#267 esq. Neptuno,
Habana Vieja
Tel. (7) 33 85 83 to 89
Fax (7) 33 85 92
Tourist hotel
*Built in 1909, the
hotel was initially
a private residence,
then home to a
daily newspaper
printing factory.
The Marquis of
Pinar del Río, who
founded the hotel,
was responsible for
its distinctive style.
It has a terrace, with
a bar and café.
188 rooms ($60/$80)*
🏠

Hotel Riviera★★★★★
A E2
Paseo e/ Malecón
y 1ra Vedado
Tel. (7) 33 40 51
Fax (7) 33 37 39
Tourist hotel
*Dating from the late
1950s, this slightly
old-fashioned and
recently restored
one-time palace
houses the former
Palacio de la Salsa
(where the most
famous Cuban bands
once performed).
The latter has been
converted into a
cabaret ◆ 237.
310 rooms ($60/$89)
and 20 suites*
🎬 🖥 📶

Hotel Santa Isabel★★★★★
E F3
Calle Baratillo #9
Habana Vieja
Tel. (7) 33 82 01
Fax (7) 33 83 91
Hotel with character
*The former
Santovenia palace
built on the Plaza
de Armas in the
18th century was
converted into
a hotel in 1867.
Renovated in 1996,
it is now the
most luxurious
establishment in*

HOTEL INGLETERRA

LA BODEGUITA DEL MELIA

*the old city. The El
Condado restaurant
serves Creole and
international cuisine.
17 rooms
($113/$137) and
10 suites*
🎬 🖥

Hotel Sevilla★★★★
E C3
Calle Trocadero #55
Tel. (7) 33 85 60
Fax (7) 33 85 82
Tourist hotel
*Built in 1880 in
Moorish style, the
Sevilla was so-
named in honour
of the Andalusian
capital, Columbus'
point of departure.
Reopened in late
1993 after large-
scale building work
and now run by the*

*Accor group, this is
one of the nicest
hotels in the
colonial city.
188 rooms ($52)*
🎬 📶

Hostal Valencia★★★
E F3
Calle Oficios #53
esq. Obrapía
Habana Vieja
Tel. (7) 62 38 01
Fax (7) 33 56 28
Hotel with character
*The former palace
of the Count of
Sotolongo (18th-
century) has now
been converted
into a lavish colonial-
style hotel with
garden, patio and
terrace. Nicely
furnished rooms.
Spanish cuisine in
La Paella restaurant.
Friendly staff and
service.
14 rooms ($46)*
🏠 🍴

→ RESTAURANTS
El Aljibe
A D2
Ave. 7 e/ 24 y 26
Miramar
Tel. (7) 24 15 84
Typical restaurant
*In the Miramar
quarter, this
restaurant has a
spacious terrace,
where the only
dish on the menu*

*is chicken prepared
in a variety of
different ways.
Popular with
Cubans. Inexpensive.
À la carte: $12*
🏠

✪ La Bodeguita del Medio
E E3
Calle Empedrado
#207 Habana Vieja
Tel. (7) 61 84 42
Fax (7) 33 88 57
Typical restaurant
Establishment
*founded in 1942, not
on a crossroads, as
was the practice at
the time for business
custom, but in the
middle of a street,
hence its name. La
Bodeguita would
have remained a
modest canteen
frequented by
workers from the
nearby printing
press, had it not
been for Ernest
Hemingway, Julio
Cortázar and many
movie stars who
gradually wove a
legend around the
restaurant. Its walls
are covered with
graffiti and tourists
now sit at tables
once occupied by
the pride of South
American literature;
but the atmosphere
in this historical
eatery is no less
magical. Legendary
food: the tasty
ajiaco, a meat and
vegetable stew
simmered in a Creole
pot, combines
Spanish influences
with far-off
memories of
Africa. The menu
includes moros y
cristianos (black
beans and rice), and
succulent grilled
pork whose flavor
is beyond compare.
It is served with a
clear sauce and
black beans.
A trio of guitarists
wanders from table
to table, singing
melancholy ballads.
À la carte: $20/$30*

✪ : the editors' choice

The grid references (for example: Hotel Inglaterra **E** B4)
refer to the maps at the end of the guide ◆ 265.

La Cecilia
A D2
Ave. 5ta e/ 110 y
112, Miramar
Tel. (7) 24 15 62
Luxury restaurant
*In the midst of a
lovely tropical
garden, customers
dine in two
African-style halls.
Creole cuisine,
shellfish and
seafood, several
meat dishes and a
fine Spanish and
French wine cellar.
Fairly prompt
service.*
À la carte,
$20/$25
✪

La Ferminia
A D2
Ave. 5ta #18207,
e/ 182 y 184
Playa
Tel. (7) 33 65 55
Luxury restaurant
*A former patrician
house converted
into a beautifully
furnished
restaurant, with
dining rooms and
terraces where the
best catering
students finish
their training.
Shellfish, fish,
excellent service.*
À la carte, $18/$25
⊡

✪ La Finca
A D2
Ave. 19 e/ 134 y 140,
Reparto Cubanacán,
Playa
Tel. (7) 23 58 38
Closed Sun.
*The two best
restaurants in
Havana are now
El Ranchón (Creole
cuisine by the
excellent Cuban
chef Erasmo) and,
nearby, La Finca,
a new restaurant
under the same
management. Its
chef is the young
Manuel Elías, who
spent five years
training in Paris.
Freshly-caught fish,
shrimps, simply
prepared fresh
lobster. Several*

*European wines.
Excellent cocktails.
Stylish service.
Enjoyable pianist.
The only drawback is
the sky-high prices.*
À la carte, $35/$40

El Floridita
E C4
Calle Obispo #557
esq. Monserrate
Habana Vieja

HOTEL LOS JAZMINES

Tel. (7) 63 10 63
Fax (7) 33 88 56
Luxury restaurant
*Founded in the early
19th century and
frequented by
Hemingway, this
historical venue was
listed among the
seven best bars in
the world. The
restaurant serves
seafood specialties.
Musical ambiance.*
À la carte, $30/$35

El Patio
E E3
Plaza de la Catedral
Tel. (7) 57 10 34
Typical restaurant
*A shady patio with
fountain, always very
busy. Savor a mojito
on the terrace,
before sampling the
Creole menu of pork,
chicken or fish.*
$10–12

**WESTERN CUBA: PINAR
DEL RÍO PROVINCE**
SIERRA DEL ROSARIO
A C–D3
→ **ACCOMMODATION**
Hotel Moka
A D3
Autopista 32 miles
Las Terrazas
Tel. (7) 33 55 16
Hotel with character
*The Sierra del
Rosario is a historic
area once devoted
to coffee farming.*

*This undulating
landscape of hills
and valleys was
designated a
Biosphere Reserve
by UNESCO.
The comfortable,
colonial-style hotel
is surrounded by
luxuriant tropical
vegetation.*
26 rooms ($58/$72)
⊡ ▥ ▣ ▣ ⊠

→ **RESTAURANTS**
Buena Vista
A D3
Las Terrazas
Reached by a
gentle hiking trail
and by car.
Typical restaurant
*Go on foot, from the
Hotel Moka, through
the tropical flora of
royal palms, orchids,
hibiscus, tree-ferns.
This region,
breathtakingly
beautiful in the
summer, is called
'Little France': the
ruins of the
Buenavista
plantation have
been converted into
a bar and restaurant.
On the menu, pollo
brujo (a chicken
dish), eaten under
the trees.*
À la carte: $8–12
▨ ▢

SAN DIEGO DE LOS BAÑOS
A C3
→ **ACCOMMODATION**
Hotel Mirador*
A C3
Calle 23 final
San Diego
de los Baños
Tel. (85) 33 54 10
Tourist hotel
*The waters
(between 85°F
and 105°F) and the
warm mud of this
spa have been*

*famous since
1632. The spa is
modern (offering
dermatology and
rheumatology)
and is very close
to the hotel.*
30 rooms ($27/$34)
▣ ⊠

VIÑALES VALLEY
A C3
→ **ACCOMMODATION**
Hotel La Ermita**
A B–C3
Carretera de la
Ermita, 1 mile,
Viñales
Tel. (8) 9 32 04/3208
Fax (8) 93 60 91
Tourist hotel
*Recent colonial-style
establishment.
Spacious and well-
equipped rooms,
reached by
gangways. From the
swimming pool and
the rooms, you can
enjoy a view of the
Viñales Valley and
the sensational play
of light and shadow
over the mogotes
(small limestone
hillocks).*
64 rooms ($38)
▨ ⊠ ▣

✪ Hotel
Los Jasmines ***
A B3
Carretera de Viñales
16 miles
Tel. (8) 9 3205
Tourist hotel
*Leaving the
languid charm
of Pinar del Río,
the road winds its
way northward to
a narrow pass
overlooking one
of the most
breathtaking
landscapes on the
island. Below, the
hotel affords one
of the finest
viewpoints over the
Viñales Valley,
patterned with
mogotes. When
the sun gradually
burns off the early
morning mist,
the sight is awe-
inspiring.
Comprising several
low buildings,
connected by*

gangways, the hotel is attractive and extremely comfortable. The quality of the restaurant, on the other hand, depends on supplies and the tour groups staying the night. 78 rooms

→ RESTAURANTS
✪ Casa de Don Tomás
A B–C3
Calle Cisneros, #141 Viñales
Tel. (8) 93 114
Typical restaurant
Viñales is the center of production for the tobacco leaves that give Havanas their distinctive aroma. It has the manner of a sleepy town, especially on either side of the main street, near the small church. In the valley, workshops (despalillos) prepare the leaves that will be sent to the factories in Havana. At mealtimes, the city comes alive, children return home from school and American classic cars, legacies of a bygone age, venture out for a short spin. Enjoy a leisurely lunch or dinner in the oldest wooden house in the city (1889) or on the terrace; the patron cooks a dish called, somewhat pompously, Las Delicias ($8), a variation on the theme of paella, rice with pork, chicken, sausage and lobster.
À la carte: $10/$15

A B–C3
→ ACCOMMODATION
Hotel Pinar del Río***
endpaper 1/B5
Calle Mart, final, esq. Autopista
Tel. (82) 50 707
Tourist hotel
Large characterless

hotel opposite the University. It is just as easy to rent a room in a family home. Restaurant. 149 rooms ($27–32)

→ RESTAURANTS
✪ Rumayor
A B3
Carretera de Viñales (just over half a mile out of the city)
Tel. (82) 3507
Closed Thu.
Typical restaurant
*This is a sort of large African straw hut, which serves a wonderful specialty: pollo ahumado, smoked chicken à la Rumayor.
An adjacent cabaret performs two shows nightly.*
À la carte: $12/$15

A A–B4
→ ACCOMMODATION
Villa Turística
A A–B4
Laguna Grande
Tel. (82) 2430
Holiday cottage complex
On the road to the peninsula, a couple of miles from Isabel Rubio, small individual chalets near the lake of Laguna Grande (fishing); beach at Punta Colorada and María la Gorda (scuba-diving)
12 bungalows

A B–C–D3
→ ACCOMMODATION
Puero Esperanza
A B3
Dora Gonzales Fuentes, Pelayo Cuervo #5
Puerto Esperanza
You will feel as if you are at the end of the world here. Rent a room in a family home just 100 yards from the ocean.
$15 with dinner

A E2
→ RESTAURANTS
La Terraza
A E2
Calle Real #161, y Candelaria, Cojímar
Tel. (7) 65 3471
Daily 10am to 11pm
Typical restaurant
East of Havana, the suburbs are still steadily spreading, lining up barrio after barrio. In Cojímar, nothing seems to have changed since the days when Ernest Hemingway and his friend Gregorio Fuentes, the fisherman, would plan their fishing expeditions here. La Terraza, with its superb wooden bar and dining room suspended over the bay, recalls those legendary times. Countless photos on the walls attest to the exploits of the author of the Old Man and the Sea. There are still fishermen here who knew 'Papa' Hemingway. The food also pays tribute to the writer's legend: fresh lobster, shrimps and other shellfish, and dish of the day are specialties.
À la carte: $15/$18

A E2
→ ACCOMMODATION
Aparthotel Atlántico
A E2
Ave. de Las Terrazas e/ 11 y 12 Santa María del Mar
Tel. (687) 2560 to 69
Fax (687) 33 51 58
Tourist hotel
Rooms and small studios with fridge and balconies in a hotel complex that stands a stone's throw from the beach. Restaurant.
108 rooms ($35)

Aparthotel Las Terrazas
A E2
Ave. de las Terrazas e/ 10 y Rotonda, Santa María del Mar
Tel. (687) 38 29/38 59
Fax (687) 80 23 96
Tourist hotel
The appearance of this building may leave much to be desired but it has good facilities. Its strong point is its beachside location. Two restaurants.
154 rooms ($45/$55)

Villa Los Pinos****
A E2
Ave. de las Terrazas, #21 e/ 4ta y 5ta Santa María del Mar
Tel. (687) 97 13 61
Fax (687) 80 21 44
Tourist hotel
In addition to the beachside hotel situated at the entrance to the sea side resort, this complex offers several two-room cottages.
70 double rooms
26 houses ($200)

Villa Trópica***
A E2
37 miles Via Blanca Playa Jibacoa
Tel. (687) 33 80 40
Fax (687) 66 75 85
Tourist hotel
Part of the Gran Caribe group, run by Villaggi del

LA TERRAZA

◆ **HOTELS AND RESTAURANTS**
CENTRAL CUBA

✪ : the editors' choice
The grid references (for example: Hotel Inglaterra **E** B4)
refer to the maps at the end of the guide ◆ 265.

Ventaglio, this hotel offers all the recreational activities to be had in the Gulf of Mexico: fishing, swimming, water sports.
128 double rooms
26 triples
▥ ▣ ≋

Tropicoco Beach Club
A E2
Ave. Sur y Las Terrazas
Santa María del Mar
Tel. (687) 25 31 to 39
Fax (687) 33 51 58
Tourist hotel
Modern building surrounded by gardens and attractively decorated. Close to the sea, there are several cabarets and restaurants nearby.
188 rooms ($50)
🔲 ≋ 🎵

MATANZAS

A F2
→ **ACCOMMODATION**
Hotel Velasco
endpaper 1/D4
Calle Contrera, Plaza Libertad
Tel. (52) 4443
Hotel with character
A testament to the colonial past of this city, once a flourishing musical center because of its famous opera house. Modest establishment in the city center, but full of character.
18 rooms ($25)
🅲

VARADERO

A F2
→ **ACCOMMODATION**
Hotel Acuazul
endpaper 1/D4
Ave. 1ra y 13
Tel. (5) 66 71 32
Fax (5) 66 72 29
Tourist hotel
In the center of Varadero, near the beach, a nine-story building with every comfort for an enjoyable stay.
78 rooms ($35)
≋

Bella Costa ★★★★
A F2
Carretera Las Américas, 3 miles
Tel. (5) 66 72 10
Tourist hotel
Well-kept hotel near a fine sandy beach with pleasure garden. Efficient service, sports and a program of special events. Comfortable rooms with large bay windows. Good restaurant serving fish specialties.
▥ ≋ 🔲

Hotel Coral★★★★
A F2
Carretera Las Américas e/ H y K, Reparto la Torre
Tel. (5) 66 72 40
Tourist hotel
On one of the loveliest beaches of the peninsula, this recently built hotel also has a huge swimming pool and a comprehensive range of leisure facilities. Comfortable rooms and stylish restaurant.
230 rooms ($155/$310)
≋

Aparthotel Mar del Sur
A F2
Ave. 3ra esq. Calle 30
Tel. (5) 66 74 81 to 82
Fax (5) 66 74 81
Tourist hotel
Restaurant, two bars, a snack-bar and a café. Ideal for families.
318 rooms including 48 two-bedroom apartments, 98 one-bedroom apartments, 42 studios and 130 hotel rooms ($35)

Meliá Varadero★★★★★
A F2
Autopista Sur Playa de las Américas
Tel. (5) 66 70 13
Fax (5) 66 70 12
Luxury hotel
One of the best modern hotels on

the island, as much for its luxurious rooms and prime position on a promontory as for its quality service and well-motivated staff. Lovely setting of lush vegetation and fountains; the star-shaped layout of the rooms means that they all enjoy a sea view.
497 rooms ($57/$120)
▥ ≋ 🔲 🎵

Super Club Tuxpán★★★★
A F2
Carretera Las Morlas Playa de las Américas
Tel. (5) 66 75 60
Fax 66 75 61
Tourist hotel
Recent establishment on a fine sandy beach, shaped like a Mayan pyramid simlar to those in Cancún, Mexico. The restaurant's excellent reputation is well earned.
234 rooms ($155/$195 for full board)
🔲 ≋ 🎵

CÁRDENAS

A F2
→ **RESTAURANTS**
Las Palmas
A F2
Ave. Céspedes y Calle 16
Open Tue.–Sun.
Typical restaurant
In an old building that stands monument to the glittering past of the colonial city. Creole and Spanish cuisine. Music in the evenings.
À la carte: $10/$12
🎵

CENTRAL CUBA
CIÉNAGA DE ZAPATA

A E–F4
→ **ACCOMMODATION**
Villa Guamá
A F4
Laguna del Tesoro
Tel. (59) 2979
Tourist hotel
Attractive bungalows on stilts in a garden at the center of the

lake; wooden structures with palm roofs. Perfect for nature-lovers. The restaurant serves chicken, fish and crocodile.
59 rooms ($34/$44)
▥ 🎵 🔲 🏠

Hotel Playa Larga
A F4
Playa Larga, Península de Zapata
Tel. (59) 7225/94
Tourist hotel
Around fifty well-equipped bungalows.
57 rooms ($20/$25)

→ **RESTAURANTS**
La Boca
A F4
Open 10am–6pm
Typical restaurant
Near the crocodile farm, good wholesome food in a relaxed atmosphere. Chicken, pork, fish and occasionally crocodile served with a smile.
À la carte: $12/$18

CIENFUEGOS

B B3
→ **ACCOMMODATION**
Hotel Jagua
B B3
Calle 37 #1 e/ ave 0 y 2
Tel. (432) 30 214
Fax (432) 66 74 54
Tourist hotel
At the entrance to Punta Gorda, the residential quarter of Cienfuegos, this late 1950s hotel, run by Accor, has a superb view over the bay. Meals nearby at the Palacio del Valle.
145 rooms ($35/$50)
▥ 🏊

Hotel Rancho Luna
B B3
Carretera de Rancho Luna, Cienfuegos
Tel. (432) 4 8 120
Fax (432) 33 50 57
Tourist hotel
Ten miles from the center of Cienfuegos, this is a good hotel for

lazing on the beach or scuba-diving. Excursions into the hills of Escambray. Two restaurants. 225 rooms ($28/$34), ⛆

TRINIDAD

B C4
→ **ACCOMMODATION**
Hotel Ancón
B C4

Playa Ancón, 9 miles from Trinidad
Tel. (419) 66 74 24
Tourist hotel
Recommended for its fabulous view of the sea and white sandy beach rather than for its rather off-putting architecture; this hotel also has quality bungalows. Scuba-diving, water sports and mountain-biking. Restaurant.
279 rooms ($60/$80)
⛆

Hotel Costa Sur
B C4

Playa María Aguilar, Casilda
Tel. (419) 3180/3491
Tourist hotel
Next to the previous hotel, smaller, with friendly staff. Dive sites in front of the hotel. Also an ideal base for enjoying the mountain scenery of the south coast or the Sierra del Escambray. Restaurant.
131 rooms ($35/$45)
⛆ 🎵 ◭ ⛆

Motel Las Cuevas
B C4

Calle Finca Santa Ana (10 mins. walk from the center)
Tel. (419) 4013/9
Tourist hotel
On the hillside above this small colonial city, boasting a sea view, this motel run by Horizontes offers functional accommodation, 10 mins from the center.
114 rooms ($45)
60 bungalows
⛆ 🎵 ⛆ Ⅲ

→ **RESTAURANTS**
☺ **El Mesón del Recogidor**
B C4

Calle Simón Bolívar, #424
Tel. (419) 3756
Open 11am-10pm
Typical restaurant
A visit to Plaza Mayor, the Museo de Arquitectura and the Iglesia de la Santísima Trinidad will plunge visitors into the Spanish colonial atmosphere of this unique city, one of the three oldest cities in Cuba. Avoid breaking the spell by eating at this restaurant, which offers the best food near Plaza Mayor, with its small bar and gorgeous leafy patio. You will be served traditional Cuban cuisine,

EL MESÓN DEL RECOGIDOR

grilled pork with or without sauce, accompanied by cabbage, but with a great deal of cheer and a complete lack of pretension.
À la carte: $12/$16.

SANCTI SPÍRITUS

B D4
→ **ACCOMMODATION**
Villa Rancho Hatuey
B D4

Carretera Central, 239 miles (2 miles from Sancti Spíritus)
Tel. (41) 2 6015
Typical hotel and restaurant
This has been converted into a hotel with cabañas

(bungalows). The stylish, sophisticated restaurant is a cut above the rank and file of 'official' restaurants. One of the few good restaurants in the region.
38 rooms ($60)

SANTA CLARA

B C3
→ **ACCOMMODATION**
Hotel Santa Clara Libre
B C3

Parque Vidal #6 e/ Trista y Padre Chao
Tel. (422) 7548
Tourist hotel
Huge building (1956) in the city center, which was one of the landmarks in the Castroist Revolution. Rooms are quite small, but some have double beds. Decent restaurant.
168 rooms ($25–30)
🎵 ⬆ ◭

Hotel Mascotte
B C3

Parque Martí, Santa Clara
Tel. (422) 5481
Tourist hotel
One of the few hotels in this old Spanish colonial city, which was the site of one of the last episodes in the war for independence of 1895. Typical lobby. Moderate prices.
10 rooms ($15)

FROM MORÓN TO CAYO GUILLERMO

B E2–3
→ **ACCOMMODATION**
Hotel Tryp Cayo Coco**
B E3

Tel. 33 53 88
Fax 33 51 66
Luxury hotel
Magnificent recently built hotel complex representing a colonial-style village, with every

comfort and a wide up-to-date range of sports and water sports facilities. One of the restaurants specializes in fish and shellfish.
458 rooms ($141/$204 full board)
⛆ 🎵

Meliá Cayo Coco**
B E3

Tel. 30 12 80
Fax 30 12 85
Tourist hotel
On the superb Playa de las Coloradas, this new Sol Meliá complex offers a comprehensive range of facilities bound to guarantee an enjoyable stay, including good service and cuisine (Italian food and beachside restaurant).
270 rooms ($92/$97 full board)
Ⅲ ⛆ ⬆

Villa Cojímar
B E2

Cayo Guillermo
Tel. (33) 30 17 12
Fax (33) 30 17 27
Tourist hotel
West of Cayo Coco, this resort abounds with memories of Hemingway and his fishing expeditions beyond the coral reefs and the mangroves of the south coast, colonized by pelicans. This hotel is recommended for fishing enthusiasts.
167 double rooms ($100/$120 full board)

Villa Vigía**
B E2

Cayo Guillermo
Tel. (33) 30 17 60
Fax (33) 30 17 48
Tourist hotel
This is the most recently built tourist complex; it is also haunted

✪ : the editors' choice
The grid references (for example: Hotel Inglaterra **E** B4)
refer to the maps at the end of the guide ◆ 265.

by the ghost of
Hemingway.
*Run by Gran Caribe,
it is a must.*
264 double rooms
Restaurant

CAMAGÜEY

B F5
→ ACCOMMODATION
Hotel Colón
B F5
Calle República
#72 e/ San José
y San Martín
Tel. (322) 83 346
*Former colonial
house, converted
into a hotel in 1920.
The rooms are
arranged around
a tiny patio.
Restaurant.*
$10–20
▥

→ RESTAURANTS
**La Campaña del
Toledo**
B F5
Plaza San Juan
de Dios
Tel. (322) 95 888
Typical restaurant
*The tables of this
restaurant are
arranged under the
arches around the
patio of a former
colonial house,
in the heart of the
city. The specialty
(boliche de
mechado) comes
from the cattle
farms of Camagüey.
Attentive staff.*
À la carte: $10
🄒

ORIENTE
HOLGUÍN

C C4
→ ACCOMMODATION
Villa el Bosque
C C4
Ave. Jorge
Dimitrov
Tel. (24) 48 10 12
Tourist hotel
*Bungalows
situated in a tree-
lined park in the
city center; a
pleasantly relaxed
atmosphere.
Moderate prices.*
69 rooms ($32)
Bungalows with
shower, patio.
🄳 🌊

GUARDALAVACA

C D5
→ ACCOMMODATION
Villa Turey
C D5
Tel. (24) 30 195
Fax (24) 30 265
Tourist hotel
*Hotel complex
comprising
comfortable
villas near the
sea (300 yards).
Quite pricey for
the quality of
the facilities.*
2 restaurants.
136 rooms ($50–75)
3 suites

HOTEL CASA GRANDA

BAYAMO

C B5
→ ACCOMMODATION
Hotel Sierra Maestra
C B5
Tel. (23) 45013
Tourist hotel
*Despite its size
and lack of
character, the only
hotel in Bayamo
is a comfortable
stopover for
travelers passing
through. Fairly good
cuisine. Restaurant.*
207 rooms ($30–40)
▥ 🌊

MANZANILLO

C B5
→ ACCOMMODATION
Hotel Guacanayabo
C B5
Ave. Camilo
Cienfuegos
Tel. (23) 54 01 25
Fax (23) 4139
Tourist hotel
*At the entrance
to the city, on a
promontory jutting
out over the sea.
Well-kept, if
characterless,
establishment, with
friendly staff; also
used by Cubans.*

*The restaurant serves
seafood specialties.*
103 rooms ($30–35)
🌊 ▥

SIERRA MAESTRA

C B5
→ ACCOMMODATION
Villa Santo Domingo
C B5
(15 miles south of
Bartolomé Masó)
Tourist hotel
*This is the point of
departure, along the
River Yara, at an
altitude of 2500 ft,
for 'ecotourists'
wanting to make
the ascent of Pico
Turquino (6476 ft),
the highest point in
the Sierra Maestra.
Pony trekking.*
20 bungalows
($25/$35)

SANTIAGO DE CUBA

C D5
→ ACCOMMODATION
✪ **Hotel Casa Granda**
C D5
Calle Heredia #201
Santiago de Cuba
Tel. (226) 88 600
Fax (226) 86 035
Typical hotel
*In 1914, Santiago
de Cuba, then the
second largest city
in the country,
celebrated the
inauguration of a
colonial-style hotel,
which was to make
it one of the leading
resorts on the island.
Now, after a
complete facelift,
Hotel Casa Granda
has again opened its
doors. In the city
center, opposite the
Plaza de Armas, now
Parque Céspedes
and on the corner by
the cathedral, the
hotel is ideally*
placed near Calle
Heredia, the city's
cultural center. A
rooftop bar, on the
sixth story, overlooks
the park and the
bay. You can get one
of the best mojitos
here. Since it
reopened, a special
effort has been
made to ensure the
high quality of the
food.
58 rooms ($52/$82)
🄳 📷 ▥

Hotel Santiago
C D5
Ave. Las Américas,
esq. Calle M,
Santiago de Cuba
Tel. (226) 42 612
Fax (226) 41 756
Luxury hotel
*The most recently
built hotel in
Santiago combines
metal and
polychrome
structures, the work
of a Cuban architect.
A striking contrast
with the colonial
atmosphere of the
rest of the city. Very
comfortable, but the
furniture is not very
robust. La Cubana
Restaurant.*
302 rooms ($67)
🌊 🎵 🄳

→ RESTAURANTS
Balcón del Caribe
C D5
Carretera del Morro
(5 miles from the
center of Santiago)
Tel. (226) 91 011
Hotel and restaurant
with character
*The rooms are so
bare that they are
virtually empty, but
visitors will enjoy the
lovely swimming
pool, surrounded
by palm trees
overlooking the
sea. Bar (fabulous
panoramic view of
the bay at sunset)
and restaurant
serving Creole and
international cuisine.
Well-trained and
friendly staff.*
72 rooms ($28–32),
bar, restaurant.
🌊 🄳 ⛷

Restaurant 1900
C D5
Calle San Basilio,
#354 Santiago de
Cuba
Tel. (226) 23 507
Open from 7pm
to midnight
Luxury restaurant
*The former
residence of Emilio
Bacardí with its
flamboyant decor
is probably the
best restaurant
in the city. Varied
Creole cuisine
(pork, seafood) and
efficient service.
Expensive.*
À la carte: $20

El Morro
C D5
Carretera del Morro
(4 miles from the
center of Santiago
de Cuba). At the
foot of the fortress
Tel. (226) 91 576
Open from noon
to 10pm.
Typical restaurant.
*Magnificent
terrace at the foot
of the fortress,
where you can savor
fish, shrimp and
other shellfish, and
several Creole dishes
at any time.
Excellent staff.*
À la carte: $8-12

PARQUE BACONAO
C D5
→ ACCOMMODATION
Hotel Bucanero
C D5
Tel. (226) 28 130
Tourist hotel
*Hotel complex
comprising eight
small buildings,
with a wonderful
seaside location
near a cove.*
200 rooms
($50 including
meal)

Hacienda Montesur
C D5
Carretera de
Baconao (6 miles
from Santiago)
Tel. (226) 86 213
Tourist hotel
Situated in Parque

*Baconao, the hotel
is perfect for
relaxing,
scubadiving and
bathing. Restaurant.*
20 rooms
($24/$30)

GUANTÁNAMO
C E5
→ ACCOMMODATION
Casa de los Ensueños
C E5
Calle Ahogado,
esq. Calle 15
Norte, Reparto
Caribe
Tel. (21) 32 63 04

VILLA LINDAUAR

Hotel and
restaurant with
character
*Small family
hotel which serves
the best food in
the city. You can
even choose your
own menu, as long
as you arrange
it in advance. This
custom is completely
at odds with the
practices of state-
owned restaurants.*
3 air-conditioned
rooms.
($12–15)

BARACOA
C F5
→ ACCOMMODATION
Hotel el castillo
C F5
Calle Calixto
Garcia
Tel. (21) 42 103
Hotel with character
*On the site of the
former fortress of
Seboruco (1740),
this establishment
occupies a
strategic position.
The view from some
of the rooms is
exceptional and
the architecture,*

*for once, respects
the site it is built
on. Beautiful
swimming pool at
the heart of the
former Spanish
fortress.
An excellent
restaurant is also
situated on the
hillside, serving
meat specialties
and Creole cuisine.
Very friendly
staff add to the
atmosphere.*
35 rooms
($40–50)

ARCHIPIÉLAGO DE LOS CANARREOS
ISLE OF YOUTH
A C–D4–5
→ ACCOMMODATION
Hotel el Colony**
A D5
Carretera de
Siguanea, 10 miles
Tel. (61) 9 8181
Tourist hotel
*Southwest of the
island, beside a
white sandy beach
lined with coconut
palms, this slightly
old-fashioned hotel
was the first diving
center in Cuba.
The restaurant
serves turtle
fricassée.*
83 rooms. ($60/$80)

CAYO LARGO
A F5
→ ACCOMMODATION
○ **Villa Lindamar**
A F5
Cayo Largo del Sur,
Archipiélago de los
Canarreos
Tel. (5) 4 8111 to 118
Fax (5) 4 8160
Leisure complex
*The Villa Lindamar
(Gran Caribe),
situated on the*

*beach, comprises
a row of buildings
reminiscent of
tobacco barns,
with roofs covered
in palm leaves.
International and
Creole cuisine is
served in the
restaurant.*
63 rooms

PALADARES & CASAS PARTICULARES
HAVANA
Cocina de Lilian
Miramar
Allow around $20
Paladar Huron Azul
Calle Humboldt,
#153, esq. P
Tel. (7) 79 1691
Open daily
from noon to
midnight
Amparo Lopez
Línea 53
between M y N
Tel. (7) 32 7003
Allow $25
Maritza
Calle principe
#140
Espada y Hospital
Tel. (7) 78 6842
Paladar Aladino
Calle 21 #55 e/
M y N

SANTIAGO DE CUBA
**Jorge Abdala and
Haydé Haber**
Calle J #65
e/ 2da 3ra
Reparto Sueño
Tel. (226) 25 196
3 rooms ($25)
**Hermez Dominguez
Family and Dalgis
López Sablón**
Feliz Peña (altos)
Tel. (226) 20 060
Allow $25
Paladar el Amanecer
Calle 10 #224
Bravo Corrioso
Reparto San
Barbara
Double rooms.

TRINIDAD
Maritza Hernandez
Calle Francisci
Cadahia #223
e/ Colon y Lino
Pérez
Tel. (419) 3160
Allow $18

BIBLIOGRAPHY

GENERAL

Barclay, Juliet, *Havana: Portrait of a City*, Cassell, 1993

Black, A, and S. McBride, *Cuba Yesterday and Today*, Abbeville Press, 1998

Cabrera Infante, G., *Holy Smoke*, Faber and Faber, 1985

Cabrera Infante, G., *Mea Cuba*, Faber and Faber, 1985

Cuba's Representative Machinery, Human Rights Watch, 1999

Carley, R., Cuba, *400 Years of Architectural Heritage*, Whitney, 1997

González-Wippler, Migene, *Santería: African Magic in Latin America*, Doubleday/Anchor, 1973

González-Wippler, Migene, *The Santería Experience*, Prentice-Hall, 1982

Kohli, Eddy, Cuba, Rizzoli, 1997

Lechthaler, Ernst, Amiel Pretsch and August F. Winkler, *Rum Drinks and Havanas*, Abbeville Press, 1999

Llanes, Lilian, *The Houses of Old Cuba*, Thames and Hudson, 1999

Murphy, Joseph M., *Santeria: African Spirits in America*, Beacon Press, 1988

Nichele, Franc, and Michel Renaudeau, *Cuba*, Evergreen, 1999

Núñez Jiménez, Antonio, *The Journey of the Havana Cigar*, Cubatabaco, Havana, 1988

Ortiz, Fernando, *Cuban Counterpoint: Tobacco and Sugar*, Alfred A. Knopf, Inc., 1947

Raffaele, H., et al., *Birds of the West Indies*, Christopher Helm, 1998

Silva Lee, A., *Natural Cuba*, Pangaea, 1996

HISTORY AND POLITICS

Bethell, Leslie, ed., *Cuba: A Short History*, Cambridge University Press, 1993

Brenner, Philip, and Daniel Siegal, eds. *The Cuba Reader*, Grove, 1988

Brugioni, Dino A., *Eyeball to Eyeball: The Inside Story of the Cuban Missile Crisis*, Random House, 1991

Castañeda, Jorge, *Compañero - the Life and Death of Che Guevara*, Bloomsbury, 1998

Castro, Fidel, *Face to Face with Fidel Castro: A Conversation with Tomás Borge*, Ocean Press, 1993

Che: The Photobiography of Che Guevara, Thunder's Mouth Press, 1999

Fursenko, Aleksandr, and Timothy Naftali, *'One Hell of a Gamble'*, Pimlico, 1999

Geyer, Georgie Anne, *Guerrilla Prince: The Untold Story of Fidel Castro*, Little, Brown and Co., 1991

Higgins, Trumbull, *The Perfect Failure: Kennedy, Eisenhower and the CIA at the Bay of Pigs*, W.W. Norton, 1987

Hinkle, Warren, *Deadly Secrets: The CIA-Mafia War Against Castro and the Assassination of J.F.K.*, Thunder's Mouth Press, 1992

Lockwood, Lee, *Castro's Cuba*, Westview Press, Boulder, Co., 1990

Martí, José, *Our America*, Monthly Review Press, 1977

Miné, Gianni, *An Encounter With Fidel*, Ocean Press, 1991

Moreno Fraginals, Manuel, *The Sugarmill: The Socioeconomic Complex of Sugar in Cuba*, Monthly Review Press, 1976

Pérez, Louis A., *Cuba: Between Reform and Revolution*, Oxford University Press, 1988

Pérez-Stable, Marifeli, *The Cuban Revolution*, Oxford University Press, 1993

Quirk, Robert E., *Fidel Castro*, W.W. Norton

Suchlicki, Jaime, *Historical Dictionary of Cuba*, Scarecrow Press, 1988)

Thomas, Hugh, *Cuba, or The Pursuit of Freedom*, Eyre & Spottiswoode, London, 1971

LITERATURE

Cabrera Infante, G., *Infante's Inferno*, Harper & Row, 1984

Cabrera Infante, G., *Three Trapped Tigers*, Harper & Row, 1971

Cabrera Infante, G., *View of Dawn in the Tropics*, Harper & Row, 1978

Carpentier, Alejo, *The Chase*, Farrar, Straus and Giroux, 1989

Carpentier, Alejo, *Explosion in a Cathedral*, Harper & Row, 1979

Carpentier, Alejo, *Reasons of State*, Writers and Readers, 1977

Fuentes, Norberto, *Hemingway in Cuba*, Lyle Stuart, 1984

Greene, Graham, *Our Man in Havana*, William Heinemann Ltd., 1958)

Guillén, Nicolás, *Patria o Muerte!, The Great Zoo and Other Poems*, Monthly Review Press, 1972

Hemingway, Ernest, *Islands in the Stream*, Scribner's, 1970

Hemingway, Ernest, *The Old Man and the Sea*, Jonathan Cape, 1952

Lezama Lima, José, *Paradiso*, Farrar, Straus and Giroux, 1974

Martí, José, *Major Poems*, Holmes & Meier, 1982

Michael Palin's Hemingway Adventure, Weidenfeld and Nicolson, 1999

Montejo, Esteban, *The Autobiography of a Runaway Slave*, Pantheon, 1968

Robles, Mireya, *Hagiography of Narcisa the Beautiful*, Readers International Inc., 1996

Simbel, Wendy, *Havana Dreams*, Virago, 1999

Valdés, Zoé, *Yocandra in the Paradise of Nada*, Allison and Busby Ltd, 1995

TRAVELLERS' TALES

Cardenal, Ernesto, *In Cuba*, New Directions, 1974

Chadwick, Lee, *A Cuban Journey*, Dobson, 1975

Gébler, Carlo, *Driving through Cuba*, Simon & Schuster, 1988

Miller, Tom, *Trading with the Enemy*, Atheneum, 1992

Smith, Stephen, *The Land of Miracles: A journey through modern Cuba*, Abacus, 1998

Terry, T. Philip, *Terry's Guide to Cuba*, Houghton Mifflin, 1929

DISCOGRAPHY

COMPILATIONS

Made in Havana: 30 Years of Cuban Rhythms, Music Collection International Ltd, Nascente, NSCD012

Casa de la Trova, Erato disques SA, 3984.25751-2, 1999

La Musica Cubana, Arc Music Productions Int. Ltd, EUCD 0313, 1999

The Cuban Danzón: Before there was jazz, 1906-29, Arhoolie Productions Inc. CD032, 1999

Retro Officielle des musiques cubaines, Fremeaux & associés, FA176

Cuadernos de la Habana, Winter, 910 030-2, 1999

The Golden Age of Son, EMP Musique, 995482, 1994

Rhythm and Smoke, The Cuba Sessions, Global Disc Records, Platinum Entertainment, 1998

Cuba Tradicion, Ayra Musica/Rata Records, pa'ti pa' mi 71016

Cuba 1923-95 (with English notes), Fremeaux & Associés, FA157

Cuba Now, EMI Records Ltd, 7243 4931562 4, 1998

Real Cuba, Universal Music, 012153838-2, 1999

A Carnival of Cuban Music, Rounder Records, CD5049, 1990

A Night in Havana, Charly Schallplaten GmtH CDHOT 617, 1997

Cuban Roots, OPW Records, PWK 83635, 1999

Cuban Gold: Que se sepa, yo soy de la Habana, Qbadisc, QB9006

Cuban Gold: Bajo con Tumbao, Qbadisc, QB9016

Cuban Gold: El Mambo me priva - the '60s, Qbadisc, QB9024

Cuban Gold: Fuego Candela -the Smokin' '70s, Qbadisc, QB9025

Cuban Gold: Ipa' Bilari - the '80s, Qbadisc, QB9027

From Cuba to Cuba, Edenways, EDE 1057-2, 1996

Sacred Rhythms of Cuban Santeriá, Smithsonian Folkways, SFCD 40419, 1995

Alma Cubana, A

Collection of Popular Songs, sung by Bobby Jiménez, Elan, CD 82294

ARTISTS' RECORDINGS

Albita, *Una Mujer como yo*, Epic, Sony Music Entertainment, 489 002 2, 1997

Antonio Arcaño y sus Maravillas 1944-51, *Danzón Mambo*, Tumbao Cuban Classics, Dist. Camarillo Music Ltd, TCD-029, 1993

Bakuleyé, *Fiebre del ula ula*, Ahi-Namá Music, 1091, 1998

Banda Gigante with Benny Moré, *Locas por El Mambo*, Harmonia Mundi, Iris Musique, HMCD 79, 1993

Banda Gigante with Benny Moré, *El Barbaro del Ritmo*, Javelin Promotions Ltd, PSCCD 1004, 1995

Adelardo Barroso con la Orquesta Sensación, *No Hay Como Mi Son* 1954-56, Caney, CCD 514, 1996

Elena Burke Trio, *Matamoros*, Orfeon Videovox, 9944130102, 1997

Malena Burke and NG La Banda, *Salseando*, IMP, Son 023 212

Pupi Campo and his orchestra, *Rhumbas and Mambos*, Tumbao Cuban Classics, Dist. Camarillo Music Ltd, TCD-007, 1991

Caravana Cubana, *Late Night Sessions*, Dreamer Music Productions, DMCD 0562, 1999

David Calzado and La Charanga, *Grandes Exitos*, Universal Music, LATD-40058, 1997

Clave y Guaguaricó, *Songs and Dances*, Green Linnet Records Inc., Xenophile GLCD 4023, 1990

Conjunto Casino 1941-46, *Rumba Quimbumba*, Tumbao Cuban Classics, Dist. Camarillo Music Ltd, TCD-030, 1993

Conjunto Casino, *Mambo con cha-cha-cha*, Tumbao Cuban Classics, Dist. Camarillo Music Ltd, TCD-080, 1996

Conjunto Casino, *Cancion del alma*, Tumbao Cuban Classics, Dist. Camarillo Music Ltd, TCD-040

Compay Segundo, *Cien Anos de Son*, Warner Music International,

39842 66932, 1999

Cantinero de Cuba, *Cubamar*, Pacific Toyama Inc., Global Disc Records, 15095 957 42, 1999

Cuba LA, Narada Productions Inc., VND CD18, 1998

La Bella Cubana, *Questa de Camara de Madrid*, Orfeon Videovox, CDL-13113, 1997

Maestro Richard Egües y La Orquesta Aragon, *Homage Postumo a Rafael Lay*, ODEA, 01103, 1996

Maestro Richard Egües, *Aguardiente de Caña*, ODEA, 01104, 1996

Richard Egües and friends, *Cuban Sessions*, Latin World Productions, CD-99001, 1999

Familia Valera Miranda, *Caña Quema*, Nimbus Records, NI 5517, 1997

Juan Formell and Los Van Van, *Te Pone la Gabez Mala*, Metro Blue, Caribe Productions Inc., 7243 821307 27, 1997

Celina González & Reutilio, *Desde la Habana te traigo*, Tumi CD 074, 1998

Celina González, *Rich Harvest*, Tumi CD 066, 1996

Celina González, *Fiesta Guajira*, World Circuit, WCD 034

Grupo Afro Cuba, *African Roots*, Shanachie Entertainment Corps, 66009, 1998

Grupo Afro Cuba, *Smooth Jazz Moods*, Universal, RMD82233

Grupo Changui de Guantanamo, *Llegaron los Changüiceros*, Lucho 7713-2, 1994

Changui, Traditional Crossroads, CD4290

Grupo Oba-Ilu, *Santeriá, Songs for the Orishas*, Soul Jazz Records, CD38

Liuba Mariá Heria, *Alguien me espera*, Eurotropical, EUCD2

Iluyenkori, *Cuban Drums*, Playasound, PS 65218, 1999

Homenaje al Ernesto Lecuona, Seeco Tropical, STR 90528, 1991

Ernesto Lecuona, *Cuban Originals*, BMG Music, RCA, 74321-69937-2, 1999

Lecuona Cuban Boys, Vol. 1, Harlequin, HQCD11, 1989

Lecuona Cuban Boys,

Vol. 2, Harlequin, HQCD07, 1991

Lecuona Cuban Boys, Vol. 3, Harlequin, HQCD21, 1992

Lecuona Cuban Boys, Vol. 4, Harlequin, HQCD26, 1993

Liviam, Eurotropical, EUCD 5, 1997

Orquesta de Belisario López, *Prueba mi Sazón*, Tumbao Cuban Classics, Dist. Camarillo Music Ltd, TCD-069

Antonio Machin, *Cancionero de Oro*, Alma Latina, ALCD-505, 1995

Antonio Machin, *El Manisero*, Tumbao Cuban Classics, Dist. Camarillo Music Ltd, TCD-026, 1993

Antonio Machin, *Lamento Esclavo*, Tumbao Cuban Classics, Dist. Camarillo Music Ltd, TCD-053, 1995

Antonio Machin, *Cuarteto and Septeto*, Harlequin, HQCD 122, 1998

Celeste Mendoza, Rise International Music Ltd, LM82058

Celeste Mendoza y Benny Moré, *La Reina y el Barbaro*, CD 0022, Egrem, 1992

Celeste Mendoza, *con la Or de Bebo Valdés*, Musica del Sol, MSC 7203

Celeste Mendoza, *Le Reina del Guancanco*, Sonido and Déclic, 506962, 1999

Mariano Mercerón y sus Muchachos Pimienta, *"Negro Ñañamboro"*, Tumbao Cuban Classics, Dist. Camarillo Music Ltd, TCD-050, 1994

Mariano Mercerón, *"Yo tengo un Tumbao"*, Tumbao Cuban Classics, Dist. Camarillo Music Ltd, TCD-064, 1995

Los Muñequitos de Matanzas, *Rumba Caliente 88/77*, Qbadisc QB9005, 1992

Los Muñequitos de Matanzas, *Congo yambumba*, Qbadisc QB9014 1984

Rita Montaner, *La Unica*, Alma Latina, ALCD 004, 1995

Orquesta America, *Charanqueando*, 73138 35802-2, Egrem 1996, Milan Entertainment Inc., 1997

Manny Oquendo y su conjunto libre incredible, Bethlehem Music Co. Inc., CDGR 154, 1994

Orquesta America, with Cuban All Stars, Tumi TMG CD4, 1997

Orquesta America, with Chucho Valdes and Felix Revia, Tumi, TMG CD5, 1997

Orquesta Americana, with Celina González, Caridad Cuervo, Roberto Sanchez and Felix Baloy, Tumi, TMG CD6, 1997

Orquesta Revé, *La explosion del momento!* Realworld/Virgin Ltds, RW CD4, 1989

Orquesta Revé y su Charangon, IMP, SON 022, 1993

Isaac Oriedo, Routes of Rhythm Vol. 3, Rounder Records Corp, CD 5055, 1992

Guillermo Portabales, *Romance Guajiro*, Musica Latina Nostalgia, MLN 55009

Guillermo Portabales, *Al Vaiven de mi carreta*, Tumbao Cuban Classics, Dist. Camarillo Music Ltd, TCD-084, 1996

Guillermo Portabales, *Promesas de un campesino*, Tumbao Cuban Classics, Dist. Camarillo Music Ltd, TCD-804, 1999

Perez Prado, Cuban Originals, BMG Music, 74321 70046-2, 1999

Nico Saquito y sus Guaracheros de Oriente, *Alborada*, TCD 094, 1998

Nico Saquito, *Goodbye Mr Cat*, Egrem 1982, WCD 035, 1993

Septeto Anacaona 1936-7, Harlequin, HQCD27, 1993

Sexteto Habanero, Son Cubano, Tumbao Cuban Classics, Dist. Camarillo Music Ltd, TCD-001, 1991

Sextetos Cubanos, Arhoolie, CD7003, 1991

Sintesis, Ancestros QB9001, 1992

Sintesis, Ancestros 2, QB9015, 1994

Roberto Torres y Sigo Oriollo, Guarjiro Records, SAR 1046, 1988

Trio Matamoros, Harlequin, HQCD69, 1997 Trio Yagua, *The Trova*, Nimbus Records, NI 5565, 1998

Merceditas Valdés, *Ay que bueno!*, 43051-2, Egrem 1997, Milan Ent. Inc.1990

Los Van Van, Best of Los Van Van, 73138-357999-2 9 Egrem 1996, Milan Entertainment Inc. 1999

© P. Hausherr.
Bell of La Demajagua,
© P. Hausherr.
Street in Manzanillo,
© P. Hausherr.
206 Fresco charting
the History of the
Revolution,
© P. Hausherr.
The Morro and the
harbor entrance, 19th-
century lithograph,
Paris, BNF,
© BNF.
206/207 Fresco
charting the History of
the Revolution,
© P. Hausherr.
207 Fresco charting
the History of the
Revolution,
© P. Hausherr.
Drawing,
© Titouan Lamazou.
208 Roof of
the convent,
© T. Deschamps/Diaf.
Balcony of the city hall,
© B. Perouse/ Hoa Qui.
209 Compay Segundo,
© E. Lobo/Hoa Qui.
Inside the Casa de la
Trova, © P. Hausherr.
El Guayabera,
© G. de Remuzat/
Yemaya Productions.
210 Patio, © Sablon/
Publicitur Balcony,
© P. Hausherr.
211 Detail of the
decorative woodwork,
© B. Lenormand/

Gallimard.
Bedroom,
© B. Lenormand/
Gallimard.
Drawing room,
© P. Hausherr.
Dining room,
© P. Hausherr.
212 Early 20th
century postcard,
Havana, BNJM,
© BNJM/Gallimard.
212/213 View
of Santiago,
© M. Renaudeau/
Hoa Qui.
213 Store in the 1920s,
© Fototeca de Cuba
Tumba Francesa
dancers, © D. Laisné/
Cosmos.
214 The harbor,
© G. Boseo/
Hoa Qui.
Statue in honor of
Antonio Macéo,
© P. Hausherr.
215 Bacardí factory,
1930s/40s, © Fototeca
de Cuba.
Street barber,
© P. Hausherr.
216 Castillo el Morro,
© P. Hausherr.
217 Number plate,
© J.C. Pratt/Diaf.
Classic car,
© P. Hausherr.
Street in Santiago,
© M. Renaudeau/
Hoa Qui.
218 The Basilica

of El Cobre,
© P. Hausherr.
Pilgrimage to the
Basilica P.
Hausherr.
id, © P. Hausherr.
220 Joseíto Fernandez,
Havana, MNM,
© MNM.
Changüí band,
© P. Hausherr.
221 Packets of
cucurucho,
© P. Hausherr.
Street in Baracoa,
© P. Hausherr.
*The Execution of
Hatuey*, anonymous
engraving, © P. Alibert.
222 House in
the country,
© T. Deschamps/Diaf.
Portrait of La Rusa,
© P. Hausherr.
Hotel La Rusa,
© P. Hausherr.
223 Cayo Rico,
© G.A. Rossi/Altitude.
224 Isle of Youth,
© Ph. Beuzen/Scope.
225 José Marti's prison,
© Ph. Beuzen/Scope.
Pirates Anne Bonny and
Mary Read, 18th-
century engraving,
© P. Newark's Historical
Picture.
226 Church of Nuestra
Señora de los Dolores,
© P. Hausherr.
226-227 The
Penitentiary,

© P. Hausherr.
Castro's cell,
© P. Hausherr.
228 Beaches at
Cayo Largo,
© G.A. Rossi/Altitude/
Hoa Qui.
229 © E. Valentin/
Hoa Qui.
230 Propaganda,
© T. Deschamps/Diaf.
Children,
© M. Renaudeau/
Hoa Qui.
Man from behind,
© P. Cheuva/Diaf.
Homme smiling,
© M. Renaudeau/
Hoa Qui.
232 Coco Taxi,
© M. Peainchau.
235 © M. Renaudeau/
Hoa Qui.
236 © M. Debatty/
Photocéans.
237 © C. Sarramon.
247 Hôtel Inglaterra,
© C. Sarramon.
Bodeguita del Medio,
© M. Renaudeau/
Hoa Qui.
249 La Terraza,
© C. Sarramon.
251 Meson del
Recogidor,
© C. Sarramon.

Thank you to Vivian
Montane, José Goïtia
and Ion de la Riva for
their valuable
assistance.

259

The headings within the 'Practical Information' section, such as climate and entry requirements, appear in the index. The numbers that refer to this section are in italics.

◆ INDEX

Map section

A

GULF OF MEXICO

ARCHIPIÉLAGO DE LOS COLORADOS Y DE SANTA ISABEL

CAYO LEVISA
El Morillo
Bahía Honda
Manuel Sangully
La Palma
SIERRA ROSARIO
SOROA
Niceto Pérez
CUEVA DE LOS PORTALES
PARQUE LA GÜIRA
Entronque de Herradura
Consolación del Sur
Los Palacios
Herradura
Cubanacán
Playa Dayaniguas
PUNTA CARRAGUAO

CAYO INÉS DE SOTO
Puerto Esperanza
VIÑALES VALLEY
Santa Lucía
CAYO JUTÍAS
Viñales
Minas de Matahambre

DE GUANIGUANICO

CAYO RAPADO GRANDE
Dimas
SIERRA DE LOS ÓRGANOS
Sumidero
Pinar del Río
Puerta de Golpe
CORDILLERA DE

CAYO DE BUENAVISTA
Arroyos de Mantua
Mantua

PUNTA TABACO

VUELTA ABAJO
San Juan y Martínez
San Luis
Alonso de Rojas
La Coloma

PUNTA DE ÁBALOS
Guane
GOLFO DE GUANAHACABIBES
Bolívar
Sandino
Isabel Rubio
PLAYA BAILÉN
Punta de Cartas
Cortés

PUNTA LA FIJA

CAYOS DE LA LEÑA
GUANAHACABIBES PENINSULA
La Balada
BAHÍA DE GUADIANA
La Fé
Manuel Lazo
CABO FRANCÉS

Las Tumbas
BAHÍA DE CORRIENTE
María La Gorda
CABO CORRIENTES
CABO DE SAN ANTONIO

PINAR DEL RÍO

CAYOS DE SAN FELIPE

CAYO LOS INDIOS
ENSENADA DE LOS BARCOS
ENSENADA DE LA SIGUANEA
CABO FRANCÉS
COSTA DE LOS PIRATAS
Cocodrilo

CARIBB

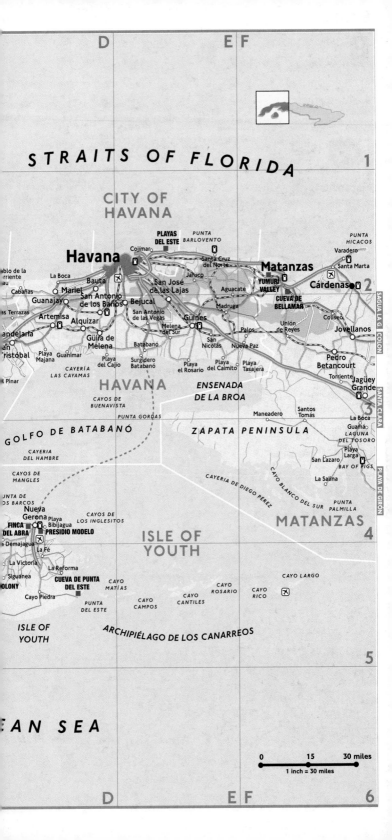

B

A B C

GÜINES/LA HABANA

LA HABANA

ARCHIPIÉLAGO DE SABANA

CAYO MORO
CAYO CRUZ DEL PADRE
PUNTA HICACOS
CAYO PUNTA ARENAS
CAYO BAHÍA DE CÁDIZ
CAYO BLANQUIZAL
BAHÍA DE SANTA CLARA
CAYO PIEDRA DEL OBISPO

Varadero
Santa Marta

1

Matanzas **Cárdenas**

Máximo Gómez

Coliseo

Jovellanos Périco

Valdivieso

Baños de Elguea

Corralillo Sierra Morena

Hoyo Colorado EMBALSE PALMA SOLA

Martí

San José de Ramos

San Pedro

Caharatas

Quintín Banderas

Quemado de Güines

CAYO ESQUIVEL DEL NORTE

Isabela de Sagua

Playa Uvero

Sagua la Grande

VILLA

CAYO DROMEDARIOS

CAYO DE PAJON

Pla
Ju
Emilio Francis
Córdoba
El Sant

Calabazar de Sagua

EMBALSE ALACRANES

Cifuentes

Encrucijada

Pedro Betancourt Agramonte

Torriente

Jagüey Grande

Seis de Agosto

Colón

San Pedro de Mayabón

Los Arabos

Cascajal

Santo Domingo

San Diego del Valle

Camajua

EMBALSE MINERVA

2

Céspedes

Santos Tomás

Australia
La Boca

Guamá

LAGUNA DEL TOSORO

Aguada de Pasajeros

La Victoria

Cartagena

Esperanza

Santa Clara

Placetas

San Lázaro

Playa Larga

BAY OF PIGS

Covadonga

Real Campiña

Rodas

Ranchuelo

CAYO BLANCO DEL SUR

PUNTA PALMILLA

La Salina

Playa Girón

Yaguaramas

Constancia

Ariza

Palmira

Cruces

San Fernando de Camarones

Agabama

Foment

Horquitas

Cienfuegos

Cumanayagua

Manicaragua

3

MATANZAS

CAYO LARGO

Juraguá

Castillo de Jagua

JARDÍN BOTÁNICO DE LA SOLEDAD

La Sierrita

San Juan

EMBALSE HANABANILLA

Topes de Collantes

Gunínia de Miranda

Condado

Trinidad

CIENFUEGOS

Casilda

TORRE MANACA IZNAGA

PLAYA ANCÓN

VALLE DE LOS INGENI

San Pedro

SANCTI

4

5

CARI

6

A B C

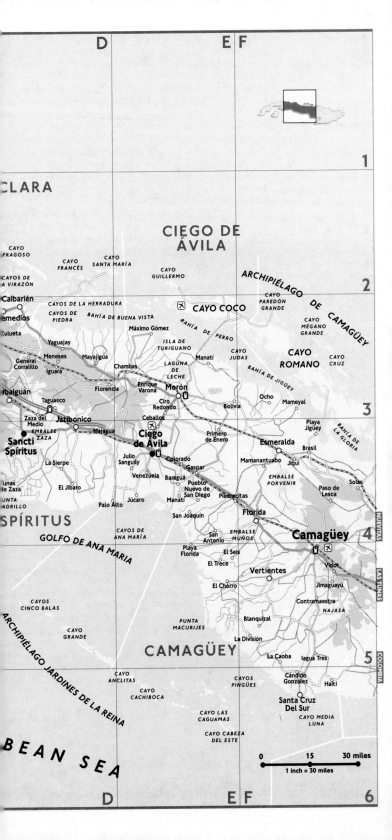

C

A   B   C

ARCHIPIÉLAGO DE CAMAGÜEY

CAYO CRUZ

1

ROMANO

SANTA

BAHÍA DE LA GLORIA

CAYO GUAJABA

PUNTA CRUZ

Piloto

CAYO SABINAL

Solas   Mola

ESMERALDA

2

Paso de Lesca

Senado   Lugareño   Nuevitas   Santa Lucia

PUNTA DE PRÁCTICOS

LAS TUNAS

CIEGO DE Á

Minas

Camagüey

EMBALSE MAÑANA DE SANTA ANA

PUNTA BRAVA

Vidot

Sibanicú

Camalote   Puerto Manati   Playa Jibara

Playa La Herradura

Jimaguayú

Martí

Rincón   Manati   Guinea   Vázquez   Delicias

Puerto Padre

Playa de Caletones

NAJASA

Najasa

Guáimaro

Jesús Menendez   Gibara

SANTA CRUZ DEL S

3

Colombia

Las Tunas

Naranjo

Velasco   Potrerillo

San Andres

Floro Pérez

Holguín

Amancio Rodriguez   Jobabo

Calixto

Buenaventura

Haiti

Ojo del Agua

Dormitorio

Mir

Maceo

Cacocum

Báguano

Guayabal   Playa El Habanero   Zábalo

Guamo Embarcadero

EMBALSE LEONERO

Río Cauto

EMBALSE CAUTO DEL PASO

Cauto Cristo

Babiney

Urbano Noris

4

ENSENADA DE BIRAMA

GOLFO DE GUACANAYABO

Cauto Embarcadero

CAYOS DE MANZANILLO

GRANMA

Manzanillo   Yara

Bayamo

Jiguaní

Contramaestre

Campechuela

Bartolomé Masó

Buey Arriba

Guisa

EMBALSE CANTILLO

Los Negros

Palma Soriano

CAYOS BALANDRAS

Media Luna

Las Mercedes

Yao del Medio

Victorino

Dos Palmas

Niquero   Vicana Arriba

Santo Domingo

SIERRA

San Lorenzo

MAESTRA

La Marsellesa

Pozo Redondo

Río Nuevo   Pilón

Marea del Portillo

PICO TURQUINO 1974 M

La Magdalena

Uvero   Chivirico

PUNTA TABACAL

5

CABO CRUZ

Alegría de Pío

SANTIAGO DE CUBA

6

A   B   C

CARI

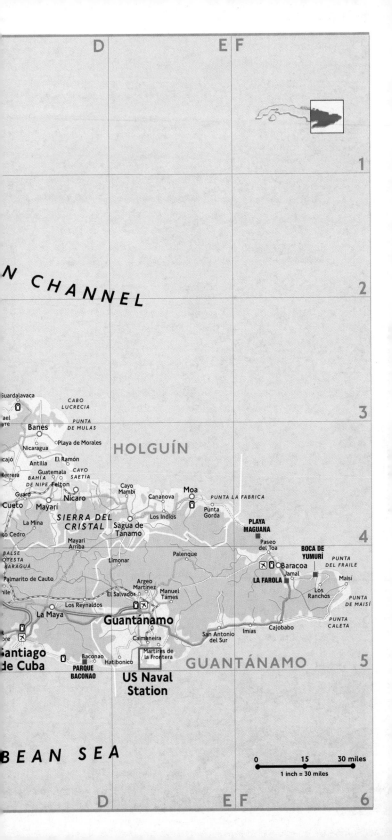

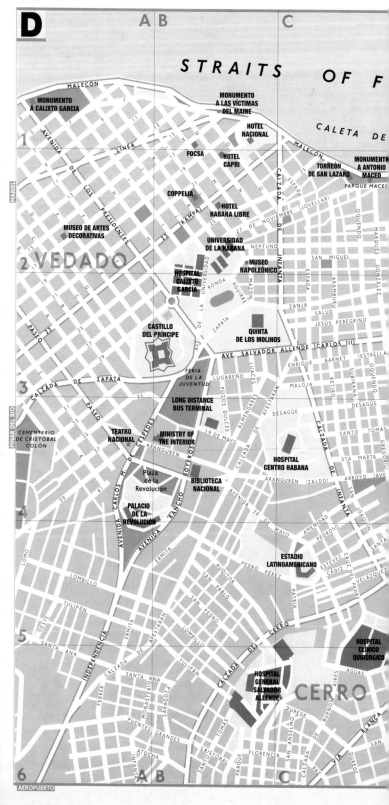

D

STRAITS OF F

MALECÓN

MONUMENTO A CALIXTO GARCIA

MONUMENTO A LAS VÍCTIMAS DEL MAINE

CALETA DE

HOTEL NACIONAL

MALECÓN

AVENIDA

LÍNEA

FOCSA

HOTEL CAPRI

TORREÓN DE SAN LÁZARO

MONUMENTO A ANTONIO MACEO

PARQUE MACEO

COPPELIA

HOTEL HABANA LIBRE

CALZADA

ESPADA

OQUENDO

MARQUÉS GONZÁLEZ

(RAMPA)

DE NOVIEMBRE (JOVELLAR)

MUSEO DE ARTES DECORATIVAS

MUSEO DE LOS PRESIDENTES

NEPTUNO

SAN MIGUEL

INFANTA

SAN MIGUEL

ARAMBURU

UNIVERSIDAD DE LA HABANA

MUSEO NAPOLEÓNICO

ESPADA

VEDADO

HOSPITAL CALIXTO GARCIA

AGUIRRE

MAZÓN

ZANJA

SALUD

JESÚS PEREGRINO

DE LA UNIVERSIDAD

RONDA

ZAPATA

QUINTA DE LOS MOLINOS

ENRIQUE

BARNET

(ESTRELLA

OQUENDO

CASTILLO DEL PRÍNCIPE

AVE. SALVADOR ALLENDE (CARLOS III)

PASEO

23

LUACES

SUBIRANA

RETIRO

FERIA DE LA JUVENTUD

LUGAREÑO

MALOJA

CALZADA

DE

ZAPATA

PASEO

POZOS DULCES

DESAGÜE

DESAGÜE

LONG DISTANCE BUS TERMINAL

AVESTARAN

SANTO TOMÁS

CEMENTERIO DE CRISTÓBAL COLÓN

19 DE MAYO

CALZADA

STA. MARTA

GREGORI

TEATRO NACIONAL

MINISTRY OF THE INTERIOR

ARANGUREN

BOTEROS

HOSPITAL CENTRO HABANA

ARROYO (AVE

Plaza de la Revolución

BIBLIOTECA NACIONAL

RANCHO

ARANGUREN (ZALDO)

INFANTA

PALACIO DE LA REVOLUCIÓN

AVENIDA 20 DE MAYO

SAN JOAQUÍN

LOMO

AVENIDA CARLOS M. DE CÉSPEDES

AVENIDA

DE MAYO

AMENIDAD

PEDROSO

LOMBILLO

ERMITA

AUDITOR

SAN PABLO

PEDRO PÉREZ

ESTADIO LATINOAMERICANO

ESTÉVEZ

CÁDIZ

PATRIA

SANTA

CRUZ DEL PADRE

VELAZQUEZ

TULIPÁN

SAN PEDRO

INDEPENDENCIA

LOMBILLO

OESTE

CALZADA DEL CERRO

HOSPITAL CLÍNICO QUIRÚRGICO

SANTA ANA

AVESTARAN

TULIPÁN

AGUAS

FERRER

SANTA ANA

MONASTERIO

ZARAGOZA

CALZADA DEL CERRO

HOSPITAL GENERAL SALVADOR ALLENDE

CERRO

BUENOS AIRES

SAN ANSELMO

DUREGE

BLANCA

PUENTES GRANDES

SANTO TOMÁS

SAN CRISTÓBAL

PARQUE

FLORENCIA

CALZADA

VÍA

SAN

ATOCHA

INFANTA

DUREGE

A   B   C

CASTILLO DE
LOS TRES REYES
DEL MORRO

CASTILLO DE
SAN SALVADOR
DE LA PUNTA

FORTALEZA
DE SAN CARLOS
DE LA CABAÑA

CANAL DE ENTRADA

RIDA

N LÁZARO

PARQUE DE
LOS MÁRTIRES

AVE. CARLOS M. DE CÉSPEDES (DEL PUERTO)

Parque Céspedes

CASTILLO
DE LA REAL
FUERZA

SAN LÁZARO

MALECON

SAN LÁZARO

TROCADERO

CAMPANARIO

AVENIDA DE ITALIA (GALIANO)

AGUILA

INDUSTRIA

PASEO DE MARTÍ (PRADO)

ZULUETA

AVE. DE LAS MISIONES

CUARTELES

TACÓN

CUBA

TEJADILLO

EMPEDRADO

Plaza de
la Catedral

VIRTUDES

VIRTUDES

NEPTUNO

NEPTUNO

AVE. DE BÉLGICA

AGUACATE

VILLEGAS

O'REILLY

OBISPO

Plaza
de Armas

CENTRAL
HAVANA

ESCOBAR

TUÑO

SAN MIGUEL

PARQUE
CENTRAL

LAMPARILLA

HABANA
VIEJA

MERCADERES

Plaza
de San
Francisco

OFICIOS

ZANJA

AGRAMONTE

TENIENTE REY

Plaza
Vieja

GERVASIO

SALUD

DRAGONES

CAPITOLIO
NACIONAL

BRASIL

MURALLA

HABANA

SOL

SANTA
CLARA

INQUISIDOR

AVE. SIMON BOLÍVAR (REINA)

PARQUE DE LA
FRATERNIDAD

LUZ

LUZ

ESPÍRITU
SANTO

CUBA

SAN PEDRO

ENRIQUE

BARNET

CAMPANARIO

RAYO

ANGELES

GÓMEZ (MONTE)

CORRALES

PICOTA

JESÚS MARÍA

MERCED

MALOJA

INDIO

AGRAMONTE

FACTORIA

EGIDO

LEONOR PÉREZ (PAULA)

CASA NATAL
DE JOSÉ MARTÍ

FIGURAS

MÁXIMO

TENERIFE

GLORIA

CENTRAL
STATION

DESAMPARADOS

(BELASCOAÍN)

GLORIA

CORRALES

DIARIA

NGLARI

MATADERO

GÓMEZ (MONTE)

ARROYO (AVE. MANGLAR)

AVENIDA DEL PUERTO

ENSENADA DE ATARÉS

VEZ

MÁXIMO GÓMEZ

FABRICA

CASTILLO
DE ATARÉS

OMO

FERNANDINA

CERRADO

SAN FELIPE

SAN FRANCISCO

SAN JOAQUIN

RAMÓN PINTO (C. DE CONCHA)

CES

CALZADA DEL

ENNA

VIA BLANCA

MARINDO

ENSENADA

MUNICIPIO

LUYANÓ

ROSA ENRIQUEZ

SAN

SAN LEONARDO

DE 10 DE OCTUBRE

VILLANUEVA

FABRICA

PEREZ

MELONES

JUAN ALONSO

RAMÓN PINTO

CALZADA DE LUYANÓ

SANTA FELICIA

ANTOS
UAREZ

COMPROMISO

0   1000   2000 feet

1 inch = 2000 feet

D   E   F

CENTRAL HAVANA

E

A B C

1

CASTILLO DE SAN SALVADOR DE LA PUNTA

PARQUE DE LOS MARTIRES

ANTIGUA CÁRCEL DE LA HABANA

MAXIMO GÓMEZ

CÁRCEL

PALACIO VELASCO

C A L E T A   D E   S A N   L Á Z A R O

GENÍOS

MORRO

MACEO (MALECÓN)

SAN LÁZARO

REFUGIO

MUSEO DE LA REVOLUCIÓN

AVENIDA

COLÓN

REFUGIO

CRESPO

INDUSTRIA

PASEO DE MARTI (PRADO)

COLÓN

2

SAN LÁZARO

BLANCO

TROCADERO

CONSULADO

GRANMA MEMORIAL

CAMPANARIO

MANRIQUE

LAGUNAS

BERNAL

ZULUETA

MUSEO NACIONAL DE BELLAS ARTES

ÁNIMAS

ITALIA (GALIANO)

SAN NICOLÁS

AGUILA

ÁNIMAS

AVE. DE LAS MISIÓN

PERSEVERANCIA

VIRTUDES

AMISTAD

VIRTUDES

PALACIO DE LOS MATRIMONIOS

EDIFICIO BACARDÍ

3

CONCORDIA

AVE. DE

MANZANA DE GÓMEZ

O'REILLY

NEPTUNO

NEPTUNO

PASEO DE MARTI

HOTEL INGLATERRA

PARQUE CENTRAL

CENTRO ASTURIANO

AVE. DE BELGICA (MONSERRATE)

CENTRAL HAVANA

SAN MIGUEL

SAN MIGUEL

TEATRO FEDRICO GARCÍA LORCA

AGRAMONTE

OBRAPÍ

SAN RAFAEL

SAN RAFAEL

OFFICINA DE CORREO

BERNAZA

(SAN JOSÉ)

SAN MARTÍN

SAN MARTÍN (SAN JOSÉ)

INDUSTRIA

BRASIL

4

ZANJA

ITALIA (GALIANO)

BARCELONA

BARRIO CHINO

AMISTAD

CAPITOLIO NACIONAL

MARTI

DRAGONES

AGUILA

FÁBRICA PARTAGÁS

CAMPANARIO

MANRIQUE

SAN NICOLÁS

SALUD

DRAGONES

PARQUE DE LA FRATERNIDAD

AGRAMONTE

5

AVENIDA   SIMÓN   BOLIVAR   (REINA)

(MONTE)

CARDENAS

ECONOMÍA

PALACIO DE ALDAMA

ENRIQUE

BARNET

(ESTRELLA)

ANGELES

GOMEZ

APONTE (SOMERUELOS)

CIENFUEGOS

GLORI

SAN NICOLÁS

RAYO

CORRALES

SITIOS

AGUILA

REVILLAGIGEDO

APODACA

FACTORIA

MISIÓN

CAMPANARIO

MANRIQUE

MALOJA

INDIO

MAXIMO

ANGELES

GLORIA

SUAREZ

6

SAN NICOLÁS

A   B

CORRALES

GLORIA

C

MARIEL

PINAR DEL RIO

AEROPUERTO

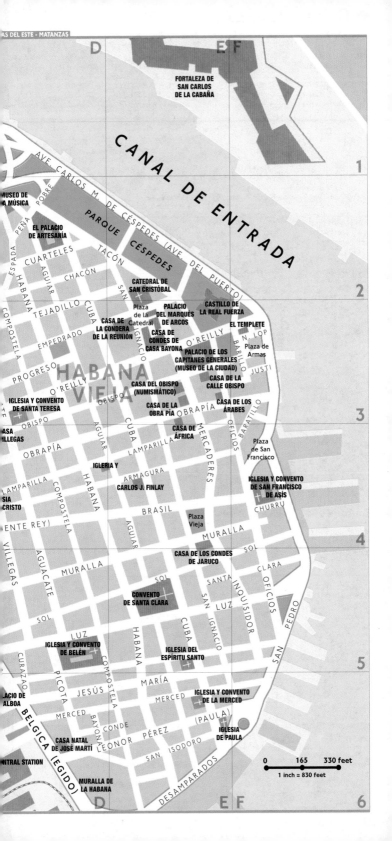

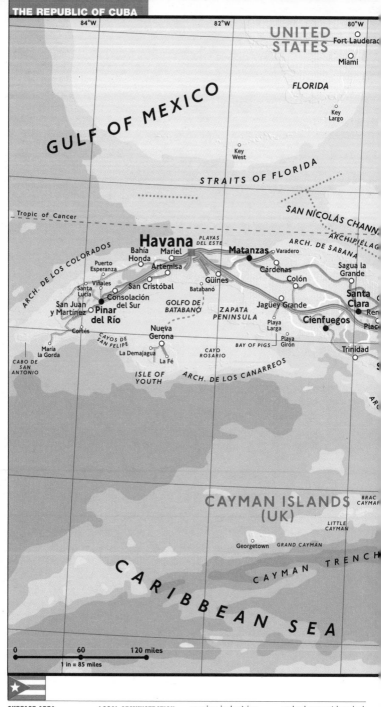

SURFACE AREA
42,803 square miles
POPULATION
11.2 million: over
2 million in Havana
and its suburbs and
more than 400,000
in Santiago.
CAPITAL
Havana

LOCAL ADMINISTRATION
14 provinces and 169
municipalities.
LANGUAGE
Spanish
CURRENCY
Peso and dollar
WORKING POPULATION
5.2 million (est. 1998).
Administration,

service industries
and commerce: 38%;
industry and
construction: 27%;
communications and
transport: 13%;
agriculture and stock
farming: 22% as at
the end of the 1980s.
Economic

redeployment has led
to a drop in the
number of employees
working for the state
(70% of staff), a rise
in cooperatives
(9.6%), and the
emergence of private
sectors (20.8%) and
mixed sectors (0.6%).